THEODORE ROOSEVELT:

Confident Imperialist

THEODORE ROOSEVELT:

Confident Imperialist

David H. Burton

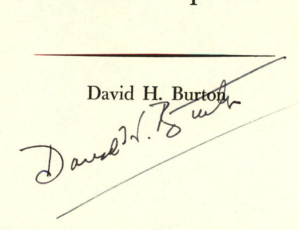

Philadelphia
University of Pennsylvania Press

This is Gerri's book

PREFACE

Theodore Roosevelt has been dead nearly fifty years. Yet his historical character continues to elude a final evaluation. The present study is intended as a step toward a definition of Roosevelt in history. Its purpose is not to rehabilitate T.R.'s reputation, if indeed it stands in need of such therapy, but to examine one dimension of the man that merits fresh consideration, his imperialist thought.

While I must assume responsibility for whatever limitations this study displays, I am in debt to others for much of whatever strengths it may possess. I especially want to acknowledge the advice of Professor William H. Harbaugh, who offered me encouragement in the formative stages of my work and who has enabled me to see the total Roosevelt more clearly. Professor M. A. Fitzsimons also watched the study grow from infancy, and I value his friendly concern as well.

The Editors of *Arizona and the West*, the *Journal of History of Ideas* and *Mid-America* have generously permitted me to quote from portions of articles that appeared originally in the pages of their journals.

I am pleased to thank St. Joseph's College (Faculty Research Program) and the American Philosophical Society (Penrose Fund) for financial assistance.

My mother's interest has never flagged, while the little ones, Antoinette, Monica, and Victoria, in the unknowing way of children, played their part. To my wife, Gerri, the book owes very much indeed, and to her it is dedicated.

David H. Burton

Petts Wood, Nr. Orpington, Kent
April 16, 1968

INTRODUCTION

Theodore Roosevelt belonged to a generation with unshakable confidence in the progress of mankind and an equal determination to further that progress. It was a generation that witnessed great breakthroughs in science and technology, a steady if uneven rise in the standards of living for most western nations, and enhanced political stability, reflective of man's increased skill in ruling himself. His was a generation that, as it came to maturity at the beginning of the new century, dared on occasion to dismiss as unlikely future wars between the Great Powers, now too civilized to entertain the prospect of mass destruction. Western imperialism, one of the prominent features of the era, typically enough evinced this mood of confidence wherever it went and by whomsoever it was taken. Britain's white man's burden, the French mission to civilize, imperial Germany's ambitions were variants of a constant: progress through civilization.

Even though conquest and military occupation were often the cruel preliminaries to the spread of western civilization, optimism that the movement worked to the welfare of mankind was everywhere evident. Such optimism was basic to Theodore Roosevelt's imperialist thought and action, and in a great measure it can be applied to the total of American overseas expansion as well. At heart Roosevelt was confident because he viewed expansion by the Great Powers as productive of far more good than harm to conquerors and conquered alike. Acknowledging the evils accompanying imperialism, he looked upon them as a price man had to pay for improvement. In the course of years he was to elaborate a philosophy and policies of imperialism rooted in this principle. If his conviction was in some ways unwarranted by the facts or if it was at times a particularly specious rationalization, there remained much in American expansion abroad that persuaded Roosevelt to look with confidence on the imperialism of his time.

In what way can it be argued that the significance Roosevelt ascribed to American imperialism was characteristic of the attitudes of his fellow citizens? How much did this one man shape the thinking of his era? Indeed, is there any nexus worthy of serious consideration between systemized thought and action? And if so, can it be convincingly demonstrated? To such questions perhaps no certain answers can be given. They are fruitful questions to ask nevertheless. They can serve as guidelines for inquiry into the phenomenon of Theodore Roosevelt that was not the "pure act" of Henry Adams' judgment but a man, after all, in whom thought and action mingled naturally. For him imperialism constituted action needing human values to sustain it. Because Roosevelt has not usually been understood as a man of ideas, much less as one who systemized his thought, to speak of his imperialist "philosophy" may seem excessive if not misleading. Yet there does not appear to be a much more accurate way of referring to his logically reasoned explanation and defense of imperialism in modern history. A second party, such as the historian, may tend to order or systemize Roosevelt's ideas somewhat more formally than he himself did. However, his "philosophy" consisted not simply in the discernibility of a system of thought in his imperialist outlook, but in his deliberate adherence to a whole set of principles, drawn from diverse sources and brought by him to the level of a distinctive rationale.

There has never been a lack of books about Theodore Roosevelt, and recent scholarly and popular accounts of his life attest to the durability of his appeal to authors and readers alike. The studies of Howard K. Beale—*Theodore Roosevelt and the Rise of America to World Power*—and William H. Harbaugh's *Power and Responsibility: The Life and Times of Theodore Roosevelt*, as well as the first volume of Carleton Putnam's projected multivolume biography, *Theodore Roosevelt: The Formative Years, 1858–1886*, are all notable scholarly treatments in recent years. Any future historian who would better understand Roosevelt and his imperialism will be especially conscious of the remarkable contribution to that end found in the analysis of the late Howard K. Beale. Still, such is the fascinating complexity of Roosevelt's life and his influence on his era that one may be justified in saying the last word on T.R. is some books distant. Because of the extent of the Roosevelt bibliography any new book must make its peace with the authorities, however. For a study such as the present one the choice is fairly clear: Either one includes a good deal of familiar data by drawing on the various published sources to provide a context for a fresh interpretation of his imperialism; or one may prefer a leaner, more direct approach and include only those details of the Roosevelt biography that seem to bear directly on the discussion at hand, thereby placing the major reliance on his *Letters* and *Works*. Out of respect for the impressive body of Roosevelt scholarship, the present work elects the sharper focus, with the emphasis given to Roosevelt's own views. It has been a decision that, once taken, has not been easy to adhere to, for the colorful, "bully" side of T.R. is not always neglected happily. What emerges is, one hopes, not an interpretation of Roosevelt's imperialism having limited reference or relationship to the total Roosevelt, but a study that adds to the intelligibility of him as a leading figure of his America, affirming him as a living figure as well.

In this book on Roosevelt's confident imperialism I have intended to write in the genre of intellectual history and not as a historian of American diplomacy. The study is not archives oriented; the raw materials are Roosevelt's own correspondence and writings. Diplomatic affairs have been treated largely as the settings for the expression of his ideas and the statement of his views. Only occasionally have I gone beyond broad discussions of American imperialism like Walter LaFeber's *The New Empire* and Ernest May's *Imperial Democracy* to expand or clarify a point. Similarly, in Roosevelt's relations with others I have turned only to the biographies and special studies that are pertinent, in the conviction that Roosevelt was largely if not totally a self-contained imperialist, with a self-generating imperialist outlook. Perhaps the results can be described as "Roosevelt on Roosevelt's imperialism." My purpose has not been to offer a defense of Roosevelt, but rather by an examination of his imperialist thought to know better how he conceived of the world movement of imperialism and thus to understand better Theodore Roosevelt's part in it. The study is limited to that specific but not inconsequential point of view, for T.R. was one of the formulators and guardians of the imperialist democracy.

CONTENTS

THEODORE ROOSEVELT:

Confident Imperialist

1

Family and Frontier

Much of Theodore Roosevelt's imperialism lies rooted in his formative years, long before he left his desk in Washington for the command in Cuba that was, in a way, the beginning of his imperialism and the imperialism of his America. Both the man and the people had been capriciously endowed for affairs of empire. Roosevelt possessed a fine mind in a weak body, which, his father warned him, he must work to strengthen. America had been equipped just as strangely: energy and ambition enough to gain and hold a continent but no real taste for foreign conquests. Young Roosevelt sought manfully to overcome his physical frailty and succeeded well enough, though as he admitted his athletic triumphs were not really numerous. Meanwhile, his well-equipped mind waxed strong in studies of nature and her ways, in travel abroad—"a useful part of my education," and in scientific and historical reading. By the time he was ready to enter Harvard College in the fall of 1876 Roosevelt had struck the balance between intellectual range and accomplishment and physical stamina that was characteristic of him all his life.

The imperial inheritance of Theodore Roosevelt's America came out somewhat differently. Policing the Western Hemisphere was never an easy task for her, earning as much resentment as respect—and very little gratitude. Instead of finding fulfillment of ambition in overseas possessions, her conquering instincts were first sobered by the bloody business of suppressing the Aguinaldan rebellion and then transformed into a compulsion to work for the good of her "little brown children," as Roosevelt spoke of the Filipinos when they had come under the care of William Howard Taft as governor general of the Philippines. The result was that no American empire, old style, ever came into existence, and only the United States among the Great Powers remained free of most imperialist trappings. Why this is so, in the largest sense, is buried deeply in the history of the American people. But events when taken singly may explain a great historical movement; parts can be examined to make an able judgment of the whole. Theodore Roosevelt and his imperialism combined to form such a piece of history.

No statesman stood out more prominently in the years of imperial opportunity and temptation than did Roosevelt; no President exerted so much influence. Few Americans gave imperialism more serious attention than he, and certainly no public man elaborated, at times without conscious motivation, a philosophy of imperialism more nearly in keeping with the traditions of the American people. This philosophy, which was mirrored consistently in action, was itself a product of the American experience he shared in so profoundly. Its peculiar qualities were due substantially to Roosevelt's response to his America, so that its source and character should be sought primarily in his own life. The essence of it was American. When his imperialism was fully wrought and finally rendered it became clear how much he had taken from America and how richly he had given it. The United States in after days continued to display traces, and more, of Roosevelt's public career. But in his own time he stamped American imperialism with many of its distinctive markings. He could shape and direct a colonial movement only by drawing upon himself and what he had become as an American. His imperialism would be acceptable to the people and supported by them only in what was common between them and him as he reflected their formation in his own in the generation that came of age in 1898. In an outbreak of youthful exuberance for martial glory, in a hesitant and temporary commitment to empire, in a willingness to

4

utilize whatever means were appropriate to get a job done that needed doing, and in a determination to play the protector and benefactor of less able races, Roosevelt was typical of his America.

Theodore Roosevelt, who was born in 1858 in New York City, came from a long established and much respected banker-merchant family; his mother was Martha Bullock, the daughter of a well-to-do Georgia planter. The family of the senior Theodore Roosevelt occupied a fine home at No. 28 East 20th Street, and "Teedie" was raised there in an atmosphere that bespoke security of future and propriety of manners. Distinction of lineage and upbringing, while they offer no certain clue to Roosevelt's destiny or to his contributions as an imperialist statesman, were nonetheless inseparable from him as boy and man. The Dutch ancestry of his forefathers, he wrote in his *Autobiography*, had been all but effaced by the "next seven generations from father to son every one of us . . . born on Manhattan Island." His description of his family tree as set forth there proclaimed him, with the blood of Englishmen and Welshmen and Irishmen mingled with the Dutch, an archetypical American. A love for America echoed in the family's past. His forebears fought in the Revolution, he had relatives on both sides in the Civil War, grandfathers contributed by their genius to the growing prosperity of New York City, his own father had been concerned personally with the social problems accumulating as a consequence of that growth. A patriotic dedication was embedded in Roosevelt's ways of thinking and acting, a presupposition of his public work and personal principles. America's best interest and doing one's best were hardly distinguishable in his ancestors or, in his own judgment, in himself.

According to one of the rules operating in American public life in the post-Civil War decades Theodore Roosevelt probably should not have had the chance to become a powerful politician and thence a statesman of imperialism. That he made such an opportunity for himself and helped open the way for others of his social background to feel at home in politics and to become influential the more easily is a tribute to the persuasions he as an individual managed to impart to the course of American growth. For in his younger days men of birth and breeding avoided politics—that inevitable preliminary to rule in a republic—as a low art, distasteful to them and their class, though in truth party organization was frequently closed to them by the machine professionals. This was particularly true of New York politics where the political boss in America had attained classic proportions. Such a paradoxical state of affairs Roosevelt found contrary to his own ambitions and contrary to the welfare of the country. He was determined to join the "ruling class," as he but half smilingly termed the organization men, by overcoming the obstacles of wealth and position. Thus it was that in 1880, fresh from Harvard, he joined the Twenty-first District Republican Association which held its meetings at Morton Hall on 59th Street, "a large, barn-like room over a saloon." In coming to know and like the "heelers" of the 21st District and in learning to respect Jake Hess, the "big leader," young Roosevelt thought of himself as a member of an elite who had entered politics both to deny power to men he deemed unworthy to exercise it and to possess power that was rightfully his. The strong sense of *noblesse oblige* evident in the elder Roosevelt's numerous charities and civic pursuits was passed on to his son, to be expressed in his early political purposes.

An odd mixture of idealism and practicality in his approach to active politics persisted years after Roosevelt's baptism of fire. In his *Autobiography* he ventured the opinion that a man should not, if wise, make politics his only occupation, particularly because a choice of other work would enable him to leave politics at any time rather than compromise his conscience. As a member of a prominent family Roosevelt always had several courses of action open to him should these awkward circumstances arise. He strangely failed to appreciate that the average man in politics might be neither so fortunate nor so honest. At any rate, a consciousness of this freedom to depart politics if it came to a choice between principle and promotion helped give him a deep belief that right must always prevail and that a man must, whatever the cost, persevere in the attainment of right. In his years of public office events often demonstrated that Roosevelt was not only convinced of the rightness of his policies but that he considered himself free to pursue them with unrestrained determination, his own individual success or failure—not to mention the prospects of his livelihood—hardly contingent on the outcome. The result was the enduring presence in his attitudes of the kind of confidence common to an elite that was sure of its power and responsibilities.

"My father . . . was the best man I ever knew," Theodore Roosevelt recalled in after years.[1] The directness of his words and the conviction they carry have a uniqueness and a charm difficult to resist. At the same time, they suggest the secure position Theodore Roosevelt, Sr., retained as an influence on his son. His father always had been so much with him that, as he wrote to a close friend a few days after the elder Roosevelt's death, "it seems as if part of my life has been taken away."[2] The father as the President remembered him was "an ideal man," combining strength and courage with tenderness and purity.[3] This good man was worshipped by his son, though their affectionate association led young Theodore to respect and emulate the spirit of his father's religious persuasions and ethical principles rather than the letter of his faith. The senior Roosevelt was a frankly religious man, fond of church attendance, concerned with the message of the sermon, conscious of being in the service of God, of whom he was personally aware, and entirely willing to wait upon His divine mercy for salvation.[4] His intense religious conviction expressed itself in a long list of charitable endeavors: the Mission

1. *Theodore Roosevelt: An Autobiography*, (New York, 1913), p. 7; hereafter cited as *Autobiography*.
2. Roosevelt to Henry D. Minot, February 20, 1878, *The Letters of Theodore Roosevelt*, 8 volumes, (Cambridge, 1951–1954) edited by Elting B. Morison *et al.*, II, p. 31; hereafter cited as *Letters*. His father had died February 9, 1878.
3. To Edward S. Martin, November 26, 1901, *ibid.*, I, p. 1443.
4. Carleton Putnam, *Theodore Roosevelt: The Formative Years, 1858–1886*, (New York, 1958), p. 42.

Church among New York's destitute, the Children's Aid Society, the State Charities Aid Association, the Orthopedic Hospital, the Newsboys' Lodging-House. He was, in the judgment of one who knew him and worked with him in these undertakings for over twenty years, possessed of "so much of all that goes to make up the true Christian manhood." [5] Altogether an imposing legacy of public service to leave a son and heir.

Even more apropos, the elder Roosevelt's unaffected goodness dominated his household, touching the family and everyone in it. If the young Theodore adored his father it was partly because he managed to make goodness attractive, something happy, almost gay, and easily cherished. His son responded favorably in this atmosphere. His own character he modeled in great measure upon that of his father. In his own family life years afterward he deliberately sought to re-create for his children the warmly affectionate but always proper upbringing he had known while growing up, whether he was about the serious duty of instructing his children in right living or bringing them to appreciate the happiness of a holiday.[6]

Unlike his father, Theodore Roosevelt was not by instinct drawn toward an acknowledgment of the saving grace of God or to denominational religion. He worshipped variously and apparently with equal ease in Episcopalian, Presbyterian, and Dutch Reform churches. While a Harvard undergraduate he once wrote his father of attending a Unitarian service with a friend and of being edified by the sermon because it was based on attributes of Christianity.[7] According to Lyman Abbott, "he did not endeavor to explain the Godside of Jesus but was attracted to and imitated the manward side of service." [8] What his father did suc-

---

5. *Ibid.*, p. 45.
6. Roosevelt, *Theodore Roosevelt's Letters to His Children,* (New York, 1919). See, for example, "A Preaching Letter" (to Kermit), pp. 60–61 and "The Supreme Joy of Christmas" (to Corinne, his sister), pp. 81–82.
7. To Theodore Roosevelt, Sr., April 15, 1877, *Letters,* I, p. 27.
8. Edward Wagenknecht, *The Seven Worlds of Theodore Roosevelt* (New York, 1958), p. 183. That Roosevelt had sympathy for the figure of Christ as a youngster was conveyed in a letter to his sister, Corinne, written from Paris just after he had wandered through the Louvre. Remarking on the paintings of Gustave Doré he wrote that Doré "alone represents Christ so that your pity for him is lost in intense admiration and reverence." Corinne Roosevelt Robinson, *My Brother, Theodore Roosevelt* (New York, 1921), p. 117.

cessfully impress on him, and this remained securely a part of him even after he ceased pursuing good merely out of respect for his parent, was a strict code of behavior toward himself and toward other men. One day this would be translated into the rule of righteousness of his imperialist philosophy. His moral code was grounded on the traditional Christian premises of good to be sought and evil to be avoided, though Roosevelt was more concerned with temporal sanctions than rewards or punishments in the hereafter. The virtues of selflessness, purity, gentleness, and self-control and the vices of untruthfulness, cowardice, cruelty, and idleness composed the most typical elements of his code of honor. It had a single uncompromising standard for all, and when he referred it to people and to nations his moral code received a universal application.

This sense of proper conduct instilled in Roosevelt in his early years was undeniably real. It played a leading part, for example, in his decision not to pursue a legal career. Legalism did not, to his way of thinking, seem to promote justice but rather to be set against justice. To him "the *caveat emptor* side of the law [was] repellent; it did not make for fair social dealing," and encouraged the sharp practice rather than the honest bargain.[9] Roosevelt was not prepared to identify himself with any career that did not promise to satisfy his insistent urge to make real the virtuous way of life his father had inspired in him. In the politics of the Gilded Age, on the other hand, there was every prospect that a young man of high ideals would find plenty of wrongs to be set right, virtue to be re-claimed, and the whole spirit of public life regenerated unto justice. The purposes that the elder Roosevelt experienced in a more spiritual realm Theodore found altogether congenial to the mundane world of American politics. His thirst to redeem politics, if not the political spoilsman—he was inclined to hate the sin and revile the sinner—was combined powerfully with his instinctive will to action, producing a formidable advocate of *character* in public life.

The critical place that character occupied in his philosophy of imperialism was foreshadowed in his judgment that character was the great objective worth striving for by individual men. He

9. *Autobiography*, p. 54.

wished it for every race and nation as he wished it for every person. A nation having the capacity for self-rule had this attribute of character; self-rule required self-discipline and restraint of a high order, courage, and devotion to the right. In a sociopolitical grouping such as a nation this was the equivalent of virtue in the individual.

History and observation of the contemporary scene suggested to Roosevelt that not every race or people at a given time was capable of self-rule or the exercise of political freedom. The social evils that his father had fought against in New York slums and sought to alleviate through the church the older man no doubt would have admitted derived in part at least from the sinfulness of men, a lack of goodness. The son was convinced that inability to rule was the great social liability a people might incur, attributable to a real if not inherent infirmity in certain races. A people might indeed overcome this handicap but to do so demanded effort and sacrifice. Such a people would have to struggle to learn how to rule themselves, thereby reaching that level of political maturity that entitled them to free government. Further, they had to struggle with no guarantee of success within a predeterminable time. It had been thus with Theodore Roosevelt in his personal attempts to overcome the physical infirmities bequeathed him by nature. In this regard Roosevelt seemed to discern a certain unity in the affairs of men. His success in building up bodily strength may have convinced him in part that those nations called backward would have to make an analogous effort to come forward. It certainly convinced him that anything worth having—and democracy was to him "much the highest form of government"— was worth the patient labor necessary to achieve it.

The attempt on Theodore Roosevelt's life that took place in Milwaukee on October 14, 1912, was the most sensational episode of the Bull Moose campaign. As the former President left the Gilpatric Hotel, where he had been staying, to attend a local political rally, he was shot and wounded by an insane fanatic.

Fortunately for him the folded manuscript of the speech he was to deliver and a steel spectacle case combined to slow the bullet; the massive muscles of his chest did the rest. The lung remained unharmed. "It was largely due to the fact that he is a physical marvel that he was not dangerously wounded," summed up the judgment of the attending physician after surveying the damaged area; "he is one of the most powerful men I have ever seen laid on an operating table." [10] A notable verdict and one hardly predictable of a man who as a child was unusually troubled by illness. Asthma was prominent among his ailments, though colds, fevers, coughs, and stomach upsets were included on the list. His health as a youngster was of genuine concern to his family and himself, the more to be lamented because it could well mean that the potential of his mind might remain unfulfilled. "Teedie's" poor health not infrequently dominated family plans for travel and holiday and the routine of the household as well. This helps account for the rare degree of love and respect between child and parents. His father knew what it was to walk a baby son at night trying to relieve his congested breathing, and in later years he frequently took the child on long carriage rides in the open air for his comfort. Frailty of health persisted into boyhood, and while it did not shadow his sunny disposition for long, still it was a fact to be lived with.

Or was it? The exact circumstance of change was easy to mark. It came dramatically in the autumn of 1870 in a memorable conversation between father and son. With loving concern the elder Roosevelt sternly pointed out to his son, "Theodore, you have the mind, but you have not the body, and without the help of the body the mind can not go as far as it should. You must make your body. It is hard drudgery to make one's body but I know you will do it." The lad's reply to the challenge came swiftly and with confidence: "I'll make my body." [11] He took up a regimen of exercises with weights and worked on the parallel bars to enlarge his chest and thus improve his breathing. The results of this deter-

10. Quoted in Stefan Lorant, *The Life and Times of Theodore Roosevelt,* (New York, 1959), p. 573.
11. Robinson, *op. cit.,* p. 50.

mination to prevail over physical handicaps were astonishingly good, but they were not miraculous. Though he was no longer "unhealthy" after months of Spartan routine, asthmatic attacks did recur. Roosevelt only looked upon these as part of the continuing challenge to him to "make his body."

Out of the circumstances occasioned by one such attack came another small but instructive incident that is a familiar tale of Theodore Roosevelt's boyhood. He recounts it with engaging candor in the pages of his *Autobiography*. He was journeying alone to Moosehead Lake, sent there by his father to help relieve a siege of asthma. He was thirteen at the time. On the stagecoach he encountered two other boys of his own age who proceeded to rag him unmercifully. Exasperated, he thought to defend himself more than his honor by fighting them. To his chagrin he discovered that he was no match for either boy.

Determined not to allow such a situation to occur again and recognizing that he lacked the natural prowess to protect himself, he firmly resolved to train himself. The struggle to "make his body" took a new and exciting turn. Boxing lessons under former prizefighter John Long, pursued with his father's hearty approval, continued over a three-year period before Roosevelt felt he had acquired any real skill in the manly art. This was another occasion for the student pugilist to learn that accomplishment in life does not always come easily; perhaps he even concluded that the strong survive and that in physical strength there is a tangible and meaningful superiority. From victories, however small, he likewise came to know that the feeling of success could be exhilarating—a pewter mug won at boxing in John Long's gymnasium became the token of success born of struggle. Other forms of physical activity that Roosevelt turned to as part of his program of healthful vigor held the same lesson. It took him a long while and much effort to become a respectable horseman, for example. As he aptly remarked, "Any man, if he chooses, can gradually school himself to the requisite nerve, and gradually learn the requisite seat and hands. . . ." [12] But he must *choose*, as Theo-

12. *Autobiography,* p. 29.

dore Roosevelt had very deliberately chosen to make his body
and reverse the verdict of nature.

The struggle to acquire the physical strength proper to his
needs forms a colorful part of Roosevelt's youth and relates in an
important way to his character, because it constituted achievement
of the one prize he was born without. Had such a contest not been
necessary, he would have been the T.R. of neither fact nor fiction.
Perhaps in no other way could the scion of a well-to-do family experience so painfully the rough edge of life, a sense of inade-
quacy, and an opportunity to meet a challenge that most boys
might not have faced so bravely. Roosevelt called upon reserves
of moral strength that he transformed into physical vigor. The experience went far to reinforce and confirm the sense of confidence
he possessed as his birthright in the elite class. The acquisition of
physical strength and endurance may have meant even more to
him, since it not only stood for something that he was able to win
in his own right, but also sustained him on that day in Milwaukee
in the year of the Bull Moose.

The childhood frailties of Theodore Roosevelt and the
physical inhibitions they produced encouraged him to become a
bookish boy; he remained a man who loved books and who was
seldom away from them. Reading in his youth provided an outlet
for a naturally inquisitive mind made the more so by poor health.
Adventure tales, history, books on nature—he devoured one and
all. But it was reading in natural history that provided him with
his first sustained and fruitful intellectual experience. It all began when as a small boy he caught a glimpse of a dead seal in a
marketplace along Broadway. He was plainly fascinated by the
sight and tried to discover everything about the seal, from its
measurements to its place of origin and habits. His father, noting
the boy's genuine interest, provided him with books and they
whetted his appetite for more information. He read avidly in the
works of J. G. Wood and Spencer Baird, studied taxidermy for a

while under an old gentleman, Mr. Bell, "who had been a companion of Audubon's" at one time, and collected numerous if ordinary natural specimens for mounting in a collection. His subjects included wildlife gathered from the banks of the Hudson and the Nile, for at the height of this enthusiasm, 1872–73, the Roosevelt family toured Europe and the Middle East. In fact bird collecting, he wrote, lent the "chief zest" to his Nile journey.

All of this might be dismissed lightly as no more than a boy's passing fancy for the unusual except that it complemented so well the total self emerging. A glance through his later writings shows how appealing and instructive nature continued to be for him. *African Game Trails, The Wilderness Hunter, Ranch Life and the Hunting Trail* are among the most notable examples, but no mere mention of them can adequately convey the image of a man forever fond of nature. Throughout these writings the hard lessons that nature offers man stand out. He saw the romance of it, it is true. But a more persistent theme is that of the struggle always present in nature, the rule of tooth and claw whereby the strong survive.

For many men there comes a time in life when the experiences of mind and body, long building up, harden into fixed if not completed form, constituting the basis of later attitudes and action. In a public man it may be years before such attitudes are evidenced in policies, though the principles of action have been laid down long since. For some this may come slowly, and the particular set of experiences that acts as the hardening agent or the approximate time of occurrence is not easy to determine. For others it may happen, if not suddenly, at least in a marked and distinguished fashion. By the time Roosevelt left Harvard in 1880, though his life had been more varied and stimulating than most, there still had not taken place that experience that would knit together the different principles he had come to accept and was determined to live by and out of which would come a philosophy of imperialism.

14

The months Theodore Roosevelt spent in Dakota country in the early 1880's were destined to serve as the unifying force of his lifetime, one that determined the outlines of his imperialist philosophy. He later spoke of his western days as "the most important educational asset of all my life," [13] and under the spell of his frontier adventure he wrote his notable study *The Winning of the West*, the fundamental first statement of his confident imperialism. Over-all, the American West was secondary only to his father's influence, and coming as it did at a later time it seemed to bring together the elements of character and virtue, of duty and struggle, in a structured whole, placing each in an intelligible and sympathetic relationship to the other.

More surely than any other undertaking in his world of action these western days primed him for empire. He thereby identified himself personally as a part of the great western movement led by the Anglo-American race whose glory he was to sing in *The Winning of the West*. This was very much the way he viewed the world movement, the imperialism of his era, as he himself became caught up in it. Life in the West gave him an elemental contact with this movement and the experience enthralled him. The West captured the imagination of Theodore Roosevelt the American and enabled him to place the frontier history of his country in the context of the modern world. Addressing an audience at Colorado Springs in 1901 he reminded his fellow westerners:

You and your fathers who built the West did even more than you thought; for you shaped thereby the destiny of the whole republic and as a necessary corollary profoundly influenced the course of events throughout the World.[14]

On another level Theodore Roosevelt had nothing less than an affair of the heart with the American West. The description of "Cowboy Land" opening the chapter of his *Autobiography* that deals with his western adventures is memorable. It speaks of a

13. Speech at Sioux Falls, S.D., September 3, 1910, quoted in Hermann Hagedorn, *Roosevelt in the Bad Lands,* (New York, 1921), p. 2.
14. Roosevelt, "Manhood and Statehood," *The Works of Theodore Roosevelt,* Memorial Edition, 24 volumes, (New York, 1922–1926), XV, p. 322; hereafter cited as *Works.*

love, a wistful longing for the West, and a sadness that it is gone forever. His description is romanticized, but he knew the West in its rawest habits; having voluntarily entered upon a contest with its primitive power, he prevailed in that struggle.

Somewhat ironically it was a recurrence of his asthma complicated by an attack of cholera morbus in the late summer of 1883 that prompted him to take refuge in the clear dry air of the Dakotas.[15] It seemed like a perfect reason and opportunity to enjoy fully the vigorous outdoor life that had long beckoned to him. Little did he then realize what a personal solace the Badlands would afford when in February of the next year his wife and mother died within hours of each other. Partially because of this but mostly out of a genuine desire to be part of the West Roosevelt, who had gone out to see the prairie country and hunt buffalo as a tourist-sportsman, committed himself wholeheartedly to ranch life. In September 1883 he bought property there, investing over $14,000 in the enterprise, and entered on the serious business of cattle raising.[16]

With the death of his loved ones the next year he threw himself ever more intently into the life of a Dakota rancher. Out of this time of travail and loneliness, out of the adventure of the roundup and the wild humanity of the West, Theodore Roosevelt emerged a westerner and in many ways that stamp was indelible. Years later, while on safari in Africa, he talked warmly of the settlers he encountered there: "They remind me so much of my beloved Westerners that I feel absolutely at home amongst them." [17] These white settlers in Africa, like the plainsmen of the American West, were in his view part of the same world movement of the superior western races over the waste spaces that had reached a new expression in the imperialism of the late nineteenth century. But Roosevelt had grasped the meaning of the West for

15. The effects on his health were favorable. "I have never been in better health than on this trip. I am in the saddle all day long either taking part in the round-up of the cattle or else hunting antelope." To Anna Roosevelt, June 17, 1884, *Letters*, I, p. 73.

16. Eventually he invested $40,000 and experienced a loss of over $20,000 when he liquidated his holdings in 1886.

17. To Arthur Hamilton Lee, October 6, 1909, *Letters*, VII, p. 32.

him much before his trip to Africa in 1909. In the preface to *The Wilderness Hunter*, Sagamore Hill, 1893, he wrote:

In hunting, the finding and killing of the game is after all but a part of the whole. The free self-reliant adventurous life, with its rugged and stalwart democracy; the wild surroundings, the grave beauty . . . all of these unite to give the career of the wilderness hunter its peculiar charm.

And he went on in this introspective vein:

The chase is among the best of all natural pastimes; it cultivates that vigorous manliness for the lack of which in a nation, as in an individual, the possession of no other qualities can possibly atone.[18]

The western experience gave lasting form to Roosevelt's mind and so acted to provide for his philosophy of imperialism.

Experiences as rancher and hunter in the West, renewing as they did a boyhood love for nature's challenge, were part of the making of Theodore Roosevelt, the historian of the West and imperialist statesman. In his frontier days he learned firsthand the reality of primitive aborigines thwarting the progress of civilization, as they had done for centuries. He became aware of what it was to face the savage alone, save for his wits and his gun, and he shared in a rare and intimate fashion the sense of danger and mastery that belong to the conqueror.[19] He came also to appreciate deeply the significance of conquest: the creation of the West he loved and a western spirit that to him was the perfect embodiment of America. The frontiersman became the "archetype of freedom" whose image was reproduced and enlarged many times in the expansion of the western nations.

The Winning of the West, the multivolume account of the early American frontier, was the literary counterpart of Theodore Roosevelt the westerner. It combined his thirst for the active life and

18. In "Frontier Types" he wrote: "The Hunter is the archetype of freedom. His well-being rests in no man's hands save his own." *Works*, IV, p. 458.
19. Roosevelt, "Red and White on the Border", *ibid.*, IV, pp. 480–490.

his equally compelling need to understand himself and his times. At the outset of this frontier history he stated his fundamental viewpoint of modern history:

During the past three centuries the spread of the English speaking peoples over the world's waste spaces has been not only the most striking feature in the world's history but also the event of all others most far-reaching in its effects and its importance.[20]

The consequences of this expansion were of incalculable advantage to mankind; through it many peoples of the world had come to know and to value the premier civilization of the age.[21]

Since the beginning of the modern era of expansion European civilization had been taken to backward areas by many of the western powers. Roosevelt looked upon the Russification of Turkistan and French penetration of Algeria as expressions of progress through imperialism that resembled English occupation of Burma and Egypt.[22] It was only that in the expansions after 1500 the most notable efforts were made by "men speaking English." [23] This process of conquest and control was a world movement toward a composite civilization that derived its explanation from the political and technological superiority of the European or white race. This was not a conventionalized social Darwinism in that Roosevelt was ready to welcome to the ranks of the superior peoples those other than European, provided they emulated the West. In due course the Japanese were judged superior by T.R., for they seemed to adapt to western ways quite readily. In any comparison of the accomplishments of the non-English and the English peoples, however, Roosevelt held that those of the latter were of a different and higher quality. The

20. Roosevelt, *The Winning of the West,* Allegheny Edition, 4 volumes, (New York, 1894), I, p. 1.

21. *Ibid.,* IV, pp. 2–4. It can be argued that Roosevelt was an exponent of what has been termed "continentalism," that is, the extension of American power into the Pacific as an outgrowth of settling the frontier. This was in keeping with his Americanism. See Charles Vevier, "American Continentalism," *American Historical Review,* Vol. LXV, No. 2 (January 1960), pp. 323–335.

22. To Carl Schurz, September 8, 1895, Roosevelt *Manuscript;* see also to Henry White, August 14, 1908, *ibid.;* and to Sidney Brooks, November 20, 1908, *Letters,* VI, p. 1370.

23. To Sir Cecil Spring-Rice, August 11, 1899, *ibid.,* II, pp. 1049–1053.

triumphs of the English, generally ethnic in nature, gave birth to new commonwealths in Australia, Canada, and the United States and stood in instructive contrast to the political occupations resting on force that typified European domination in Asia and Africa. Under English inspiration the ideas of western man were better able to take root and to reproduce, at times on an even grander scale, superior institutions. The conquest of the American continent, as Roosevelt emphasized in *The Winning of the West,* was the "crowning and greatest achievement of these world movements." [24]

The frontiersman, individually and in the sum of his achievement, was central to Roosevelt's interpretation of how the West was won. To Frederick Jackson Turner he explained that the aim of *The Winning of the West* was "to show who the frontiersmen were and what they did as they gradually conquered the West." [25] Such a purpose was characteristic of Roosevelt's historical world; the frontier had had a profound influence in Americanizing people because it had "invariably beaten all the frontiersmen of whatever stock into one mould." [26] As the frontier was won again and again the American nation was made. And its people, constantly expanding across a continent, carried with them English principles of law and justice that in the course of but a few years became established American principles in stable communities.

The Winning of the West, along with other of his historical writings in the 1880's, represented an attempt by Roosevelt to describe in an honest and frankly patriotic fashion what might be learned by his own and later generations from the North American phase of the world movement and by implication how the lessons could be applied to contemporary imperialist problems. In his judgment research, however painstaking and complete, should never obscure the decisive contributions of the great thinker in the writing of history. The genius of a Parkman or a Macaulay, historians Roosevelt especially admired, derived from their insights and not merely from a factual knowledge of the subject

24. Roosevelt, *The Winning of the West, Works,* X, p. 8.
25. To Frederick Jackson Turner, April 10, 1895, *Letters,* I, p. 440.
26. To Ernest Bruncken, March 1, 1898, *ibid.,* I, pp. 786–787.

matter.[27] Thus the study of the West appealed powerfully to his sense of the purpose of writing history, for in the conquest of the frontier he found both the great fact and proof of American life and the methods whereby American principles of society and government could be taken to backward races across the world.

The hero of frontier conquest—and Roosevelt's historical appreciations were congenial to heroes and villains—was the individual settler. He might be English, Scotch, Irish, German, or even Huguenot by extraction, it did not matter. Within a generation the individual living a frontier existence became an American in race and outlook.[28] These people were more than farmers; they were also warriors without whose skill and courage no agricultural settlement could have been sustained. Far superior to any regular army of conquest, they lived not off the land but on it, making it their home.[29] Such were the typical frontiersmen that Roosevelt described crossing the Appalachians to settle the Northwest Territory, move down the Mississippi, and eventually conquer the Spanish borderlands and the Great Plains. Conquest and settlement were achieved largely by the "dogged frontier farmers, each skilled in the use of rifle and axe, each almost independent of outside assistance, and each with a swarm of towheaded children. . . ."[30] Here then was a "masterful race" composed of individuals of superior resourcefulness and daring whose accomplishments depended not upon statesmen and generals but upon the whole people.[31]

But these "masterful Americans" did not occupy a continent that was uninhabited or unclaimed. Any history of the settlement of the West must deal with these considerations, as indeed any imperialist philosophy must define in terms of principles not only the validity of rival claims of the Great Powers but also the rights of the natives subjected to conquest. In his various writings on the West Roosevelt treated both claims and rights in such a manner as

27. To Sir George Otto Trevelyan, January 25, 1904, *ibid.*, III, pp. 707–708; see also Roosevelt, "Francis Parkman's Histories," *Works*, XIV, pp. 286–294.
28. Roosevelt, *Thomas Hart Benton*, (Boston, 1891), pp. 1–4 *passim*.
29. Roosevelt, *The Winning of the West*, Allegheny Edition, II, p. 24.
30. To Frederick C. Selous, March 19, 1900, *Letters*, II, p. 1233.
31. Roosevelt, *The Winning of the West*, Allegheny Edition, II, p. 221.

to predicate on his historical interpretations important aspects of his world outlook. He held that the great feature of American history, next to the very preservation of the national life itself, was the settlement of the "vast and fertile spaces" of the frontier. But before the West could be settled it had to be won; having been won it became American by right of conquest.[32] Yet some amplification of this simple Darwinian formula is required to understand Theodore Roosevelt's true attitude.

In Roosevelt's view the western regions were "peculiarly our heritage . . . [and] the property of the fathers of America which they held in trust for their children."[33] The nation, once established along the seaboard, had a singular claim to the lands lying to the west. The validity of this claim was not simply in the ability to conquer but in the ability to conquer and to settle—to establish new communities where men were free to govern themselves. To Roosevelt's mind, for example, it was not the negotiations of Jefferson and his fellow statesmen that removed the French claim to Louisiana; the claims of the Spanish and the French had effectively been undermined by the great westward movement of Americans begun before the Revolution and by the free communities that were quickly founded.[34] Conquest and settlement by their very nature strengthened the American right to new areas contiguous to earlier settlements. For this reason, rather than the law of "might makes right," Roosevelt maintained that "the region west of the Mississippi could become the heritage of no other people save that which planted its populous communities along the eastern bank of the river."[35]

Similarly, the controversial claims to the Oregon country were only as good as conquest could make them—successful conquest would be followed by settlement. "The real truth," Roosevelt observed in his biography of Thomas Hart Benton, "is that such titles are of very little practical value and are rightly enough disre-

---

32. *Ibid.*, III, p. 1, see also Roosevelt, "George Rogers Clark and the Conquest of the Northwest," *Works*, IX, p. 21.
33. Roosevelt, *Gouverneur Morris, ibid.*, VIII, p. 524.
34. Roosevelt, *The Winning of the West*, Allegheny Edition, IV, p. 258, p. 261; to Frederick Jackson Turner, November 4, 1896, *Letters*, I, p. 564.
35. Roosevelt, *The Winning of the West*, Allegheny Edition, IV, p. 261.

garded by any nation strong enough to do so. . . ."[36] Oregon legally belonged to no one and it was sure to become valuable. Because Americans were in a natural position to develop it, Roosevelt recognized their claims to the area as the most legitimate.[37] The acquisition of Texas and the Southwest was explained and justified by much the same argument, but this conquest was complicated by the counterclaims of the Mexicans, a people he considered inferior. Whatever the territorial rights of the Mexicans had been at one time, the Texans abrogated them by settlement. To expect these transplanted Americans to accept rule from a people incapable of governing themselves, much less others, was to Roosevelt unreasonable.[38] Frontier Americans of the early nineteenth century, he wrote approvingly, "looked upon all the lands hemming in the United States as territory which they or their children should some day inherit."[39] The claims of other nations meant little enough to them.

If the territorial ambitions of rival nations struck the average American settler as unwarranted, the presence of the Indian was to him a source of immediate and constant danger. By the end of the nineteenth century, Roosevelt once reminded Sir George Otto Trevelyan, people no longer realized what "formidable and terrible" enemies the Indians had been.[40] Men were unable therefore to understand the justice of war against the savages. Roosevelt's attitude regarding these wars was one in which the barbarian character of the Indians was prominent—an authentically Western frontier attitude.[41] Writing of the conquest of Tennessee he stated his general judgment on the Indian wars: "In its results and viewed from the standpoint of applied ethics, the conquest and settlement by the whites of the Indian lands was necessary to the greatness and the well-being of civilized man-kind. It was as ultimately beneficial as it was inevitable."[42] The inevitability of

36. Roosevelt, *Thomas Hart Benton*, p. 51.
37. *Ibid.*, pp. 51–52.
38. *Ibid.*, pp. 176–177.
39. *Ibid.*, p. 20.
40. To Sir George Otto Trevelyan, January 1, 1908, *Letters*, VI, p. 881.
41. Hagedorn, *op. cit.*, p. 355.
42. Roosevelt, *The Winning of the West*, Allegheny Edition, II, p. 175; Roosevelt, *Thomas Hart Benton*, pp. 5–7 *passim*.

this warfare stemmed from two conditions: the expansive quality of the superior frontier people and the refusal of the Indians to give up their lands. The wars that ensued were notable for their ferocity and terror; the Indians were tenacious foes fighting a war they considered both just and holy. White men quickly found themselves battling the Indians on the latter's terms, sinking to a level of viciousness that Roosevelt admitted was uncivilized.[43] But he was also ready to explain and defend the brutal treatment accorded the savages. Much of the injustice, he reasoned, came from a loosening of social bonds that frequently gave the vicious person opportunities for evil. Moreover, the long continuance of the warfare and its horrors tended to condition all men, good and bad, to accept bloodshed as normal and eventually to look upon the Indians not only as inferior but also as less than human.[44]

Roosevelt did not sanction harsh behavior for its own sake, as his discussion of Senator Benton's role in the Indian removals well illustrates. Benton was one of the great advocates of the systematic settlement of the Indians of the South on reserves west of the Mississippi. But "so far as was compatible," Roosevelt wrote, Benton "always endeavored to have them kindly and humanely treated." [45] The Senator admitted that cruelty was involved but he did not see how it could be avoided, as the Indians held millions of acres of fertile farm land. In both *The Winning of the West* and *Thomas Hart Benton* Roosevelt digressed to scold those humanitarians who were scandalized by the record of relations between the Indian tribes and the United States, pointing out that the Government had erred as often through sentimentality as it had through willful wrongdoing.[46] A different standard of international morality applied to savages from that applied to stable and cultured communities, and it was idle to hold otherwise.[47]

Roosevelt approached his histories of the West with the pur-

---

43. Roosevelt, *The Winning of the West,* Allegheny Edition, IV, p. 9.
44. *Ibid.,* II, pp. 147–148; IV, p. 9.
45. Roosevelt, *Thomas Hart Benton,* p. 56.
46. Roosevelt, *The Winning of the West,* Allegheny Edition, III, pp. 42–43; Roosevelt, *Thomas Hart Benton,* pp. 172–173; Roosevelt, "Red and White on the Border," *Works,* IV, p. 485.
47. Roosevelt, *The Winning of the West,* Allegheny Edition, III, p. 44.

pose of instructing his own generation. This aim was implicit in the conception of *The Winning of the West,* was woven subtly into the narration, and on occasion was stated unequivocally. In one reference to Indian-white conflict for example he declared:

> The most ultimately righteous of all wars is war with savages, though it is apt to be also the most terrible and most inhuman. The rude fierce settler who drives the savage from the land lays all civilized mankind under his debt. Americans and Indians, Boer and Zulu, Cossack and Tartar, New Zealander and Maori—in each case the victor, horrible though many of his deeds are, has laid deep the foundations for the future greatness of a mighty people. . . .[48]

and later in the same volume:

> Many good persons seem prone to speak of all wars of conquest as necessarily evil. This is, of course, a short-sighted view. In its after effects a conquest may be fraught either with evil or with good for mankind according to the comparative worth of the conquering and the conquered peoples. It is useless to try to generalize. . . . The world would have been halted had it not been for the Teutonic conquests of alien lands; but the victories of Moslems over the Christians have always proved a curse in the end. . . . This is true generally of all victories of barbarians of low racial characteristics over gentler, more moral and more refined peoples, even though these people to their shame have lost the vigorous fighting virtues. Yet it remains no less true that the world would probably not have gone forward at all, had it not been for the displacement or submersion of savage and barbaric peoples as a consequence of the armed settlement in strange lands of races who held in their hands the fate of the years.[49]

Roosevelt concluded that the American backwoods conqueror had to be judged like other conquerors of savage people, whether they be Greeks in the Po Valley or Boers in the Transvaal.[50] Nor did he refrain from lecturing the American people—the "educated

48. *Ibid.,* pp. 45–46.
49. *Ibid.,* pp. 175–176.
50. *Ibid.,* p. 176.

classes in particular"—on the need to realize that although war was evil it was a far greater evil not to fight if the cause was a just one.[51]

The great westward movement was not merely a conquest that brought with it millions of fertile acres for agricultural use. Rather it brought English-speaking communities to the interior of the continent,[52] and resulted in the extension of civilization based on Anglo-Saxon concepts of justice and law. Roosevelt spoke of it as the "first duty" of the backwoodsmen to institute civil government.[53] These frontier sovereignties, he thought, were sure to reflect two ingredients: a democratic spirit typical of all that westerners undertook[54] and a representative system derived from their British and colonial forebears.[55] The communities that emerged were economically, socially, and politically self-sufficient. As Americans took possession of a new country they had to work out the precise form of government under which they would live; but as a matter of course this form included elective officers, a democratic franchise, and rule by the majority. Roosevelt did not suggest that these frontier governments operated perfectly or that they had not blundered sometimes in serious fashion. Such imperfections simply were to be "accepted as part of the penalty" paid for free government, the birthright of a superior people.[56]

In particular instances, Roosevelt explained, the political progress resulting from the westward movement involved more than the establishment of free governments for a homogeneous population. The French inhabitants encountered in some areas were more welcome and were more likely to remain in their holdings than were the Indians. American leaders in the West occasionally faced the task of governing an alien people like the French and the problem of striking a just and workable balance between conquerors and conquered. In *The Winning of the West* Roosevelt re-

51. *Ibid.,* IV, p. 97.
52. Roosevelt, *Thomas Hart Benton*, p. 1.
53. Roosevelt, *The Winning of the West*, Allegheny Edition, II, p. 381.
54. *Ibid.*
55. *Ibid.*, p. 383.
56. *Ibid.*, IV, p. 218 *passim*.

lates how the French in Illinois reacted to the opportunity to become full-fledged Americans.[57] Since Virginia then claimed the region Governor Patrick Henry urged his agent, John Todd, to pay special heed to the customs of the French and the French-Indians in order that they might be more easily induced to give loyalty to the conquerors.[58] But these people, unaccustomed to the Anglo-American processes of free government, were unable to adjust to their proper use. Like any race unfamiliar with the practice of self-rule, the French had to be governed until they were more politically mature.[59] The political problem in Illinois was epitomized in Roosevelt's description of the administrative responsibility of George Rogers Clark, who had to rule a vast area and keep content and loyal a population alien in race, creed, and language—a task that demanded a rare combination of energy and executive ability.[60]

With regard to the Louisiana Territory after its acquisition from France, Roosevelt emphasized that even Jefferson saw no inconsistency between the principle of "consent of the governed" and the establishment of a government on grounds of common sense until the people there were ready for self-rule.[61] Free men, after all, had to rule others whom they conquered until such time as the less progressive people were prepared to participate directly in their own government. All these elements in the conquest and settlement of the American frontier led Roosevelt to declare that the winning of the West was "the great epic feat in the history of our race" [62] and to assure his countrymen that in the new age of imperialism and world frontiers the need for the old pioneer virtues remained unchanged.[63]

Theodore Roosevelt knew the American West in the raw as well as in the realm of thought, and the impact of the total experience on his philosophy of imperialism was clear. The West con-

57. *Ibid.*, II, pp. 47–48.
58. *Ibid.*, p. 169.
59. *Ibid.*, p. 170.
60. *Ibid.*, pp. 49–50.
61. Roosevelt, "The Issues of 1900," *Works*, XVI, p. 552.
62. Roosevelt, "Manhood and Statehood," *ibid.*, XV, p. 323.
63. Roosevelt, "Address at Alliance, Nebraska," April 25, 1903, *ibid.*, XV, p. 324.

tributed to its general orientation, conditioned its judgments, and accounted for much of its content. The lessons of the West combined naturally and powerfully with Roosevelt's character. The western principle of action was congenial to his personal vitality; its purpose and achievement fitted in well with his code of values. The frontier interlude and its literary counterparts confirmed in Roosevelt's thinking the serviceability of the virtues his family life and in particular his father had instilled in him, and his philosophy of imperialism would reveal that indebtedness to family and frontier in a conscious and consistent fashion.

2

The Nineties and the Navy

The neoimperialism of Benjamin Disraeli and Leopold of the Belgians was ranging at large in the world as Theodore Roosevelt turned from ranching to writing in the years after 1886. Professor Seeley's book *The Expansion of England,* published in 1883, converted Lord Roseberry and his generation of Englishmen to a new belief in their own destiny. Leopold II, acting more surely on instinct, possessed himself of the substance of Central Africa and thereby offered the lesson that any power, large or small, had a place and a right in the world movement if it was willing to exercise the proper initiative. Most of the powers were as quick to act. France underwent what has been termed a colonial renaissance with Jules Ferry as its apostle. Hesitant at first, Germany succumbed to the blandishments of empire once colonialism offered advantages consonant with economic growth at home. Italy would have what she could take and hold in Africa. The Russians and the Austro-Hungarians were able to identify their imperialisms with age-old expansionist ambitions. And in the Orient Japan bore witness to the exportability of imperialism as she developed along industrial, commercial, and financial lines. The United States did not remain immune to this new imperialist surge, nor could she afford to be indifferent to the implications it held for her world position. It remained to be seen if the American Republic would enter into the competition for empire and, should the move come about, whether it would arise from conscious motivation or accidental involvement.

Any number of forces were at work in *fin-de-siècle* America, some merely contemporary and others more profoundly a part of the nation's history, that rendered imperialism a logical if not an inevitable step. The American people were in this way conditioned for empire, whether of design or circumstance. Whatever the sources of this imperial commitment, they were part of the American past and present. Americans favored imperialism insofar as they were to experience it because the very considerations preparing them for acceptance were consistent with important elements of their national traditions. The nation was much like the man in this respect. Just as the early years of Theodore Roosevelt witnessed the formulation of a set of principles that would one day determine his imperialist outlook, likewise the earlier history of his people, in combination with whatever interpretations contemporaries made of it and its destiny, revealed tendencies toward imperialism that circumstances in the 1890's readily drew out into overt action.

The sources of American imperialism were a complex of the humanitarian, the racial, the religious, the strategic, and the economic; of subtle emotional drives and barefaced nationalistic craving. All in all, it was a mixture of varied and conflicting ingredients. The nation was large in population and extent, its society heterogeneous, its economy both diverse and expanding, its history a record of conquest and self-rule. No simple argument would possibly serve to explain the phenomenon of United States expansion abroad and no single individual, however complex or thoroughly American he might be, can be expected to mirror faithfully its total image. By no means did Theodore Roosevelt produce a full effect. There were certain important aspects of the image he simply did not reflect. He lacked Albert Beveridge's appreciation of and sympathy for the economic possibilities of empire, for one thing, and the mission of spreading spiritual Christianity as advocated by religious leaders like Josiah Strong he instinctively diluted and diverted to humanitarianism. Despite such prominent lapses one can discover a remarkable alignment between the generally recognized sources of United States imperialism and Roosevelt's own views, which prior to 1897 were necessarily of a nonpolicy nature. In short, Roosevelt was generally in tune with the imperialist serenade of the nineties, lending his voice to it and having his own imperialist convictions refined and strengthened in turn.

The movement Roosevelt committed himself to was not, according to his own view, imperialism in any established sense but the same kind of expansion that had typified American continental growth. He disavowed the old style of conquest, insisting that

the simple truth is there is nothing even remotely resembling imperialism or militarism involved in the present [1900] development of that policy of expansion which has been part of America from the day she became a nation. The words mean absolutely nothing as applied to our present policy in the Philippines.[1]

The basis of his judgment was the positive nature of the results of such expansion. The backward races profited by contact with more advanced peoples and civilizations, learning among other things the techniques of self-rule, while the expansive nations grew stronger as they demonstrated their superiority. Such was Roosevelt's definition of American imperialism. The strong political complexion of his mind was likewise displayed in the humanitarianism he discovered in American expansion. The supreme contribution that an advanced people made to another was to provide the conditions out of which the lesser races grew to political maturity. For Roosevelt there was no more effective way to help one's fellow man.

In Theodore Roosevelt's personal evolution as an expansionist, as with the nation at large, the most tangible expression was navalism. It amounted to a passion in him that the United States join the ranks of the naval powers, for the possession of a great

1. To E. O. Wolcott, September 15, 1900, (letter of acceptance of the Vice-Presidential nomination), *Letters*, II, pp. 1403–1404.

fleet was the most obvious and elemental means of achieving national stature in the modern age. His delight with the implements of war, an expression of his martial instincts, was readily apparent. Nationalism rather than navalism was the underlying feeling, however, unifying as it did the sense of Anglo-Saxon racial and political superiority, the means of spreading Christian ethical principles, and the tide of history in a single creed. In the world of the 1890's the nationalistic faith was made manifest most surely by the deeds of a truly powerful navy. In his appreciation of the role of a navy in the history and destiny of nations Roosevelt came markedly under the spell cast by Captain Mahan whose books, beginning with *The Influence of Sea Power in History* (1890), he read with consuming interest and discussed enthusiastically. By the time of his appointment as Assistant Secretary of the Navy in the McKinley Administration in April 1897 Roosevelt had become one of the most determined spokesmen for an enlarged American fleet, exposing further his own militarist inclinations.

His concern for the Navy as a power political factor began with his study of naval strategy in the War of 1812. He entitled his first book, an analysis of that strategy, *The History of the Naval War of 1812*. In it he argued implicitly that had the Navy been ready to fight, there would have been no war, for the British would have avoided taking on a well-fitted and well-manned American fleet. The policy of naval neglect pursued by Jefferson and Madison had, to his way of thinking, directly encouraged the War of 1812 and its attendant calamities.[2] In Mahan with his sweeping interpretation of sea power as the decisive force in modern history Roosevelt found a mentor, friend, and confidant. When in the course of time Roosevelt assumed a position of influence relative to naval policy and statecraft the ideas of Mahan won an eloquent and gifted exponent in an Assistant Navy Secretary and a President of the United States.

2. Roosevelt, *The History of the Naval War of 1812, Works*, VII; see also Roosevelt, "The Influence of Sea Power on the French Revolution," *ibid.*, XIV, p. 324. William E. Livezey has an enlightening treatment of the thought of A.T. Mahan in *Mahan on Sea Power*, (Norman, 1947).

Roosevelt could not have been more sympathetic to the teachings and preachings of Mahan's first and major work, *The Influence of Sea Power in History,* with its argument that from the Punic Wars of Rome to the contemporary era military success or failure at sea had extensive formative effect on the ultimate triumph or defeat of nations.[3] He agreed with Mahan that England's sea power which made possible her empire in North America, India, Australia, and South Africa, combined with the jealous division of her two most formidable opponents in the quest for European leadership, gave England her world political power. Had it been otherwise, had England not maintained a strong navy or had France and Holland submerged their mutual antagonisms and united their fleets against England, "it might have changed the fate of the world; and if so, would probably have changed it much for the worse." [4] Race superiority and navalism combined in the same argument was a common feature of Roosevelt's imperialist thought, pointing up how one principle served to buttress another or to make a conclusion the more understandable.

As interested as Roosevelt was in the lessons that naval history offered, he was more eager that these lessons be made intelligible to his fellow Americans. The time might be all too short for him, and others who were conscious of America's destiny, to explain that destiny and the place a great navy perforce would occupy in its accomplishment. As early as 1890 he began firing salvos in favor of a naval establishment second to none. In his review of Mahan's first book, which appeared in the *Atlantic Monthly,* he vigorously advocated proper forts with heavy guns for coastal defense, bases of supply for offensive operations, and above all "the greatest need, a fighting fleet . . . a squadron of heavy battleships able to . . . attack; ships, the best of their kind, and plenty of them; a large navy, not merely cruisers but a full proportion of power-

3. Roosevelt, "The Influence of Sea Power on History," *Works,* XIV, p. 309.
4. *Ibid.,* p. 310; Roosevelt, "The Influence of Sea Power on the French Revolution," *ibid.,* pp. 323–324.

ful battleships." [5] Thus began Roosevelt's public campaign to sell the American people on the indispensability of a big navy.

One of the strongest and most effective selling points was the Mahan-Roosevelt contention that the era of hurried naval construction—in a word, improvisation—had been brought to an end by the emergence of the heavy, technically complicated, and altogether imposing modern battleship. Ingenuity and enthusiasm, they argued, could no longer substitute for or offset the existence of many well-constructed ships and the long training and the strict discipline needed to transform them into a fighting fleet. Conclusions drawn from the naval wars of the French Revolution were clear and undeniable. "No amount of fiery enthusiasm or talent could take the place of cool methodical courage, and of the skill acquired in the course of long years employed solely in the handling of such formidable and delicate engines of war." [6] In consequence, Roosevelt went on, America should be alert to what it had to do. The steady technological improvement of fighting ships since Copenhagen (1801) and Trafalgar (1805) made a patriotically inspired and intelligently conceived long-range plan of naval construction and training imperative. The whole concept of naval strategy was being rethought and the details of naval tactics and training restudied. The United States could not allow itself to be caught off guard in a position of permanent naval inferiority by neglecting to move in new directions. [7]

In his appeal for a strong navy Roosevelt stressed the fighting qualities of the captains and naval ratings, qualities that seemed to be summed up admirably, if in a facile way, by the character of the English sea captain Horatio Nelson. To Roosevelt, Nelson was a "proper combination of strict obedience to orders with liberty of individual action among his subordinates . . . [showing] the necessity of initiative and self-reliance. . . ." [8] Without true fighting men no amount of exertion in the interests of naval construction would be worthwhile. The Navy must be manned by those

5. Roosevelt, "The Influence of Sea Power on History," *ibid.*, pp. 315–316.
6. Roosevelt, "The Influence of Sea Power on the French Revolution," *ibid.*, p. 321.
7. *Ibid.*, p. 322.
8. *Ibid.*, p. 323.

who would fight, for the fighting man epitomized for Theodore Roosevelt the very highest ideal. The "fighting edge" was the sign of a mighty and masterful people. In his discussion of Mahan's *Life of Nelson* he contended almost fanatically that "no merchant, no banker, no railroad magnate, no inventor . . . can do for any nation what can be done by its fighting men. No triumph of peace," he went on, "can equal the armed triumph. . . . It is better for a nation to produce one Grant or one Farragut than a thousand shrewd manufacturers or successful speculators." [9] The extremes of this denunciation, Roosevelt must have judged, were warranted by the urgency of his purpose. For while every effort had to be made to procure superiority in force and equipment, in battle fortune still favored the brave.[10]

Roosevelt's apparent reluctance to accept the struggles common in the business world as part of the greater struggle of life reveals more than his economic obtuseness. Despite the commercial background of the Roosevelts in New York City, he had a mixture of contempt and suspicion toward those who devoted themselves to the accumulation of wealth. His father's philanthropic career partly accounted for this, and in addition the conquering frontiersman and the lone hunter exhibited for him a glamour altogether wanting in the countinghouses. The misuse and ostentation of wealth that characterized American society during Roosevelt's formative years were added considerations. It amounted to a matter of temperament. "I am simply unable to understand the value placed by so many people upon great wealth," he once observed with a sense of perplexity to Sir Cecil Spring-Rice.[11] Environment may also help to explain temperament. The ample means of the Roosevelt family—the contest that had been waged for its wealth was part of the ancestral past—prevented T.R. from respecting economic struggle, just as it relieved him of the necessity of participating in the businessman's determined battle for success.

9. Roosevelt, "Captain Mahan's *Life of Nelson*", *ibid.*, p. 330.
10. *Ibid.*, p. 332.
11. To Sir Cecil Spring-Rice, April 11, 1908, Roosevelt *Mss.*

The ever more strident navalism Theodore Roosevelt personally harbored and frequently gave expression to should be seen
against the background of steadily mounting imperialist agitation
in the United States dating from the late 1880's. Particularly following the defeat of the cautious Cleveland in 1888 and Harri-
son's appointment of James G. Blaine—"Jingo Jim"—as his
Secretary of State, the imperialist cadence quickened. From the
new President on down Americans talked more and more of a new
phase of manifest destiny to be fulfilled in the backward areas of
the world among backward peoples. All manner of men, though
not all men, spoke easily of an American empire, of far-off places
made contiguous by the Navy. In Beveridge's later idiom, the very
elements were in league with American destiny.

It was a movement to which Roosevelt was unreservedly committed. He believed in outright annexation of Hawaii and wanted
to see the United States construct an interoceanic canal and
vigorously uphold the Monroe Doctrine; for all these undertakings a great navy was indispensable. That these objectives could
probably be accomplished only by some kind of military action
was more a stimulant than a deterrent to him. Roosevelt thought
of American expansion in terms of the dominance of superior nations over the lesser breeds and the waste spaces of the globe.
And civilization advanced, for as expansion took place the tropical
races became civilized in the process, and relations between them
and the imperial powers could then follow the settled pattern of
international conduct and morality.[12]

England, of course, had been long in the forefront of western
expansion, doing her great work of conquest and settlement in
India, Egypt, South Africa, and Australia. The most important
single consideration about British imperialism was that it had ad-

12. Roosevelt to Lodge, October 27, 1894, *Selections from the Correspondence of Theodore Roosevelt and Henry Cabot Lodge, 1884–1918*, 2 volumes,
(New York, 1921), I, p. 319; hereafter cited as *Roosevelt-Lodge Correspondence*.
See also Roosevelt, "National Life and Character," *Works*, XIV, p. 247. John
A. Garraty's *Henry Cabot Lodge* (New York, 1953) gives recurring attention
to the Roosevelt-Lodge relationship. It was an intimate friendship but Lodge
added nothing distinctive to Roosevelt's imperialist outlook, though his friendly
agreement often reassured T.R. in his own views.

vanced the welfare of mankind. As Roosevelt observed to Henry White in 1896, "I feel it is in the interest of civilization that the English-speaking races should be dominant in South Africa," [13] even though he had undisguised admiration for the Boer farmers who stood across the path of a British Africa from Cape to Cairo. Occasionally the advance of civilization could not avoid military action, as demonstrated by the Boer War; but usually the people under British rule were the lesser races over whom a strict supervision was indispensable for international law and order.

Writing to Spring-Rice in 1897 Roosevelt remarked that he did not much like the look of things in India at that time owing to the growth of "liberalism" both in England and in India. He called the English position in India "essentially false" because they could not hope to rule justly and still subject themselves to questions and questioning by the natives. The solution he suggested was a direct and an unambiguous one: "If the English in India would suppress promptly any native newspaper that was seditious, arrest instantly any seditious agitator, put down the slightest outbreak ruthlessly; cease to protect usurers and encourage the warlike races as long as they were absolutely devoted to British rule" all would be well.[14] A decade and a half later Roosevelt was heard offering the same advice about British rule in Egypt, which he discovered lacked the firmness and resolve necessary to promote order and progress. "Govern or go" from Egypt, he told a Guildhall audience in London in 1910. In the intervening years his mind had changed little enough on the right of the superior nations to rule.

The same elements of race superiority, utilization of force, and progress for mankind—the components of confident imperialism —that Roosevelt was able to discern in British overseas success he associated with the stirrings of American imperialism toward the close of the nineteenth century. There was an instructive analogy between British domination in South Africa and the position of the United States in the Western Hemisphere, for example. The former was "exactly as the latter should be," he told Henry

---

13. To Henry White, March 30, 1896, *Letters*, I, p. 523.
14. To Sir Cecil Spring-Rice, August 13, 1897, Roosevelt *Mss.*

White.[15] To Lord Bryce he expressed the view that the United States "ought to take Hawaii in the interests of the white race," just as England would be doing her duty as a civilized nation if she overthrew the Mahdists and opened up the Sudan."[16] And somewhat later as the United States was assuming control of the Philippines, Roosevelt, reflecting on the experience of ruling over a backward people, said he believed that it would do "an incalculable amount" for American character as British governance in Egypt had done for British character.[17]

Theodore Roosevelt gave increasing attention to America's world position in the 1890's. The two areas, he concluded, where it was possible for the United States to come into some kind of political tutelage of backward peoples were Cuba and the Philippines. His thoughts about the problems of rule over these peoples, considerably before American colonialism became an actuality, show that though the American and British imperialist purposes were similar, a perfect identity did not exist between them. The difference was the more explicit intention of the Americans, when the time came, to act as political mentors of less able races in order that they might have an understanding of self-rule and thereby gain the ability to conduct their own governments freely. The whole process would take time of course, but because of their own heritage and history Americans felt strongly, even more than the British, that the effort must be made. "If we have a right to establish a stable government," Roosevelt argued, "it follows that it is not only our right but our duty to support that government until the natives grow fit to sustain themselves."[18] Yet a people cannot have civilization thrust upon it. Roosevelt insisted upon the danger of plunging a people into self-rule without adequate preparation. It was the supreme right and duty of the mentor nation to bring a backward race along. Genuinely desirous that the Cubans and the Filipinos have liberty, he held that it must be

15. To Henry White, March 30, 1896, *Letters,* I, p. 523.
16. To James Bryce, September 10, 1897, *ibid.,* p. 803.
17. To Sir Cecil Spring-Rice, December 2, 1899, quoted in Howard K. Beale, *Theodore Roosevelt and the Rise of America to World Power,* (Baltimore, 1956), p. 164.
18. To Anna Roosevelt Cowles, August 25, 1896, Roosevelt *Manuscript,* p. 73.

liberty with order, liberty guaranteed at first by the American flag, with that protection continuing until such time as that guarantee had outlived its necessity.

Like no other pre-1898 incident the Anglo-Venezuelan boundary dispute, which flared up in 1895, provided Theodore Roosevelt and a great many other Americans with a suitable occasion to give vent to the rising nationalist-navalist spirit. Roosevelt's old friend Henry Cabot Lodge had introduced a Senate resolution, as Congress opened in December of 1895, that stated in part that "any attempt on behalf of any European power to take or acquire new territory on the American continent whether under the pretense of boundary dispute or otherwise" would be considered a hostile act by the United States. Roosevelt wrote Lodge to say that he was "delighted" with this firm position.[19] A few days later when Cleveland's message to the Congress declared that the United States would defend any Venezuelan claim that, after investigation, it considered just, Roosevelt again expressed his personal satisfaction to Lodge, adding, "I think the immense majority of our people will back him [Cleveland]." [20]

To Roosevelt the issue at stake in this boundary controversy was the Monroe Doctrine. This was made clear in his support of the position taken by Cleveland and his Secretary of State, Olney, in a letter by Harvard man Roosevelt to the editors of the *Harvard Crimson* published January 7, 1896. To oppose the Administration's stand in the dispute, he told the editors, was a betrayal of the American cause, "the cause not only of national honor but in reality of international peace." Reminding them that it had been a Harvard man, John Quincy Adams, who had formulated the Monroe Doctrine, he went on to point out that the doctrine maintains that the United States will not "acquiesce in any territorial aggrandizement by a European power on American soil at

19. To Henry Cabot Lodge, December 6, 1895, *Letters*, I, 498.
20. To Henry Cabot Lodge, December 20, 1895, *ibid.*, p. 500; to William S. Cowles, December 22, 1895, *ibid.*, p. 501.

the expense of an American state." The United States could not permit European states to decide whether they might seize territory. Such a policy, or rather the abandonment of policy that in his judgment this attitude entailed, simply served to invite European aggression and the consequent disruption of the peace of the hemisphere and the world. Nor did Roosevelt miss the opportunity of stressing that in a showdown with Great Britain or any would-be aggressor a defense of the Monroe Doctrine would depend to a critical extent on the effectiveness of the Navy. The two, the Monroe Doctrine and the Navy, were linked inextricably together. It would be militarily impossible to keep the hemisphere free of foreign intervention without a large navy and diplomatically very foolish to threaten the use of force if insufficient force was available. In closing the letter to the *Crimson* he urged "the strictest application of the Monroe Doctrine" and "immediate preparation" to build a "really first-class fleet." [21]

Two months later Roosevelt sought a wider and more popular audience for his views in "The Monroe Doctrine," an article that appeared in *Bachelor of Arts* (March 1896). Responsive to the imperialist mood, he began by discussing the Monroe Doctrine as the touchstone of American foreign policy. His reason for reiterating his stand was not hard to fathom. As public debate had demonstrated, the American people had not rallied as a man to the firm posture assumed by the Cleveland Administration in the Venezuelan affair. The business community was split in its reaction, some elements supporting the President's stand and others suspicious and fearful that as a result of a hard policy line the international situation might become so disrupted as to thwart the commercial prosperity just then returning after the Panic of 1893. [22]

In making clear the views of those who supported Cleveland's position Roosevelt was at great pains to present the Monroe Doctrine as an instrument of national prestige and honor. To his way of thinking it was "not a question of law at all. It is a question of

---

21. To the Editors, *Harvard Crimson*, January 2, 1896, *ibid.*, pp. 505–506.
22. For an analysis of the reaction of the American business community to the Venezuelan crisis see Walter LaFeber, *The New Empire*, (Ithaca, 1963), pp. 271–276.

policy. It is a question to be considered not only by statesmen, but by all good citizens." [23] "Primarily, our action is based on national self-interest. In other words it is patriotic." [24] It was not surprising that in this frame of mind he revealed a degree of nationalism and national pride of an extreme kind. It was somewhat more indicative of the roots of his imperialist philosophy, however, that he saw a direct comparison between the useful individual and the useful nation, with usefulness measured by a yardstick of individual accomplishment. "The useful member of a community," he observed, "is the man who first and foremost attends to his own rights and his own duties. . . . The useful member of the brotherhood of nations is that nation which is most thoroughly saturated with the national ideal, and which realizes most fully its rights as a nation and its duties to its own citizens." [25]

Yet such an attitude did not in Roosevelt's mind preclude the responsibilities that attend the possession of power. There must always be, he thought, a scrupulous regard for the rights of other nations.[26] From these premises he proceeded logically: It was in the self-interest of the United States and the other nations of the Western Hemisphere to prevent further colonial growth by Britain or by any other power. Venezuela, he emphasized, was an independent nation, not a colonial dependency, and it had already taken its first crucial steps toward freedom. In the interests of the Venezuelans themselves and for the continued peace of her neighbors Venezuela had to be protected in its development toward full freedom. In this one instance at least, where the advantages offered by England clashed with the interests of the United States, the English stood in the way of progress in Roosevelt's judgment, and American sympathy for her was "immediately forfeited." [27] He acknowledged the opposition of some bankers, merchants, and railway magnates to what he termed a truly patriotic policy, describing their attitude as "essentially ignoble." And he

23. Roosevelt, "The Monroe Doctrine," *Works*, XV, p. 225.
24. *Ibid.*, p. 228.
25. *Ibid.*, p. 229.
26. *Ibid.*, p. 229.
27. *Ibid.*, p. 234.

wrote, one feels with intentional bitterness: "When a question of national honor or national right or wrong is at stake, no question of financial interest should be considered for a moment."[28] If Roosevelt had not convinced the money men of their patriotic duty, he had nevertheless revealed that his own imperialist outlook lacked, at that point in its refinement, a specific, positive economic quality.

The position that Roosevelt espoused in the Venezuelan boundary dispute was both popular and nationalistic. By emphasizing the positive thrust of the Monroe Doctrine he advocated an alarming extension of its meaning, but by no means was he lacking distinguished company in his views.[29] It would be difficult to prove and unwise to contend that the tough line advocated by Roosevelt worked toward a solution of the Venezuelan boundary dispute without war and in such a way as to enhance American prestige. Secretary Olney presumably needed neither instruction nor encouragement in the art of hard-line diplomacy; his ultimatumlike note of July 20, 1895, to the British Government was forceful enough to have satisfied and reassured the most outspoken jingoist. And Cleveland's message to the Congress in December made firmness official Unites States policy.

Great Britain chose not to view the imbroglio so seriously. The truth is that Britain was approaching a period of crucial decisions in her over-all diplomatic commitments. The Kruger telegram (January 3, 1896) came as a grim reminder of imperial Germany's challenge in world areas of far more concern to her than Venezuela. This, combined with the close economic ties linking Britain and the United States and the sentimental attachments of the two English-speaking nations, convinced Prime Minister Lord Salisbury, that arbitration was the wisest policy. Roosevelt endorsed the American agreement to an arbitration convention to settle the dispute,[30] for in his judgment genuine arbitration would mean that

28. *Ibid.*, p. 236.
29. Dexter Perkins in *A History of the Monroe Doctrine* (Boston, 1955) has a thorough and critical discussion of the aggressive meaning given the Monroe Doctrine by American expansionism during the Venezuelan crisis; see pp. 171–185.
30. To Henry White, March 11, 1897, *Letters*, I, p. 584.

"our point is made, and hereafter European nations will recognize that the Monroe Doctrine is a living entity." [31] The practical meaning of the Anglo-Venezuelan difficulty was simple enough to T.R.: The United States must be willing to arbitrate honestly and get on with the construction of a powerful navy.[32]

In April 1897, just a year before the Spanish War and the imperial acquisitions that were its legacy, Theodore Roosevelt took office as Assistant Secretary of the Navy. It was an appointment he owed to his long-standing and well-known interest in the American Navy almost as much as to the exertions on his behalf of Senator Lodge and others. Whatever President-elect McKinley may have known or thought of his Assistant Navy Secretary when he agreed to his appointment, Lodge recognized him as a big Navy man, an avowed nationalist, and something of a racist in matters imperial. His reputation as a naval publicist was secure by that time, for over the years he had repeatedly advocated an enlarged fleet, linking it with the national interest. He once confided to Sir Cecil Spring-Rice that shock might be the best treatment after all for dispelling Americans' foolish illusions about naval preparedness. "Frankly, I don't know that I should be sorry to see a bit of a spar with Germany," he said; "the burning of New York and a few other sea coast cities would be a good object lesson on the need of an adequate system of coast defence." [33] His conviction was sincere enough, though clearly excessive.

The general tenor of the McKinley Administration and the particular attitudes of both the President and his Navy Secretary did not augur well for the policies that might be urged by a strenuous "new Navy" man like Roosevelt. McKinley himself was not much interested in the Navy and Secretary John Davis Long, cautious by nature, became dependent for advice on Rear Admiral A. S. Crowninshield, an ultraconservative officer.[34] Although Roosevelt on occasion presumed to go directly to the President in Navy matters the critical personal relationship was between the Secre-

31. To William S. Cowles, February 11, 1896, *ibid.*, p. 512.
32. *Ibid.*, p. 512.
33. To Sir Cecil Spring-Rice, April 14, 1889, Roosevelt *Mss.*
34. Harold and Margaret Sprout, *The Rise of American Naval Power, 1776–1918,* (Princeton, 1946), pp. 224–225.

tary and his Assistant. The Long-Roosevelt association did not run smoothly despite a favorable beginning. Roosevelt had protested sincerely to Lodge in March before his appointment that "my aim should be solely to make his [Long's] administration a success."[35] And Long's journal entry for April 9, 1897, bore out this impression: "Roosevelt calls. Just appointed Assistant Secretary of Navy. Best man for the place."[36]

Misunderstanding and friction set in nonetheless, a state of affairs that revealed not merely the personality clash between the young, aggressive "new Navy" enthusiast and the prudential political administrator, though there was enough of that,[37] but a fundamental conflict over official policy. By June Roosevelt was writing confidentially to Mahan of his belief that Secretary Long was "only lukewarm about building up our Navy, at any rate as regards battleships." He sought to enlist Mahan's support in "explaining to him the vital need of more battleships now and the vital need of continuity in our naval policy," adding knowingly, that "this is a measure of peace and not of war."[38]

Long for his part was disturbed by some of the warlike utterances of his young Assistant. Though he made no effort to censor Roosevelt's June address at the Naval War College, "Washington's Forgotten Maxim," he seemed to have learned a lesson from that omission. Later that summer he instructed Roosevelt to make certain modifications to tone down his article entitled "The Naval Policy of America Outlined in the Messages of the Presidents of the United States from the Beginning to the Present Day." This paper, which was published in the *Proceedings* of the United States Naval Institute in the autumn of 1897, consisted of excerpts from the writings of the Presidents from Washington to Cleveland, all of which expressed demands for a powerful navy.

35. To Henry Cabot Lodge, March 29, 1897, *Roosevelt-Lodge Correspondence,* I, p. 262. Long, of course, gave the final approval of Roosevelt's appointment partly, it appears, because Roosevelt had "a hearty interest in the navy." John Davis Long, *The New American Navy,* 2 volumes, (New York, 1903), II, p. 173.

36. John Davis Long, *The America of Yesterday as Reflected in the Journal of John Davis Long,* Lawrence S. Mayo, Editor, (Boston, 1923), p. 147.

37. Margaret Long, *The Journal of John D. Long,* (Rindge, N.H., 1956) p. 213.

38. To Alfred T. Mahan, June 9, 1897, Roosevelt *Mss.*

Its purpose was to show that naval expansion was a historic and traditional policy regardless of time, party, or President. After Long's admonition Roosevelt agreed to "adopt exactly the rule you suggest about my official publications and about my general utterances also." [39]

It would be a mistake, however, to view Roosevelt's time as Assistant Navy Secretary in terms of a challenge and response relationship with Long. He saw himself as fighting not merely the timidity of Long but the caution of the McKinley Administration, the hostility of many Navy professionals like Crowninshield, and the ignorance of the general public.[40] Furthermore, he was not merely committed to persuading others that his views were the correct ones; he was anxious to assume a controlling influence in the affairs of the Navy because they had the very largest implications for matters of state.

Shortly after assuming the Navy office in June 1897 Roosevelt delivered his first formal address, "Washington's Forgotten Maxim," to the officers of the Naval War College. He had been an advocate of the War College over the years [41] and as Assistant Secretary appreciated its potential as a strategic planning agency.[42] His speech at the college, under the circumstances, had to be interpreted as quasi-official United States Navy policy. At the very least the views expressed were the sincere convictions of a responsible Administration officer. In the address Roosevelt was at his most warlike. The talk bristled with an adventurous, militaristic spirit that contended that "no triumph of peace is quite so great as the supreme triumphs of war;" [43] it spoke of national battles of the past—Bunker Hill, New Orleans, Gettysburg—as the repositories of national greatness.[44] Roosevelt presented militarism

39. To John Davis Long, August 26, 1897, *ibid.*
40. See to Lt. William Fullam, June 28, 1897, *ibid.;* to William S. Cowles, August 3, 1897, *Letters,* I, p. 637.
41. To Alfred T. Mahan, May 1, 1893, *ibid.*, p. 315.
42. To W.W. Kimball, December 17, 1897, *ibid.*, p. 743.
43. Roosevelt, "Washington's Forgotten Maxim," *Works,* XV, p. 243.
44. *Ibid.*, p. 245.

as operating in the interests of civilization. "That orderly liberty which is both the foundation and the capstone of our civilization can be gained and kept only by men who are willing to fight for an ideal." [45] He had imbibed fully the martial spirit and through his influence wanted to help build that spirit to a national resolve. No prewar speech revealed more completely or more certainly his imperialist anticipation.

Washington's forgotten maxim, he told his Naval War College audience, was that "to prepare for war is the most effectual means to promote peace." The word arbitration had been much in use since the Venezuelan boundary trouble, so Roosevelt began his remarks by noting that though arbitration is "an excellent thing," those who sincerely desire peace for the United States "will be wise if they place reliance upon a first-class fleet of battleships rather than on any arbitration treaty which the wit of man can devise." [46] In his own phrase, "peace is a goddess only when she comes with sword girt on thigh." [47] War was seen always in the light of national honor and national greatness. "All the great masterful races have been fighting races and the minute that a race loses the hard fighting virtues, then no matter what else it may retain, no matter how skilled in commerce and finance, in science or in art, it has lost its proud right to stand as an equal of the best." [48] Yet even in such moments of patriotic catharsis, Roosevelt could not avow that might made right. "The rigid determination to wrong no man, and to stand for righteousness" was no less important than the fighting instincts.[49] A nation must have moral as well as physical courage as part of its greatness.

All of this dramatizes a dualism in Roosevelt's thought: the conflict between his passion for military force and a noble desire for human progress. His rationalization of his own ego drive cannot obscure the primitiveness of the instinct calling for the use of force as the ultimate and justifiable solution in the affairs of men. Yet his appeal to some higher ideal or to the lessons of history

45. *Ibid.*, p. 244.
46. *Ibid.*, p. 241.
47. *Ibid.*, p. 242.
48. *Ibid.*, p. 242.
49. *Ibid.*, p. 244.

was too consistent and too typical of his whole outlook to be dismissed as hypocrisy. Roosevelt was at times contradictory because he clung to diverse principles, committed to each, yet not totally so.

Roosevelt had come to his martial feelings instinctively perhaps. Yet he was careful in addressing the War College officers to make use, as Mahan did, of the lessons of history. The Romans, the Dutch, the English were all great peoples contributing to progress because they possessed moral and physical qualities of a high order. More particularly, American history had demonstrated the need for both moral and physical preparation to face national crises. The War of 1812 had proved that moral fortitude alone was not enough, that a navy was indispensable to defend national honor and reap national advantage. The lessons of 1812, he added, "apply with tenfold greater force today."

The ascendency of Mahan in Roosevelt's thinking could not have been more pronounced. Just as Mahan had argued that the era of improvisation for sea warfare was over, so Roosevelt advocated the immediate construction of battleships, cruisers, torpedo boats, and heavy coastal guns, noting how little of each the Navy had on hand and that many weeks or months would be required to provide such heavy equipment. It should be appreciated by everyone, he went on, that the United States could not wait until war broke out to make plans to build a fleet. National greatness, national survival, the welfare of mankind all were contingent upon the existence of a large navy. In particular, a great fleet of battleships was imperative if the United States intended to maintain the Monroe Doctrine.[50]

"Washington's Forgotten Maxim" was an important pronouncement by Theodore Roosevelt, essential for understanding the unifying quality that navalism imparted to his thought. For a considerable period, beginning noticeably with his exposure to Mahan's ideas and building up with increasing intensity as he became an official in the McKinley Administration, he viewed the imperialist movement in terms of an expanded role for the Navy. But despite his extraordinary emphasis on the Navy, of which his

50. *Ibid.*, p. 255.

Naval War College address was much the most impressive but by no means the only evidence, to Roosevelt the Navy was a means to an end. That end was the advance of civilization through the greatness of the American nation. A powerful navy was a tangible symbol of this and, if need be, a concrete force to achieve it with— a force for whose fighting trim he was at the time very personally responsible.[51]

Speeches and grand strategy aside, the work of assisting Secretary Long at the Navy Department went forward. In fact putting the Navy in a state of readiness and planning the wisest possible use of such a force constituted the most valuable contributions of Theodore Roosevelt to the American Navy in 1897–1898. Readiness, he realized, included provisions for reliable and effective matériel, and personnel possessing technical competence and initiative in addition to well-derived tactics. The job was a major one but Roosevelt was enthusiastic, absorbed more and more in his work, and delighted "to be dealing with matters of real moment and of great interest. . . ."[52]

Assistant Secretary Roosevelt was a painstaking administrator of the matériel and personnel under his charge, a trait that his chief, Secretary Long, appreciated but sometimes found exasperating.[53] Not content to operate from behind a desk, he made frequent inspection trips to Navy yards and to the fleet.[54] In his concern for an efficient navy he often had to deal with somewhat technical matters.[55] American adoption of the new torpedo boat

51. Roosevelt's postwar analysis of why the Navy had done so well in the Spanish War and the Army so relatively poorly was a strongly-argued brief for military preparedness. To him the difference was a difference of preparedness. See Roosevelt, "Military Preparedness and Unpreparedness," *Works*, XV, pp. 293–306.

52. To Bellamy Storer, August 19, 1897, Roosevelt *Mss;* see also to John Davis Long, August 26, 1897, *ibid.*

53. To William E. Chandler, September 23, 1897, *ibid.;* to John Davis Long, December 9, 1897, *ibid.,* Long, *The New American Navy,* II, p. 174.

54. To Admiral Montgomery Sicard, June 17, 1897, Roosevelt *Mss;* to John Davis Long, August 1, 1897, *Letters,* I, p. 651.

55. For example, to John Davis Long, August 13, 1897, *ibid.,* pp. 649–650; to Long, December 9, 1897, Roosevelt *Mss.*

was a case in point. Roosevelt studied carefully reports of French and German experience with this type of craft in order to determine United States policy regarding its usefulness. He enlisted the opinions of the Bureau of Naval Construction and line officers preparatory to rendering his own judgment as to its tactical value.[56] In the end his decisions were his own responsibility, however, and were invariably made with the ultimate strategy role of the Navy as the foremost consideration. The sinking of the *Maine* had prompted some congressmen, for example, to contend that the battleship was too vulnerable to torpedo attack. Construction on them should cease, it was argued, and the building of monitor and torpedo boats be concentrated on. Such congressional proposals worked directly against Roosevelt's conception of the Navy as an instrument of national expansion, and he opposed this viewpoint from the outset.[57] No matter how immersed he might become in the technicalities of the Navy, strategic matters were never really very far from his mind.

As Assistant Secretary Roosevelt so well said, with respect to the employment of torpedo boats, "nothing but practice will teach a man how to get the best out of them." [58] In other words, the personnel of the Navy should be proficient if the Navy was to operate effectively.[59] The center of the difficulty in the Navy of that day was the reluctance of many senior officers to recognize that the era of the sailing vessel was at an end and that modern naval vessels were so complex as to render the conventional distinction between line and engineer officers both obsolete and dangerous to the national security. "Every officer on a modern war vessel in reality has to be an engineer whether he wants to or not," he pointed out to Secretary Long. Thus "what we need is one homogeneous body, all of whose members are trained for efficient performance of the duties of the modern line officer." This was not a matter in which the United States Navy really had a choice; it

56. To Charles Davis, June 28, 1897, *ibid.;* to John Davis Long, August 1, 1897, *Letters,* I, p. 651; to Long, February 18, 1898, Roosevelt, *Mss.*
57. To John Davis Long, February 19, 1898, *ibid.*
58. To John Davis Long, February 18, 1898, *Letters,* I, p. 776.
59. Roosevelt, "The Influence of Sea Power on the French Revolution," *Works,* XIV, pp. 321–323.

was "merely recognizing and giving shape to an evolution which had come slowly but surely and naturally." [60] Well aware of the opposition that a proposal for amalgamation of line and engineer officers would encounter, he argued nonetheless that "we must disregard the prejudices of the old-style line and the old-style engineer, precisely as two centuries ago it was necessary to disregard the prejudices of those who would have kept separate the functions of the man who fought the ship and the man who sailed her." [61]

Conservative resistance to the formation of "one homogeneous body" of officers was linked in part to promotion, since it was then American naval practice to promote everyone by strict seniority. This was a method that in Roosevelt's opinion produced "long stagnation" in the lower ranks and "questionable competence in command positions"; at the same time "a positive premium is put upon the man who never ventures to take a risk." [62] Upon coming into office Roosevelt had determined to change all this and to provide properly trained and competent personnel for the new Navy wherever it was lacking. There were plenty of expert and energetic naval officers, both he and Secretary Long agreed, but promotion by strict seniority had been responsible for an officer corps of uneven caliber.[63]

The Personnel Bill of 1898 that was designed to correct this situation was drawn up for Congressional action under Roosevelt's confident, aggressive leadership. At the behest of the Secretary of the Navy he presided over the meetings of a board of eleven senior officers who were charged with the task of devising a workable method of amalgamation. As the presiding board member Roosevelt expected and got results. A plan was worked out and later set forth in the Personnel Bill that combined limitations on time in grade and service record—the latter to be evaluated by a selection board of high-ranking naval officers—as the twin criteria for promotion or retirement. Under these provisions the

60. To John Davis Long, December 8, 1897, *Letters*, I, p. 728.
61. *Ibid.*, p. 731.
62. *Ibid.*, p. 732.
63. *Autobiography*, p. 210; Long, *The New American Navy*, II, p. 173.

very strong tendency was for the best officers to advance rapidly and the less fit to retire after twenty years' service. The junior grade officers thus were encouraged to a more effective performance of their duties with an eye to advancement in rank.[64]

Significant though the Personnel Bill was as a long-range plan to improve the effectiveness of the Navy, Roosevelt's supporting it had more immediate expression in the future career of one officer in particular, George Dewey. Dewey had posted a distinguished record as a young officer in the Civil War, where his coolness and daring were a matter of official report. More recently, he had been named in 1889 Chief of the Bureau of Naval Equipment and in 1895, President of the Board of Inspection and Survey, in which positions he displayed an understanding and sympathy for advanced design battleships, cruisers, and torpedo boats. Roosevelt was impressed with Dewey's record of resourcefulness and daring on the one hand and his enthusiasm for the new Navy concept on the other. He personally encouraged Dewey's appointment as commander of the Pacific Fleet in 1897 and advised him to enlist whatever political influence he could to secure the command. Dewey's nomination was earnestly supported by Senator Proctor of Vermont, a family friend, in addition to the Assistant Navy Secretary. Roosevelt was later to write: "I urged [his appointment] upon the specific ground that whoever was sent there [the Far East] might have to go into Manila and that Dewey would certainly do it." [65] It was Roosevelt's hope that the Naval Personnel Bill would eventually bring to command positions venturesome, responsible officers, but in the meantime more expeditious means could be employed on occasion to undo the mischief resulting from promotion by strict seniority. Roosevelt knew well the man in command of the Asiatic Squadron after November 1897. His famous cablegram to Dewey the following February 25, with its instructions to destroy the Spanish fleet and undertake offensive operations in the Philippines should hostilities between Spain and the United States break out, has been termed "repeti-

64. Roosevelt, "The Genesis of the Personnel Bill," *Works*, XIV, pp. 427–437 *passim*.
65. To Colonel F. Dibble, January 17, 1899, *Letters*, II, p. 915.

tive and premature." [66] But it stood out as part of the logic of Theodore Roosevelt as Assistant Secretary of the Navy.

The value to the nation of the Navy Roosevelt helped to fashion would be measured ultimately by the strategic uses to which it was put. He came to the Navy Department with a mind full of strategy as it related to his own conception of the national interest. In two areas, Cuba and the Philippines, events were to unfold that enabled him to influence in some considerable if indirect way the final meaning of these events for the United States. Roosevelt may have been excessive when he wrote in 1897 of building a Central American canal at once and of acquiring the Danish West Indies as well—even though a canal was constructed and the Virgin Islands purchased within his lifetime. But his insistence at the same time on immediate possession of Hawaii and the expulsion of Spain from Cuba must be taken with complete seriousness. [67] The Navy would be critical in the attainment of both these objectives, a navy which Roosevelt, having helped bring it to a fighting condition, was not unnaturally disposed to make yield to his estimate of what the national interest required. [68]

At the time of his appointment as Assistant Secretary, Hawaii seemed to press most heavily on Roosevelt's concern. In a matter of days after assuming office he was prompted to write to President McKinley that "within two weeks the battleship *Oregon* could be sent to Hawaii. Her commander is thoroughly acquainted with the harbor. . . ." [69] His great fear was that Japan would act before the United States; if that occurred the results would be disastrous. [70]

66. Margaret Leech, *In the Days of McKinley*, (New York, 1959) p. 169.
67. To Alfred T. Mahan, May 3, 1897, *Letters*, I, p. 607.
68. To John Davis Long, January 14, 1898, *ibid.*, p. 759.
69. To William McKinley, April 22, 1897, Roosevelt *Mss*. William R. Braisted has pointed out that even before Roosevelt assumed the Navy position Lt. W.W. Kimball, of Naval Intelligence, had completed a comprehensive plan for naval operations in the Far East should war with Spain occur. He has suggested that Roosevelt accepted the Kimball plan of operations. See William R. Braisted, *The United States Navy in the Pacific, 1897–1909*, (Austin, 1958), pp. 21–22.
70. For example, to Alfred T. Mahan, June 9, 1898, Roosevelt *Mss;* to Captain Gaspar Goodrich, June 16, 1897, *ibid.*

This worry appeared also in an April report to Secretary Long, in which he showed further that the dispatch of war vessels to the Far East that he had suggested to McKinley would "yet leave a force which would be available at 24 hours notice in the event of things in Cuba taking an unexpected turn." [71] A two-ocean war being a possibility, it was simple prudence to plan accordingly. Neither McKinley nor Long displayed much interest in Roosevelt's particular suggestions or proddings, though the President himself was alive to American national interests in the Pacific, including the commercial advantages of annexing Hawaii.[72]

Dismayed by lack of response from his superiors and fully convinced that the Hawaiian Islands should and would be taken by the United States, Roosevelt requested the Staff and Class of the Naval War College to work out an operational plan for a problem which, he wrote, would be "of interest and importance in certain contingencies." The problem posed was as follows.

SPECIAL CONFIDENTIAL PROBLEM FOR WAR COLLEGE
Japan makes demands on Hawaiian Islands
This country intervenes.
What force will be necessary to uphold intervention and how shall it be employed?
Keeping in mind possible complications with another Power on the Atlantic Coast (Cuba).[73]

As far as Theodore Roosevelt was concerned his task as Assistant Secretary was a simple one. As he informed President McKinley in December of 1897, his duty was to help put the Navy in "the best possible shape that our means would permit when war began." [74]

The strategy for war Roosevelt had persistently advocated took on a markedly nationalistic tone as the conflict neared. Even in noncrisis situations he instinctively associated American self-

71. To John Davis Long, April 26, 1897, *ibid.*
72. To Alfred T. Mahan, June 9, 1897, *ibid.*
73. To Captain Gaspar Goodrich, May 25, 1897, *ibid.*
74. To John Davis Long, December 9, 1897, *ibid.*

interest with the highest good.[75] With frustration settling upon him because of the attitude of Secretary Long, his sense of nationalism became even more pronounced.[76] The substance of these feelings can be read in "The Need of a Navy," an article intended for popular tastes that appeared in *Gunton's Magazine* in January 1898. Roosevelt wanted to educate public opinion in regard to military matters and the national interest. Fearful that "the whole temper of our people" would have to be changed for them to be able to appreciate the value of military means in the achievement of peaceful results, he promised "I will do my part toward trying to make them understand it." [77] "The Need of a Navy" bespoke Roosevelt's desire to inform the public of the causal link existing between American interests and the Naval Service. It contained a direct appeal for a great navy as the crucial "means for carrying out any policy on which the nation has resolved." To hold otherwise was to confess ignorance or, worse, a lack of the "robust patriotism common to most Americans." He hastened to reassure his readers that in possessing a navy "we haven't the slightest intention to bluster or to commit any wrong, yet if we are perfectly ready and willing to fight for our rights . . . then chances of war will become infinitesimal." The Navy, expansion into the Pacific, and the American greatness were mutually dependent parts of the same ideal. The United States' right to become the "great power of the Pacific" and the possession of Hawaii and the building up of the Navy together would meet "the needs of American greatness." [78]

In the privacy of correspondence Roosevelt went even further in revealing the nationalistic lineament of his outlook and his own ambitions to implement it. "I should myself like to shape our foreign policy with the purpose ultimately of driving off this continent every European power," he wrote Francis C. Moore in February 1898. "I am not hostile to any European power in the

75. For example, to Sir Cecil Spring-Rice, August 13, 1897, *ibid.*
76. To John Davis Long, December 9, 1897, *ibid.*
77. To William F. Fullam, June 28, 1897, *Letters*, I, p. 633; to William S. Cowles, August 3, 1897, *ibid.*, p. 637.
78. Roosevelt, "The Need of a Navy," *Gunton's Magazine*, January 1898, pp. 1–5 *passim.*

abstract. I am simply an American first and last. . . ." [79] The attitude so crisply expressed in this letter continued to becloud his assertions in support of internationalism when he became President.[80]

Throughout his months in office, concerned though he might become with the housekeeping chores of so large an establishment as the United States Navy, Roosevelt always came back to strategic considerations. The influence of Mahan was ever apparent. Mahan's appeal was bound to be strong for almost anyone whose nationalist and martial spirits had been aroused simultaneously. "I am a bit of a jingo," Roosevelt admitted to John Hay in November 1897, an understated appraisal of his state of mind at the time.[81] And his jingoism fitted well with the expansionist mood of the moment. Thus he could observe quite candidly to Mahan himself that like Mahan he favored the outright acquisition of Hawaii as part of national expansion: "I take your views [of an Hawaiian acquisition] absolutely, as indeed I do on foreign policy generally. . . ." [82] But whereas Mahan concentrated on the *Navy* as a means, and the chief one at that, of achieving national destiny, Roosevelt was more concerned with *national greatness* itself, to be brought about by a strong navy. The difference between them was perhaps only the difference between the Navy professional and the political professional, a matter of emphasis on the end and the means—a subtle shading at times but a distinction helpful for appreciating Roosevelt the imperialist statesman. Navalism was, after all, a phase of Roosevelt's growth toward imperial statesmanship and thus a single aspect of his total imperialist makeup.

It was a vigorously militaristic stage, Roosevelt spoke of "changing the whole temper of our people before they under-

79. To Francis C. Moore, February 9, 1898, *Letters*, I, pp. 771–772.

80. To John Davis Long, February 16, 1898, Roosevelt *Mss*.

81. To John Hay, November 4, 1897, *Letters*, I, p. 707. See also to Benjamin Diblee, February 16, 1897, *ibid.*, p. 775; to Bradley Johnson, March 7, 1898, *ibid.*, p. 789.

82. To Alfred T. Mahan, May 3, 1898, *ibid.*, I, p. 607; to Mahan, June 9, 1897, *ibid.*, p. 622.

stand that in military matters our military men should be listened to," [83] with congressmen perhaps those Americans in greatest need of education concerning preparations for war.[84] Further, the prospect of a fight was a highly personal affair for him. As he told McKinley, when the shooting started he could not long remain an armchair soldier. "I myself would go to war." [85] But it remained a phase in which the Navy, however large it loomed in his thought in 1897 and 1898, was only essentially an instrument of national policy. In a letter to Secretary Long he made this point. What was the use or good of retaining Alaska or annexing Hawaii unless the United States had a navy sufficiently strong to retain them for the advantage of the nation? Equally pertinent, how could the Monroe Doctrine be maintained effectively unless the Navy was on call to back up diplomacy with force? "A great navy does not make for war," he argued to his superior, "but for peace. It is the cheapest kind of insurance." [86] The peace of the world, out of which continued moral and material progress could be realized, was to be made possible in great part by American expansion, and a powerful Navy was indispensable for that end.

In after years Theodore Roosevelt would display some awareness of the dangers arising from greatly accelerated naval construction. An element of caution, which included a willingness to support the limitation of naval forces, was part of his thinking once the European naval race commenced in earnest. While President he disavowed any wish for the United States "to lead the race for big ships." Surveying the situation in 1906 he expressed himself satisfied that the American Navy had an adequate number of ships, though if other nations insisted on increased construction it was "well-nigh criminal for us to fall behind." At the same time he took the position that the relative sizes of the world's navies were appropriate to the political power they symbolized.

83. To William F. Fullam, June 28, 1897, *ibid.*, p. 633.
84. To Anna Roosevelt Cowles, March 1, 1896, *ibid.*, p. 519.
85. To Henry Cabot Lodge, September 15, 1897, *ibid.*, p. 695.
86. To John Davis Long, September 30, 1897, *ibid.*, p. 695.

He wrote approvingly of naval restrictions, provided all the nations including the United States agreed. As the naval arms build-up continued in the years after 1906, Roosevelt returned to the more bellicose posture of the 1890's, denouncing as "well-meaning but fatuous" those who opposed a steady enlargement of the United States fleet. As in the 1890's national prestige and national security, if not the peace of the world, made a strong navy imperative.[87]

As meaningful as peace was to Theodore Roosevelt in 1898 it had to be a peace working to the advantage of the United States. Any other condition was to his mind not peaceful at all but likely to produce war, since the great nations must, in view of their very greatness, possess the power to prosper and expand. "I am not hostile to any European power in the abstract," he had written a few weeks before the sinking of the *Maine*; "I am simply an American, first and last, and therefore hostile to any power which wrongs us." [88] It would be difficult to find words that summed up Roosevelt's thinking in 1898 more trenchantly than that. When the fuse of war was lighted by the loss of the *Maine*, more and more did the mood of the nation come to resemble that of Theodore Roosevelt. The American republic was ready to take the plunge. It was the right and duty of a great nation to expand; the responsibility that expansion entailed, which Roosevelt as a private citizen and a public man experienced most sensitively, could not and should not be avoided. He did not have to be told about the nexus of power and responsibility; his formative years had bred that in him. In the new sphere of American imperialism, however, he could know it only as an abstraction, something to be accepted and believed in but not yet known from experience. The fuller meaning came to him only in the course of time and events, during which his sense of duty as well as his will to power proved remarkably durable.

The year 1898 was, however, just the beginning. The task ahead for the United States appeared a large and an important

87. To Whitelaw Reid, December 19, 1906, Roosevelt *Mss;* to Andrew Carnegie, September 6, 1906, *ibid.;* to Henry White, September 13, 1906, *ibid.*
88. To Francis C. Moore, February 9, 1898, *Letters,* I, p. 772.

one to Rudyard Kipling. Writing to Roosevelt in September of that year he commented: "Now go in and put all the weight of your influence into hanging on permanently to the whole of the Philippines [sic]. America has gone and struck a pickaxe into the foundation of a rotten house and she is morally bound to build the house over again from the foundation or have it all about her ears." [89] "Morally bound"—the phrase and the prospect suited T.R. exactly.

89. Rudyard Kipling to Roosevelt, September 23, 1898, Roosevelt *Mss*.

3

An Imperialist President

I

Theodore Roosevelt could not have known, on September 15, 1898, when he bade a sentimental farewell to his Rough Riders during mustering-out ceremonies at Camp Wikoff, what his share in the new commitments of the United States brought on by the events of 1898 would be. He spoke that day of the strong ties he felt for his horsemen, riders, and cattle-herders-turned-cavalry-men, and as he undertook to press the hand of each of them he seemed to be addressing the past, both his own and that of the nation, somewhat more than the future.

But his future had already taken on a different and not unexciting turn for him, one that appeared far removed from both the western frontier and the Spanish War in any realistic estimate of the years immediately ahead. During the summer of 1898 Roosevelt had been approved—for the very practical reason of his popularity as a war hero—by Senator Thomas Collier Platt, the all-powerful Republican boss of New York State, as the party's candidate for the governorship. Having forthrightly resigned an office with national prestige at the Navy Department, he had won nationwide fame as a soldier. And now with a politician's sure instinct for building up a home base for whatever opportunities the future held, Roosevelt literally roared his delight at Lemuel Quigg, the senatorial emissary sent to sound the depths of his political ambition. Boss Platt, after all, was entitled to some doubts as to Roosevelt's reaction to his proposal to associate formally with him. The two men had often been at odds over both power and the corruption of it in the state of New York.

Roosevelt had come to the conclusion sometime before, however, that party loyalty was indispensable to an individual's success in the American system of government. And Albany held the kind of political power unknown on the western frontier, though in reality it was akin to the physical strength the West symbolized to the colonel of the Rough Riders. He was eager to wield that power—the Assistant Navy Secretaryship and the command in Cuba having combined to sharpen his innate will to rule—even if initially on the sufferance of Boss Platt. With machine backing and despite defections from the good-government advocates who misunderstood his intentions if not his methods, Roosevelt defeated his Tammany opponent, Augustus Van Wyck, by some eighteen thousand votes. Soon he was absorbed in promoting civil service reform, controversies over corporate taxation, and other cares proper to his newly-won office.

The demands of the governorship gave Roosevelt little enough time or opportunity to remain either officially or privately concerned with America's position in the imperialist world as it then stood or to control policy as it might influence the nation's destiny. But should circumstances unexpectedly contrive to return him to some official place of responsibility for America's world role, his policies would generally be predictable, for Roosevelt's imperialist outlook had by 1898 been formulated in its major principles; only corollaries and certain details remained to be worked out. And because of his frequently practical approach to matters of state, events themselves would have a considerable influence on the application of principles and thus on the final nature of Roosevelt's imperialism.

Circumstances, of course, did make Theodore Roosevelt the twenty-sixth President of the United States, the post of ultimate responsibility for American foreign policy. There are two remarkable aspects of the train of events bringing this wholly unpredictable event to pass. At first glance Roosevelt appears as a darling of destiny, the kick upstairs to the Vice-Presidency having turned to his complete advantage upon the death of McKinley. But a closer examination suggests a second, equally important consideration, namely, his willingness to cooperate with destiny. Thus he accepted Platt's support of his gubernatorial ambitions—though he had once observed with the ring of a man pronouncing an immutable judgment that "a decent man *must* oppose" Senator Platt [1]—because to have done otherwise would have been unfavorable to his political career ambitions.

Later he was persuaded to accept the Vice-Presidential nomination because of these same career ambitions. As governor he was able to maintain a constructive if uneasy relationship with Platt, but this might well have deteriorated into an open break during a second gubernatorial term. Platt saw in the Vice-Presidency for Roosevelt the all but perfect solution to his problem, if not to Roosevelt's. As the pressures to move him out of Albany were first discernible, Roosevelt expressed the view to Lodge that "the Vice-Presidency is a most honorable office but for a young man there is not much do to." [2] T.R. was outspoken in his preference for the governorship because, as he wrote to George H. Lyman, "the fact remains that in the Vice-Presidency I could do very little, whereas as Governor I can accomplish a great deal. . . ." [3] Yet when Republican Party machinery combined with the votes of convention delegates to direct him away from the governorship and toward the seemingly empty office of Vice-President, he acknowledged the party's call and was nominated, fittingly enough, by acclamation at the Republican Convention. [4] Political power as governor now denied him, he recognized the situation

1. To Henry Cabot Lodge, May 18, 1895, *Letters,* I, p. 458. For an account of Roosevelt as governor of New York and his relations with Platt in particular see G. Wallace Chessman, *Governor Theodore Roosevelt* (Cambridge, 1965).
2. To Henry Cabot Lodge, December 11, 1899, *Letters,* II, p. 1108.
3. To George H. Lyman, December 29, 1899, *ibid.,* II, p. 1120.
4. To Henry Cabot Lodge, December 30, 1899, *ibid.,* p. 1123. President McKinley refused to endorse any Vice-Presidential candidate, though he did not especially like Roosevelt. As a war hero T.R. possessed an irresistible glamour for the nomination and McKinley gave way before it. See H. Wayne Morgan, *William McKinley and His America* (Syracuse, 1963) and John Garraty, *Right Hand Man* (New York, 1957) for arresting discussions of this aspect of Roosevelt's nomination.

for what it was and took part vigorously in the Presidential campaign of 1900.

If his presence on the ticket did much or little to insure the re-election of McKinley it mattered hardly at all. McKinley won convincingly, and Theodore Roosevelt became Vice-President of the United States. Republican strategy in the campaign had emphasized prosperity at home and the full dinner pail and had ignored as much as possible the issue of American imperialism, which the Democrats for their part had tried to focus on. Political oratory, effective though it might have been in persuading or distracting the voters, did not have the magic to conjure away the problems attendant upon imperialism. Whether McKinley or Bryan or Roosevelt held the Presidency, the American empire was at hand.

The imperialist commitments of the United States during Roosevelt's years as Chief Executive fell into two main categories: the government of the Philippines and Puerto Rico and the advocacy of the Open Door in China, which exemplified primarily the positive, constructive elements in Roosevelt's confident imperialism; and the policing of the Caribbean area, representing chiefly but not exclusively what can be termed the negative if necessary elements. These positive and negative qualities were found in varying proportions in his policies toward the Philippines, China, Venezuela, Cuba, Santo Domingo, and Colombia—a combination of progress and police typical of the total of his confident imperialism.

Roosevelt's imperialistic rationale, insofar as it had become explicit when he took over direction of affairs in 1901, was compounded of a sense of the superiority of the white race (especially the Anglo-Americans) and the persuasions of democracy, of western man's urge to dominate and his wish, often more than a pious one, to be the preceptor of less able people and less fortunate human beings. If the constituents of this compound were not entirely compatible with one another—there was a basic conflict at least at the theoretical level between race superiority and democracy, as there was between domination and protection—Roosevelt did not acknowledge it and proceeded to act as though his was an altogether consistent imperialist outlook.

In time some areas of incompatibility emerged, however, and when the resulting antagonisms promised to be of such a nature as to advise opposed lines of action, Roosevelt invariably responded with a decision in support of one definite policy. He instinctively preferred decision to drift. The justification for any action he took might be either progress or the need to police, since he respected both as bases for policy. However, some generalizations are possible. In the Philippine Islands and in Puerto Rico more often than not the positive or constructive impulses to promote the welfare of the people were dominant; in the Caribbean the negative, necessary disciplining of what were considered backward or inferior peoples in order to preserve law obtained.

Progress and order are the two critical and distinguishing norms for interpreting Roosevelt's record of imperialism during his Presidency. He himself was too close to events and too absorbed in the work of ruling to be much aware of any hypothetical conflict, much less the advisability of resolving it. In matters of state his mind simply did not operate on a theoretical plane. To his way of thinking the first step in determining policy was to act according to American national interest. Since the United States stood for progress through law and order, what was best for the United States in the long run was best for civilization. Whenever Roosevelt spoke of fostering international peace and understanding he began with this assumption, so that frequently what he had in mind was a thinly disguised nationalism—or, as he himself might have admitted to, a highly personalized version of internationalism, which he thought the only viable kind in the long run. This was an intrinsic supposition of the world movement, the fundamental first statement of Roosevelt's historical world: expansion by force on the part of the superior peoples (among whom the Americans were in the front rank) in order that some day all men would be improved morally and materially.

Without reference to theories or abstract considerations Roosevelt's policy decisions were nearly always based on a concern for national interest as that interest promoted the world movement. For there had entered into Theodore Roosevelt the public man, the imperialist statesman, a feeling for an adherence to the principles of the world movement subtle enough to be regarded as "instinctive." That the President in the all-out pursuit of a national policy objective did not take time out to deliberate studiously on the grounds for his action in order to determine some priority of motivation does not prove that there was no such priority, however unconscious, plus a blending of various motivational factors into what can be termed instinct. It merely marks him as a man of action whose motives are most truly discernible by knowing the kind of person family and experiences had helped to make of an exceptional natural talent. It points up that his policies bore a direct relationship to what he, a nineteenth-century white Anglo-Saxon Protestant born to an elite class, had become. If this contention is sound, there is nothing in Roosevelt's imperialism that is not explainable in terms of his formative years and his life's thought. The lingering popular view of him as a frenetic man of action, perhaps seeking action for its own sake—"to build one's body," "to make the dirt fly"—is made to give way to a far more accurate picture of him as one who, indulging in no attempt to escape himself, remained himself and projected his personal values into his national statesmanship.

Whatever misgivings Roosevelt had had about accepting the Vice-Presidency, his thoughts on the decision facing him had not been centered entirely on political advancement. During the last months of 1899 and early in 1900 he frequently expressed the desire to be named the first civil governor of the Philippines. In explaining his feelings to Lodge he pointed out that the Vice-Presidency would cut him off definitely from all chance of securing that position, whereas resignation from the governorship of New York was feasible should the Philippine appointment be offered him. His interest in the governorship of the Islands was clearly not politically inspired. Instead he looked upon it as a "worthwhile undertaking," a "job worth doing," "emphatically worth doing." [5] Jacob Gould Schurman, president of Cornell University and head of the First United States-Philippines Commission, suggested that he take the Philippines governorship if offered. Roosevelt readily agreed with him; because it involved work for the betterment of the islanders it was "eminently worth doing." Should he win the appointment he promised to undertake the work with "a very serious sense not only of its importance, but of its difficulty." [6]

All this does not suggest the attitude of a man who saw in the governorship of the Philippines a convenient steppingstone to higher political office. Roosevelt's ambitions were thus tempered by his idealism. His motivation was quite genuine and sincerely altruistic. Direction of Philippine affairs appealed to him as a unique opportunity to participate in an important and useful way in the world movement. The course of empire was more exciting than the course of civil service reform in New York State. Part of Roosevelt's interest in the proconsular position no doubt derived from his self-reliant belief that he could do a supremely good job of ruling these backward peoples, dispensing a firm, impartial measure of justice. It was the promotion of the western ideals of society, particularly ideas of government, under the aegis of a great proconsul given sweeping powers—"a free hand" in fact—that Roosevelt envisioned. [7] This was a romanticized image of the governorship of the Islands, but it sounded the true note of Roosevelt's appreciation of what the situation required.

Conditions in the Philippines were, however, far too complex and too prosaic to yield easily, if at all, to such a simplified formula as the one that dominated Roosevelt's thinking on the matter toward the close of 1899. The history of the Islands, even within the context of modern western experience, was a long, in-

5. To Maria Longworth Storer, December 2, 1899, *ibid.*, pp. 1101–1102; to Henry Cabot Lodge, January 22, 1900, *ibid.*, p. 1136.
6. To Anna Roosevelt Cowles, January 23, 1900, *ibid.*, pp. 1137–1138; to Henry Cabot Lodge, January 30, 1900, *ibid.*, p. 1153.
7. To Maria Longworth Storer, December 2, 1899, *ibid.*, p. 1102.

volved one, older indeed than that of the United States. The first permanent settlement had been made in Cebu as early as 1565, and less than a decade later Spanish control over Luzon, the main island of the archipelago, was complete. During the three hundred years of Spanish rule many changes took place and a great deal was accomplished. The population itself increased from 500,000 to 7,000,000, a central government was established, the Catholic religion was widely accepted. In short, a considerable degree of European civilization had come to the Philippines through Spanish rule.

In the nineteenth century the Filipinos were no less susceptible to the doctrines of nationalism and liberalism than were other peoples around the world. As national and liberal ideas penetrated more and more deeply and as increased agricultural production and trade multiplied Filipino contacts with the world at large, discontent with the established authority of Spain became increasingly widespread. Both the political authority and the Church, which was hardly distinguishable from it, were the focal points of criticism. The reaction of these twin institutions of power was one of firm opposition to all suggestions for reform.

By the 1880's the sentiment for change had produced an eloquent and dignified spokesman in the person of José Rizal. A native of the Islands, he had studied medicine in Paris and written two novels, *Noli Me Tangere* (1886) and *El Filibusterismo* (1890), appealing for social and political change. But Rizal did not propose either the use of force to attain reform or independence from Spain as a solution to the plight of his people. Undaunted by the proscription of his books in the Philippines, in 1892 Rizal organized in Manila a society devoted to economic reform called *Liga Filipina*. Because of such activities he was first exiled to Mindanao and later (December 30, 1896) executed by the Spanish authorities.

Predictably, reform groups more disposed to violence became active in the wake of Rizal's death. Confiscation of friar lands, equality before the law, and parliamentary representation at Madrid were the most persistent demands heard from the native agitators, to all of which the Government remained stoutly opposed. By late 1896 military activities between Spanish and Filipino forces directed by Emilio Aguinaldo had developed, with the insurgents operating from remote mountain bases. An armistice between the Government, who agreed to introduce certain reforms, and rebel troops was negotiated in 1897, but it failed because of the refusal of the authorities to fulfill their promises. In February 1898, some weeks before the United States entered its war with Spain, hostilities between Filipino rebels, waging their own fight for freedom, and the old mother country were resumed.

Even so brief a sketch of Philippine history down to 1898 underlines several considerations that bear directly upon the American position there, once it was taken up, and these should be borne in mind for an understanding of Theodore Roosevelt's policies toward the Islands after he came to the Presidency. First, there were notable elements in the Philippine population generally and within the reform movement itself that in fairness could not be described as typically native or backward. While it is true and necessary to point out that the Filipinos had had no particular experience in self-government, they were nonetheless a proud people, conscious of their European culture and anxious to assume direction of their own affairs. Second, the movement for Philippine freedom, grounded on the western principles of nationalism and liberalism, was a well defined one, enduring despite mounting pressure from the Madrid Government to bring it down. Unless the United States was willing to tailor its policies to the political facts in the Islands, offering either autonomy or outright independence, some serious conflict was almost certain to arise. Finally, the American reputation for anticolonialism preceded American troops and understandably encouraged the people there to expect a "Teller Amendment approach" to the Philippines. Anything less might be interpreted as a betrayal.

It is fairly easy to see why United States-Philippines relations deteriorated so rapidly in the summer of 1898. Following Dewey's naval victory at Manila American troops began landing on Luzon on June 30. They were offered no resistance by the rebels, since the insurgent army under Aguinaldo was even then preparing to lay siege to Manila, and American assistance in this endeavor was hoped for. But the policies directing American forces under Major General Wesley Merritt and the self-appointed executive of the insurrection, Aguinaldo, were not in harmony. United States troops were under orders from Washington to "protect [Filipinos] in their homes, in their employments and in their personal and religious rights," instructions that carried the ring of orders for an army of occupation,[8] whereas Aguinaldo was already busy declaring Philippine independence (June 12) and appointing a provisional government. The incompatibility of the American and the insurgent positions was spelled out unmistakably in August when Manila fell and the United States refused the rebels the right of joint occupation of the capital city.

The capture of Manila all but closed the American war with Spain, but it marked the opening of a war between the United States and the Filipino insurgents. While American and Spanish officials came together in Paris in October to discuss the terms of peace, including the fate of the Philippines, native distrust of American intentions deepened with the passing days. In January 1899, in response to the American decision to place all the Islands under some form of colonial rule to be subsequently determined, Aguinaldo openly accused the United States of betraying its pledges to free the Philippines. Some kind of self-denying principle had been inferred by the rebels from the humanitarian reasons for American entry into the war, but certain minor U.S. officials had actually made pledges without Administration clearance. The niceties of diplomatic distinctions were lost upon the Filipinos as American control of the area tightened. In the very next month, February 1899, fighting broke out between Filipinos and American regulars.[9]

Theodore Roosevelt observed these events in the Philippine

8. *Senate Document 221*, 56th Congress, 1st Session, p. 1232.
9. Background for United States-Philippines relations is well presented by Garel A. Grunder and William E. Livezey, *The Philippines and the United States,* (Norman, 1951).

Islands with the utmost interest. Though he was without official influence upon the development of American policy for retaining the Islands, he vigorously supported it and proceeded to make a series of public and semipublic statements favoring the "large policy" of President McKinley. The pattern of his argument is easy enough to appreciate, flowing as it did from the major premises of his imperialistic outlook shaped during his formative years. "Every expansion of civilization makes for peace" because "every expansion of a great civilized power means a victory for law and order and righteousness," he wrote in an 1899 essay entitled "Expansion and Peace." In this tract he sought to offer justification for America's particular contribution to peace by its expansion over the Philippine Islands. Just as the French extended their rule by force in Algeria and the English conducted campaigns against the Mahdists, and just as in the past the expansion of civilized nations over North America invariably effected progress, "the same will be true in the Philippines." Further, he contended, if the United States abandoned the Islands to the Aguinaldans, it would mean rapine and bloodshed "until some stronger, manlier power stepped in to do [our] task." Roosevelt urged the United States to "keep the islands and establish therein a stable and orderly government so that one more fair spot of the world's surface shall have been snatched from the forces of darkness." [10] The world, it seemed, had to be composed of heroes and villains.

These convictions concerning peace through expansion may better be understood if viewed in the context of certain more general ideas that sum up Roosevelt's state of mind at the time, ideas which he voiced in his widely advertised "Strenuous Life" speech at the Hamilton Club in Chicago on April 10, 1899. "Expansion and Peace" was published as one of the essays elaborating the "strenuous life" ideal. In the "Strenuous Life" address

10. Roosevelt, "Expansion and Peace," *Works*, XV, pp. 282–292 *passim*.

Roosevelt evangelized the "life of manly vigor" as an American principle for both the nation and the individual. He found no useful distinction between a personal need for a noble purpose actively pursued and the community's need to dare to do great things. The strenuosity he spoke of had to include physical stamina and moral courage. Just as an earlier generation had to face squarely the challenge of disunion so, he told his Chicago audience, Americans of that day had to face up to the responsibilities confronting them in Hawaii, Cuba, Puerto Rico, and the Philippines.

Specifically he went on to point out why the United States ought to continue to control Puerto Rico and the Philipppines. The former he pronounced "not large enough to stand alone. We must govern it wisely and well, primarily in the interests of its own people." The Philippines represented a yet graver problem. The population there he divided into two categories with respect to their political potential: people who were utterly unfit for self-government and who showed no sign of becoming so, and those who "may in time become fit but at present can only take part in self-government under a wise supervision, at once firm and beneficent." There was no question in his view that the people of the Islands taken in the aggregate were not yet ready for self-rule; the "consent of the governed" theory that opponents of American control of the Islands constantly appealed to was not pertinent. Instead, the United States was urged to look to England for a proper example regarding the governing of subject peoples. If the United States did its duty in the Islands as England had seen fit to do its duty in India and Egypt, then "we will play our part well in the great work of uplifting mankind." Should all this involve the use of force, Roosevelt concluded in his espousal of the "strenuous life," then force it must be. Resistance to American rule had to be stamped out, "no parleying, no faltering." [11]

There was no influence more critical in the formation of the explicit imperialist attitudes of Theodore Roosevelt than his personal and scholarly experience of the American West, the

---

11. Roosevelt, "The Strenuous Life," *ibid.*, pp. 267–281 *passim.*

uniquely American phase of the world movement. This influence distinguished his reaction to the crisis of affairs in the Philippines from 1899, when serious trouble first erupted, down through his own handling of U.S.-Philippine affairs while President. The frontier influence was not merely expressed by the concept of peace through expansion or illustrated by the "strenuous life"; it integrated these principles into a harmonious apologia for American dominion in the Philippines.

Roosevelt demonstrated the authority of the frontier in his thought and its notable overtones succinctly in a speech, "The Copperheads of 1900," delivered in Cincinnati on October 21, 1899. "Every argument that can be made for the Filipinos could be made for the Apaches; every word that can be said for Aguinaldo could be said for Sitting Bull," he contended. "As peace, order and prosperity followed our expansion over the lands of the Indians, so they will follow us in the Philippines." [12] The Filipinos were as ill-suited as the Apaches to work out their own problems.[13] Just as the Indians of North America blocked the path to civilization and progress and had to be removed by force from their place, so the Islands had to be pacified and then ruled justly, he argued. In addition to the justification of the use of force, American frontier history demonstrated further that there was no necessary or inevitable conflict between conquest and the consent of the governed principle. As Roosevelt pointed out in a long letter to Senator E. O. Wolcott of Colorado accepting the Vice-Presidential nomination, the doctrine of consent of the governed that Jefferson had enunciated in the Declaration of Independence "was not held by him or by any other man to apply to the Indian tribes in the Louisiana territory which he acquired." [14] Jefferson sent troops to enforce the transfer of territory and to forestall insurrection "for exactly the same reasons and with exactly the same purposes that President McKinley had sent troops to the Philippines." [15]

12. Roosevelt, "Copperheads of 1900," *ibid.*, XVI, pp. 496–504; p. 501.
13. Roosevelt, "The Strenuous Life," *ibid.*, XV, p. 279.
14. To E.O. Wolcott, September 15, 1900, *Letters*, II, p. 1401.
15. *Ibid.*, p. 1402.

The American attitude toward Florida after its acquisition by treaty from Spain carried, according to Roosevelt, the same historical lesson for current policy respecting the Philippines. The Seminoles had not been consulted about the transition (any more than the Eskimos in Alaska had been consulted before the United States assumed sovereignty there). They rebelled and waged war just as had some Filipinos, but neither Monroe nor Adams nor Jackson considered abandoning Florida and treating the nonconsent of the native Indians as a reason for turning jurisdiction over to them.

Roosevelt was not willing to make any distinction between the North American Indians in their primitive condition and the somewhat Europeanized Filipinos; nor did he allow for any changes in the operating principles of the world movement from one century to the next. The parallel between the American frontier experience and the policy the McKinley Administration proposed to the American people regarding the Philippines was, in a word, "exact." On that account it was altogether satisfying to Theodore Roosevelt, who could not take seriously anyone who failed to see in the conquest of the frontier, with its historical lessons, one of the great accomplishments for good in the whole of the modern era.

Conquest of the frontier was not a good itself, however; conquest must bring with it civilization. What had developed in North America—the spread of responsible government directing a prosperous society—Roosevelt hoped would be the sequel to pacification of the Philippines by armed might. "It is, I am sure," he remarked early in 1899, "the desire of every American that the people of each island [Puerto Rico and the Philippines] as rapidly as they show themselves fit for self-government shall be endowed with a constantly larger measure of self-government." [16] But he was convinced that "no competent witness who has actually known the facts believes the Filipinos capable of self-

16. Roosevelt, "America's Part in the World's Work," *Works,* XVI, p. 475.

government at present . . . the institutions of a free republic can not at a leap be transplanted into wholly alien soil." [17]

At the crux of the dilemma was the anti-imperialist notion about "giving the Filipinos a stable form of government." Roosevelt held that one nation could not "give" sound government to another, any more than a person could be given good character by his neighbor. In his code, character was the most important and valuable feature for an individual; character was tantamount to goodness, adherence to a virtuous way of life as defined by traditional Christian morality. For the community, especially for the pre-eminent community, the nation, character was evinced when the people demonstrated self-discipline, and adherence to the ways of law and order. Self-government was a matter of possessing certain qualities and mastering their use to render stable government viable.

Since the Filipinos were, in Roosevelt's determination, then incapable of setting up that kind of rule for themselves, it followed that it was the right and duty of the American Republic to establish such a government over them and to support it until "the natives gradually grow fit to sustain themselves." [18] A great nation could do no less. "By every consideration of honor and humanity" the United States was bound to stay in the Islands and provide a constantly increasing opportunity for responsible self-government. "Whenever the islands can stand alone," he told President Eliot of Harvard, "I should be only too glad to withdraw." [19] But as to the length of time all this might require, Roosevelt would not in 1900 hazard a guess. All he would say at the time was "when they are fit to walk alone they should walk alone, but I will not pledge myself as to a definite date for giving them independence." [20] It is worth stressing once more that the explicit aspects of Roosevelt's attitude toward the Islands was determined in great measure by his reading of American frontier history.[21] And this attitude supposed traditional moral values for the individual as

17. Roosevelt, "Free Silver, Trusts and the Philippines," *ibid*, p. 538.
18. To E.O. Wolcott, September 15, 1900, *Letters*, II, p. 1404.
19. To Charles W. Eliot, November 14, 1900, *ibid.*, p. 1415.
20. To H.K. Love, November 24, 1900, *ibid.*, p. 1441.
21. To E.O. Wolcott, September 15, 1900, *ibid.*, pp. 1402–1403.

they were expressed in community or governmental responsibility.

These are the chief considerations accounting for the optimistic character of Roosevelt's estimate of the American experiment in the Philippines as it got under way. He might have warned that such was not a romantic or a silly optimism but one grounded on the realities of the situation. The task of training the Islanders would be a stern and a demanding one; only the most dedicated could be entrusted with it. But he was sure that "we can ultimately help our brethren of the Philippine Islands so far forward on the path of self-government and orderly liberty that that beautiful archipelago shall become a center for civilization for all eastern Asia and the islands around about. A great future lies before the Philippines. . . ." [22] The United States could be expected to make some mistakes in its dealings with the Filipinos, he told a gathering at the Minnesota State Fair on September 2, 1901, just as it had been guilty of blunders and worse in certain Indian matters. But as no one would contend that "we were not right in wresting from barbarians and adding to civilization the territory out of which we have made these beautiful states," so in the Islands it must be remembered that "we are not trying to subjugate a people; we are trying to develop them and make them a law abiding, industrious and educated people, and we hope ultimately a self-governing people." [23] In light of history and the difficult business of civilizing a people this was optimism of the very highest order, the capstone of Roosevelt's confident imperialism.

Less than a fortnight after his Minnesota State Fair address Theodore Roosevelt was sworn in as President of the United States. The death of President McKinley made Roosevelt heir to both a general policy orientation toward the Philippines and a set of specific measures designed to accomplish the purposes of civilizing a backward people. Watching from the sidelines as governor of New York and then as Vice-President he had warmly seconded the direction of Philippine affairs by the Administration. As President, however, he faced the task of picking up the

22. To Raymond Reyes Lala, June 27, 1900, *ibid.*, p. 1343.
23. Roosevelt, "National Duties," *Works*, XV, p. 340.

numerous strands of policy, of deciding whether he should acquiesce in the established program or seek to improve it through some important alteration. In addition, because the situation was a fluid one Roosevelt would have to decide how to proceed in the management of new problems as they arose.

Having consistently agreed with the general propositions of McKinley's Philippine policy he was from the first disposed to maintain it *mutatis mutandis*. Examination of that policy in some detail reveals very little that Roosevelt was likely to dissent from. Yet one cannot help but think that had he been President from the inception of the Philippines imbroglio Roosevelt would have managed affairs quite differently, and that had he been the first civilian governor of the Islands a good deal more friction, misunderstanding, and perhaps even bloodshed might have occurred in spite of his many high-minded intentions.

Several considerations should be especially emphasized about McKinley's Philippines policy from Dewey's victory at Manila in May 1898 to his death in September 1901. The middle-of-the-road position of the President in the summer of 1898 regarding acquisition of the Philippines is well known, as is his own explanation of why, after all, the United States had to annex the entire archipelago. The implications of American control of the Philippines, staggering in themselves, were nevertheless the logical maturation of the McKinley Administration's "drift toward world power." [24] Thus by the end of October, after much thought and discussion in conjunction with appropriate political soundings, McKinley in prayerful judgment concluded that United States annexation was the one honorable alternative to returning the Islands to Spain, handing them over to America's commercial rivals, or allowing them a political freedom for which they were not at all prepared. The complete and unconditional sovereignty of the United States over the Islands had become the cardinal purpose of McKinley's foreign policy. Roosevelt himself pronounced it a providential turn of events when the senate completed the last step in the formal annexation procedure by

24. Morgan, *op. cit.*, p. 412; LaFeber, *op. cit.*, pp. 410–413.

approving the treaty with Spain February 6, 1899.[25] The first phase of the "large policy" of the United States relative to the Philippines stood concluded.

Since this extension of American power was unacceptable to the Filipino people as a whole, forces under Aguinaldo were almost simultaneously drawn into engagements with occupying United States troops. In the second phase of United States-Philippine relations, the pacification of the Islands, the immediate and worrisome problem was the maintenance of law and order, to be brought about by the destruction of the rebel army as an effective fighting force. Had the Filipinos undertaken a conventional war, this would have been a job that American troops could have accomplished with real though not agonizing difficulty (conventional resistance in fact ended by January 1900). As it was, the rebels waged a guerrilla campaign that required the involvement of many thousands of United States soldiers. It led to brutalities on both sides, resulting in a demoralizing, inglorious kind of war that ended only when the captured Aguinaldo took the oath of allegiance to the United States on April 19, 1901. Afterward there was scattered fighting by rebel remnants that soon deteriorated into bands of brigands. But the bitterness and suspicions engendered by the hostilities lingered on long afterward, increasing the difficulty of installing an effective civilian government.

Simultaneously with the military effort to establish physical control over the Islands, the McKinley Administration began to unfold its program for a permanent peaceful government for the Philippines. Partly at the suggestion of Admiral Dewey, whose presence at Manila enabled him to appreciate the explosiveness of the political situation there at the beginning of 1899, but mostly because of the pressing need for some concrete proposals looking to orderly liberty, McKinley assembled the so-called First United States-Philippines Commission. The President charged this body with studying "the existing social and political state," paying particular attention to local government, the administration

25. To Henry Cabot Lodge, February 7, 1899, *Letters*, II, p. 935.

of justice, and taxation. Jacob Gould Schurman accepted the chairmanship. The work of the commission was not made easier by the war that raged during its on-the-spot investigations, and the influence of the civilian members was seriously limited by the insistence of General Otis, a member of the commission, that military matters take precedence.

Schurman, refusing to allow himself to be discouraged by dissension within the commission, issued a notable proclamation on April 4, 1900, the first specific statement of long-range American intention with respect to the Philippine Islands. It began by declaring that there was no conflict between American sovereignty and the rights of the Filipino people. The proclamation went on to say that it was the purpose of the United States to "accustom" the people "to free self-government in an ever increasing measure" and "to encourage them in those democratic aspirations, sentiments and ideals which are the promise and potentiality of a fruitful national development." [26]

The friendly, reassuring tone of this pronouncement, in combination with military reverses suffered by the rebels, produced the first serious negotiations between the opposing parties since the fighting had commenced. In response to the insurgents' inquiries as to exactly what form of rule the Americans proposed to set up, the commission outlined the following plan: a government headed by a governor general possessing an absolute veto power, to be appointed by the President of the United States for an indefinite term; an advisory council to assist the governor general, to be selected on the basis of a limited franchise; a strong, independent judiciary of American and Filipino judges, also to be designated by the President. Although these negotiations of April–May 1899 failed of agreement, they weakened the native will to resist by spelling out the relatively moderate position the American Government was willing to take. For its part, the United States was by these conversations more or less committed to grant a form of rule similar to the one outlined to the Filipinos by the Schurman Commission. The commission continued its investiga-

26. *Senate Document 138*, 56th Congress, 1st Session, pp. 3–4.

tions throughout the remainder of the year, rendering a final report to the President in January 1900.

In the final statement of the commission the following points are worth noting. Illiteracy, lack of political experience, and linguistic differences were accounted the main obstacles to immediate self-rule—this despite the presence of many educated Filipinos whose loyalty to an American regime the commissioners felt should be actively cultivated. Because United States jurisdiction was a necessity, it could be successful only if the American authorities understood the character of the Philippine people and realized the seriousness of their aspirations and ideals. The Filipinos, the commission report concluded, wanted a firm guarantee of their inalienable human rights and a part in their own government, looking toward eventual independence.[27]

The submission of this last report marked the end of the work of the Schurman Commission. When Schurman himself declined further service in the Philippines, McKinley decided on a new all-civilian body and prevailed upon William Howard Taft, then a Federal judge, to preside as chairman.[28] Taft assisted Secretary of War Elihu Root in drawing up the instructions for the commission, known as the Second United States-Philippines Commission or, more simply, the Taft Commission. These instructions, approved by McKinley, authorized the transfer of all legislative power from the military command to the commission as of September 1, 1900, whereupon the commission was empowered to establish municipal and provincial governments. The selection of officials for municipal governments was to rest with the people directly, while for provincial offices natives were to be preferred as long as they were competent to perform their assigned duties. These instructions contained a further reminder that all measures adopted by the commission be designed not to satisfy certain theoretical American views but to promote happiness, peace, and prosperity in the Philippines.[29]

27. *Ibid.*, pp. 80 81.
28. Other members included Dean C. Worcester; Luke Wright, a Tennessee judge; H.C. Ide, a Vermont lawyer; and Bernard Moses, a professor of Latin-American history at the University of California.
29. *House Document I,* 56th Congress, 1st session, pp. xxxv–xxxix.

The Taft Commission arrived at Manila June 3, 1900, and immediately encountered the hostility of the American military command, especially from the newly appointed officer in charge, General Arthur MacArthur. As upsetting as Taft found this situation, it did not distract him from his job of further preparing the ground for the advent of a civilian American authority whereby the Filipinos themselves could be fitted gradually for self-rule. That it was to be a gradual process Taft quickly concluded after his arrival in the Islands. In his judgment Philippine independence was decades away. His reasons for taking this position were several. The people, at least the vast majority, were "ignorant, superstitious"; the small class of educated had acquired only "a good deal of superficial knowledge of the general principles of free government." They promised to be "difficult persons out of whom to make an honest government."

Yet for all this negative evaluation Taft found the Filipinos "a pleasant people to meet," and he began almost at once to grow fond of them. And they of him, for he refused to treat them as inferiors in any way and accepted them as his equals, however politically deficient he judged them to be.[30] This was one of the sources of conflict between Taft and the Army. The latter had quite understandably grown to cordially hate the natives as dangerous and brutal enemies; even when the fighting tapered off it was hard for the Army commanders to accept the Filipinos as equals.

Taft's farsighted attitude on the matter of race, his determination to win the confidence and respect of the masses, his refusal to publically disparage the rebel leadership, his opposition to the prohibition of the national pastime of cockfighting, however much he personally deplored the sport—these were the secrets of Taft's success as governor of the Philippines. His thoughtful reading of the prudent recommendations of the Schurman reports, advising the American authorities to respect the "prejudices" of the Filipinos as long as it was consonant with sound government, joined with Taft's own judicious outlook to set the tone for

30. Henry F. Pringle, *The Life and Times of William Howard Taft,* 2 volumes, (New York, 1939), I, pp. 171 ff.

American administration in the Philippines for years to come. No amount of schools, hospitals, or road construction could have worked to win and hold the good will and loyalty of the people had it not grown out of a sound psychology that accepted them as individuals possessing rights and dignity and fully capable of preparing for self-government. Certainly no military command was likely to undertake the moral as well as the material pacification of the Islands. Taft was convinced of his position not simply as a pious sentiment or even as a sublime statement of principle. To him it was a daily call to the hard, exhausting job of setting up numerous municipal governments, of traveling widely in the provinces in order to come to know and trust the individual local leaders and to be trusted by them in return, of determining the wise expenditure of large amounts of tax revenues. All in all, these were the routine but indispensable tasks of governmental administration at the level on which large policies were translated into detailed procedures. This work required dedication, patience, optimism, and tact; and Taft was amply provided with all these attributes.

Suitably enough, given the circumstances of successful commission rule after September 1, 1900, Taft upon direction from McKinley transformed his own official position from chairman of the commission to civil governor of the Philippine Islands, an event that took place July 4, 1901. The American principle of civilian direction of government, as well as Taft's own policies, stood vindicated.

As Theodore Roosevelt assumed presidential office in September 1901 he not only came into possession of a policy that had received enough implementation to commit the United States to a fairly definite course of action for the future, but he also inherited a governor general whose inimitable "touch" was far more potent than MacArthur's troops in sustaining American power and prestige in the Far East. Roosevelt himself had longed to be the great proconsul. But he was not well equipped by tem-permanent and training to succeed in that fondly hoped-for role. He believed no less sincerely than Taft or any man that the mission of the United States in the Philippines was one dedicated to human improvement. The measures he supported as President offer ample evidence of this. But it is more than likely that as his inclination to take things in hand when frustrations nettled him, and his sense of kinship with the military would have caused him to do less than was required to reassure the Filipinos of the good intentions of the United States. Not a trained lawyer like Taft, his reaction to the "law's delays" might not have been sufficiently forbearing. Experience in a military command in Cuba and executive positions in Washington and Albany might well have blinded him to an unfortunate degree to the "insolence of office," given all the facts of the Philippine situation.

This is not to dismiss Roosevelt's potentiality as a colonial governor altogether. Without doubt he would have brought a burning conviction, great energy, and steadfast dedication to the assignment. Had he actually come out to the Islands many of his prejudices against the "Tagal bandits" might have softened, his will to action tempered by the realities he encountered. Most men of good will are sobered by responsibility once it has settled on them, and there is no reason to believe it would not have been so with Roosevelt. A particular Rooseveltian trait might even have rendered him a reasonably patient and understanding colonial administrator. He was prone to comfortable generalizations, which on occasion led to glib judgments concerning matters about which his knowledge was incomplete and his experience vicarious or remote. But he was usually capable of learning the need for careful qualification and restrained conclusions, once he had come to grips with a real situation or had given close study to some problem. His critical distinction between evolution and social Darwinism as these figured in his imperialist outlook is a major example of this personal intellectual habit, to be discussed at length in a later chapter. There were, therefore, several considerations that might well have combined to make Roosevelt an effective colonial governor.

As it was, with Taft in Manila and later Luke Wright, a man

of similar temper, to succeed him, Roosevelt in Washington could continue to extol the American experiment in the Islands, innocent of most of the frustrations besetting the authorities out there, fully reliant upon the wisdom and dedication of his subordinates, recounting in annual messages to Congress the certain growth of stable government for the Philippine people.

In the development of Theodore Roosevelt's imperialism after he had become President, the Philippines experiment could have either confirmed or denied the confidence that typified its basic formulation. The United States might not have been able to sustain its altruistic purpose of civilizing and uplifting the native peoples as the world watched. Or the Filipinos themselves might have failed to respond to American tutelage and assistance owing to ill will or plain inability to become a self-governing people. The world movement would have faltered seriously in either case, and then cogent experiential reasons would have existed for Roosevelt and Americans generally to question the morality of empire.

It should not be forgotten that much of the opposition to the acquisition of the Islands from Democrats and Republicans alike sprang substantially from doubts that it would not work because it marked such a sharp and unfortunate departure from the American tradition. The fear was that Americans would not be good empire builders and that the experience of ruling others would lessen the spirit of republican government at home. When Beveridge spoke of duty and destiny, George Frisbie Hoar, a rock-ribbed Republican senator from Massachusetts, wondered aloud about right and justice and freedom. The imperialists generally, with Roosevelt prominent among them, dismissed such fears as shortsighted, cowardly, unworthy of a great nation whose purpose it had been historically and was then to expand and conquer, so that eventually more and more men might become free through an understanding and mastery of western political institutions.

From the viewpoint of Roosevelt's philosophy of imperialism, the American political experiment in the Philippine Islands *had* to succeed in order to justify America's continuing part in the world's work. British success in India and Egypt, French dominion in North Africa, Russian influence in Turkistan, fruitful as Roosevelt thought them for the advancement of civilization, all proved the virility and greatness of these people. America's role in the twentieth century still remained to be defined. Part of that definition, the best part, would be found in the Philippines and what the United States would be able to accomplish there. Of this Theodore Roosevelt was genuinely convinced.

At no time while President did Roosevelt presume to act directly to determine specific regulations for the Philippine Islands against the advice of his subordinates working there. As committed as he was to the task of governing the Islands, the responsibilities of the Presidency were too numerous and the Philippines too distant to encourage such a conduct of affairs. He remained satisfied to consider problems of administration and rule in the largest perspectives, leaving to his governors and their aides the details of colonial jurisdiction. Occasionally he concerned himself with a particular problem in an active way, but only if it had been thrust upon him or he happened to be especially interested in it. The very fact that he did not become deeply involved in the friar land tangle, for example, or the difficulties encountered in putting the Cooper Act into effect accounted for the all but unclouded confidence he had in the outcome of the American experiment. Confining himself to the large propositions, he kept his Philippines pronouncements at the policy level, where judgments already offered by him before he became President were likely to be confirmed without serious qualification.

At the outset of his administration he promised to give to his colonial administrators, Taft in the Philippines and William H. Hunt in Puerto Rico, "the largest liberty of action possible and the heartiest support." [31] As long as they undertook no major devia-

---

31. To William H. Hunt, September 26, 1901, *Letters*, III, p. 151.

tion from established American policy Roosevelt had no occasion to intervene, and the records of both men were more than enough to reassure him that established policies would prevail. As Vice-President he had told Taft that the "military arm should be literally an arm directed by the civil head," [32] a clear indication of the kind of government he preferred for the Islands. But to him civil government as enjoyed by Americans at home could not safely be duplicated for the Filipinos. While Vice-President he spoke of the "impossibility of working out the salvation of the Philippines, as we were forced to undertake the job, exactly on the terms of our government here at home; what does well here would work ruin there—trial by jury in all cases for instance." [33] Thus the Supreme Court's decisions in the Insular Cases of 1900 and 1901, which rejected the simple formula that the Constitution followed the flag, were much to his liking; he thought them "a great service to mankind and to the nation." [34] His large policy as President would rest upon civilian direction of a limited civil government over the Filipinos, with the U.S. Army standing by as insurance.

The most persistent early challenge to Roosevelt's endorsement of the McKinley-Root-Taft policy toward the Philippines was the perennial demand for independence by the anti-imperialists at home and ultranationalistic Filipinos. Such demands, for Roosevelt at least, reached something of a climax in the election of 1904. Thereafter, Philippine independence ceased to be a political issue of major consequence, a development confirming Roosevelt in his determination to maintain the established order of things there.

In his first annual message to Congress Roosevelt, recognizing the importance of the Philippines to the United States, spoke his views fully. "It is no light task for a nation to achieve the tem-

---

32. To William Howard Taft, March 12, 1901, *ibid.*, p. 11.
33. To Frederic Coudert, July 3, 1901, *ibid.*, p. 105.
34. To Henry Cabot Lodge, July 10, 1902, *ibid*, p. 289.

peramental qualities without which the institutions of free government are but an empty mockery. . . . Our people," he pointed
out, "are now successfully governing themselves because for more
than a thousand years they have been slowly fitting themselves,
sometimes consciously, sometimes unconsciously. What has taken
us thirty generations to achieve," he continued, "we cannot expect to see another race accomplish out of hand. . . . In dealing
with the Philippine people we must show both patience and
strength, forbearance and steadfast resolution. . . ." American
purpose in the Islands was simple. "We hope to do for them what
has never been done for any people of the tropics—to make them
fit for self-government after the fashion of the really free nations."
Perhaps, he agreed, the United States had advanced the native
peoples too far too soon, to "the very verge of safety," in hasten-
ing the process. He was sure the United States had not been lax
in granting self-rule where it was practical. "There is not a locality
fitted for self-government which has not received it." He was not
fully convinced that this experiment in government had always
worked well apparently. "It may be," he warned, "that in certain
cases it [self-government] will have to be withdrawn because the
inhabitants show themselves unfit to exercise it. . . ." [35] Generally,
however, he seemed optimistic, expressing confidence that in the
policies of Root and Taft, men who were "trying to bring the
Filipinos forward in the path of orderly self-governing liberty," [36]
the United States was cognizant of the need to mix justice and
understanding.

One reason for his optimism was his reliance on the Army's
ability to keep order, the indispensable presupposition to the
growth of free government. Army action had denied the Filipinos
their independence true enough, but in so doing it had protected
them against themselves and their own deficiencies. "Our armies
do more than bring peace," he told a Memorial Day audience
at Arlington, Virginia, in 1902, "they bring freedom. Remember
always," he cautioned, "the independence of a tribe or com-

35. Roosevelt, "First Annual Message" (1901), *Works*, XVII, pp. 128–130
passim.
36. To Edward Everett Hale, December 12, 1901, *Letters*, III, p. 209.

munity may and often does have nothing to do with the freedom of the individual." There was ample justification for using force to break the Filipino insurrection, because where it had been destroyed "there the individual Filipino enjoys such freedom, such personal liberty under our rule, as he could never even have dreamed of under the rule of an 'independent' Aguinaldan oligarchy." [37] To Roosevelt it was not a question of "might makes right," but of might making right possible to achieve.

The President wrote with considerable justification to Senator Hoar in June 1902 of "encouraging in every way the growth of the conditions which now make for self-government in the Philippines." [38] But Congress in its capacity as lawmaker was prepared to permit even more participation of the Filipinos in their Government and to specify the procedures for realizing this in the Cooper Bill, containing provisions for the further growth of Philippines self-rule. Congress passed this bill and the President signed it into law on July 2, 1902, marking the next decisive steps in United States-Philippines relations. The Cooper Act constituted a very definite advance in the American conception of proper colonial administration. A brief consideration of its genesis and its provisions shows how mutually sympathetic were the views of Roosevelt and Taft on the future of the Islands.

Governor General Taft had returned to Washington in January 1902 for reasons of both health and state. The daily grind of hard work in a difficult climate along with organic weaknesses had made him a sick man, requiring operations and a long recuperative period away from his duties. A more important reason for coming home, in Taft's own judgment, was the pending meetings of a Senate committee that was to begin hearings on Philippine matters early in the year. He believed his presence to advise the Senate on future legislation was vital. In Washington Taft was welcomed warmly by Roosevelt, and then proceeded to acquit himself well in the committee hearings. In his testimony he cautioned against any promises or even mention of independence for the Philip-

---

37. Roosevelt, "Speech at Arlington, Va.," May 30, 1902, reprinted in E.E. Garrison, *The Roosevelt Doctrine,* (New York, 1904), pp. 79–80.
38. To George F. Hoar, June 16, 1902, *Letters,* III, p. 277.

pines, hewing closely to the position both he and Roosevelt favored, the continuation of preparation for self-rule.

Taft had a large hand in drafting the Cooper Bill for submission to the Congress. Basically the law made the Islands an unincorporated territory and declared that all citizens of the Philippines were entitled to the protection of the United States. The law contained a declaration of individual rights to be safeguarded. Further, it directed the taking of a census as a preliminary to the election of the lower house of a Philippine legislature; the upper house was to consist of the Philippine Commission, with its members still being named by the President of the United States. The strong independent judiciary was continued, though the right of appeal to the United States Supreme Court was granted when the Constitution or any treaty was involved in a dispute. Finally, the Act retained the governor general as the chief executive officer. Pursuant to this law the first census was completed in 1905 and elections held on July 30, 1907. The first national Philippines Assembly met October 16 of that year. Meanwhile, of course, American tutelage remained relatively little changed, working well in Roosevelt's view. "The islands have never been as orderly, as peaceful, or as prosperous as now; and in no other Oriental country, whether ruled by Asiatics or Europeans, is there anything approaching the amount of individual liberty and self-government," he declared to an audience in Memphis in November 1902, a judgment he was to restate in his formal messages to Congress in 1902 and 1903.[39]

The presidential election of 1904 introduced a nervous, almost defensive note in Roosevelt's estimate of United States-Philippines relations. The Democrats, being ruled by partisanship rather than prudent principle in the President's judgment, announced in favor of Philippine independence in their platform. Roosevelt, who had been perennially worried over his chances of winning the Presidency on his own, felt that any one issue could be his undoing. He took the question of Philippine inde-

39. Roosevelt, "Speech at Memphis, Tenn.," November, 1902, reprinted in Garrison, *op. cit.*, p. 29; Roosevelt, "Second Annual Message" (1902), *Works*, XVII, pp. 179–180; Roosevelt, "Third Annual Message" (1903), *ibid.*, p. 223.

pendence raised by the opposition with the utmost seriousness. As he saw it, every right-thinking man recognized that independence or autonomy would come to the Islands eventually; but it should come only when adequate preparation had taken place. He wrote to President Eliot, "when Bryan or any other man for political or sentimental reasons excites false hopes of independence among the Filipinos it immediately produces a certain amount of demoralization and gives a certain set-back to the effort for their betterment." Accordingly, the "surest way to prevent them [the Filipinos] from so fitting themselves would be to promise them independence now. . . . Meanwhile they would cease from all effort to build themselves up under existing conditions and would restlessly plot as to what would happen in the future." [40] In other words, Roosevelt contended, loose talk of independence today or tomorrow or at any time in the immediate future simply worked to disrupt the whole delicate and involved process whereby the Filipinos would someday probably be ready for self-rule.

A note of probability instead of certainty was introduced by Roosevelt in writing of Philippine affairs in 1904. "I *believe* that they will gradually grow fit themselves but I am *not certain* they will so grow, and I have no idea how long the growth will take. . . ." [41] It was important to cultivate in the Filipinos not a "patriotic national sentiment" but a desire for "the sober performance of duty." "What he [the Filipino] needs is to be taught that he must first of all be able to practice justice to himself and to others." So strongly did the President feel about the foolishness of independence that he was prompted to write that the "main object of American statesmanship in the islands must be discouragement of any feeling among the Filipinos which will make them subordinate the duty of trying to become self-supporting, respecting, orderly peoples. . . ." [42]

Because of the situation, Roosevelt pleaded that the policies of his Administration be continued. To him the arguments of 1900

---

40. To Charles W. Eliot, April 4, 1904, *Letters,* IV, pp. 769–770.
41. To Jacob Gould Schurman, August 26, 1904, *ibid.,* p. 906 (italics added).
42. To Charles W. Eliot, June 20, 1904, *ibid.,* p. 839.

favoring independence had no pertinence to the facts of 1904. The United States had been in the Islands since 1899; it had undertaken the long, arduous, uncertain, but noble task of raising up the Filipinos. Now, in the midst of things, that work simply could not be put down. "We did not take the Philippines at will and we cannot put them aside at will. Any abandonment of the policy which we have steadily pursued in the islands would be fraught with dishonor and disaster; and to such dishonor and disaster I do not believe the American people will consent." [43] While perhaps no presidential election should be viewed as a mandate for a particular policy, it is hard not to interpret Theodore Roosevelt's election in 1904 as a resounding personal tribute and inevitably if indirectly as approval of his major policies. In his own estimate it was an election between a very positive man (himself) and a very negative man, Judge Parker.[44] The election, which gave Roosevelt an unprecedented popular majority of over two and one-half million votes, was a very positive endorsement of a very positive man.

Reassurance born of elective popularity plus an increasing familiarity with the situation helps to account for the more deliberate and certain tone of Theodore Roosevelt's estimate of the Philippines after 1904. The year before he had tried, unsuccessfully, to prevail upon Lord Cromer, the much respected British agent-general in Egypt, to come to Washington to discuss the problems of colonial rule and to offer the less experienced Americans his counsel. The year after he could say, as he surveyed the American empire, that Leonard Wood in Moro country had done a more difficult job than the British in the Malay Settlements and had done it better.[45] On the whole he thought the United States compared very favorably with Great Britain as an imperialist power intent on promoting human progress. "We have done more for them [the Philippines] than the English have done

43. To Jacob Gould Schurman, August 30, 1904, Roosevelt *Mss.*
44. To Kermit Roosevelt, October 26, 1904, *Letters,* IV, p. 993.
45. To Whitelaw Reid, September 11, 1905, *ibid.,* V, p. 20.

in Egypt," he wrote Lodge in April 1906. "Our problems . . . were infinitely more complex and more important, because we have [in the Filipinos] a nominally Christian population with some European blood in it, and we are now painfully endeavoring to fit these people for self-government." He went on to state that "the English are making no such effort in Egypt. The English are taking no steps and very possibly can take no steps which would give Egypt the slightest chance of permanent betterment." Further, he noted, while the British were exploiting the Malay Settlements, the cardinal doctrine of American rule in the Philippines was to avoid exploitation in any form.

By 1906 Roosevelt had entirely thrown off his deferential attitude for one of exulting confidence: "The performance of Taft," he contended to Lodge, "like the aggregate of the performances of Wood, surpasses the performance of Lord Cromer." [46] This optimism was well reflected in his fourth annual message to Congress. Pointing out that the problem in the Philippines was akin to the governing problem of other great civilized states, Roosevelt saw the American approach as unique. "More distinctly than any of these [other] powers," he informed Congress, "we are endeavoring to develop the natives themselves so that they shall take an ever increasing share in their own government, and as far as prudent we are already admitting their representatives to a governmental equality with our own. There are commissioners, judges and governors in the islands who are Filipinos and who have exactly the same share in the government of the islands as have their colleagues who are Americans, while in the lower ranks . . . of course the great majority of the public servants are Filipinos." Roosevelt garnished his optimism with caution, warning again that it would be unwise to "turn the attention of the Filipinos away from the problem of achieving the moral and material responsibility of working for a stable, orderly and just government and toward dangerous intrigues for complete independence for which the people are as yet totally unfit." [47]

46. To Henry Cabot Lodge, April 30, 1906, *ibid.*, pp. 252–257 *passim.*
47. Roosevelt, "Fourth Annual Message" (1904), *Works*, XVII, pp. 306–310 *passim.*

The annual messages for 1905 and 1906 confirmed and extended the sober optimism of the President. The government of the Islands was more and more in the hands of the people themselves and more and more efficiently conducted. Schools, roads, harbors, material improvements of all kinds continued to increase, the most encouraging feature of the whole situation being, in his judgment, "the very great interest taken by the common people in education and the great increase in the numbers of enrolled students in the public schools." Liberty and order had become commonplace, preparations for the Filipino Assembly were progressing toward fulfillment. All in all, it was a very encouraging political experiment.[48] And it was made more so, in Roosevelt's judgment, by his continued popularity. The President was a politician, sensitive to public opinion; the confidence of his imperialism, if not the theories intrinsic to it, was intimately connected with political success at home.

Roosevelt's insistence that affairs were in proper order in the Philippines and that they would improve steadily if the policy of gradualness was allowed to prevail won him some critics from both left and right. There was still sentiment in 1905 for immediate Philippine independence. To Carl Schurz and Andrew Carnegie the President emphasized both the positive and negative sides of his imperialist code. He reminded Carnegie that the United States continued to act in a spirit of genuine disinterestedness but "in a spirit wholly untainted by that silly sentimentality which is often more dangerous to both the subject and the object than downright iniquity." [49] And to Schurz he offered the warning that "hopeless and hideous bloodshed and wickedness" can be stopped "only when civilized nations expand." It was just such an expansion that had brought a boon to the Philippines.[50]

On the other hand, there were some who took the position

48. Roosevelt, "Fifth Annual Message" (1905), *ibid.*, pp. 386 ff; Roosevelt, "Sixth Annual Message" (1906), *ibid.*, p. 447.
49. To Andrew Carnegie, April 5, 1907, *Letters,* V, p. 640.
50. To Carl Schurz, September 8, 1905, *ibid.*, p. 16.

that the United States had given the Philippines too much liberty. To the plea that the Administration ought to model its policy more on the order of British rule in Egypt, Roosevelt replied by noting the critical differences between the Philippine Islands and Egypt, as there were between America and other imperialist powers. The Moslem *fellahin,* having known two and one-half millennia of tyranny, possessed far less potential for self-rule than did the partly Europeanized and partly Christianized natives of the Islands. In addition and no less significant were the ideals of the American people. "Our people do not desire to hold foreign dependencies, and do believe in self-government for them. . . . In the Philippines we found ourselves by accident in possession of the islands as the result of war. We found the islanders were wholly unable to stand alone and we have stayed there since, literally for the islanders' good and not for our own. . . ." [51]

To his critics from both sides Roosevelt was saying in effect that things in the Philippines were exactly as they should be and that his experts who knew and understood the people there should be allowed to maintain their rule without interference.

While he could not afford to appear to be quite so self-righteous with congressional leadership, Roosevelt did insist in his dealings with the legislature that the administration of the Philippine Islands was a matter for the experts. Between the passage of the Cooper Bill in 1902 and the Jones Act in 1916 congressional interest in the management of the Islands was intermittent, usually flaring up when some advantage to America seemed to be threatened. Only in 1905 and in 1907, and then due largely to the requests of Taft and others, did the Congress enact legislation specific enough to be termed regulation of the internal affairs of the archipelago. [52]

All of which suited the President well enough. Generally he felt that "a legislative body, most of whose members are elected by constituencies that in the nature of things can know nothing

51. To Silas McBee, August 27, 1907, *ibid.,* pp. 774–775.
52. The 1905 law provided for the issuance of Philippine bonds for internal improvement and railroad construction at a guaranteed 4 per cent, dealt with filing procedures on mineral claims, regulated coinage, and so forth. *Statutes at Large,* 58th Congress, pp. 689–698.

whatever of the totally different conditions of . . . the Philippines
. . . does not offer the best material for making a success of
such government." [53] He made this point rather specifically in a
letter to the Speaker of the House of Representatives with regard
to the proposed agricultural bank for the Philippines when it was
before the Congress in 1907. The bill involved the use of private
capital with certain government guarantees; its primary purpose
was to make credit available to small farmers at fair rates of
interest. Writing to Speaker Cannon to ask him to use his influence in getting the bill approved, Roosevelt commented: "In
the Philippines I feel that no one can tell what is needed (alike
from the standpoint of their material interests and from the
standpoint of sentiment) so well as those whose special business,
and the main part of whose life's work for a number of years, it
has been to attend to the needs of the Islands and shape their
development." [54]

The bill was passed into law, much to the benefit of the Filipino farmer. It was a worthy example of a constructive measure
designed to overcome a particular deficiency or evil, of which,
Roosevelt wrote Sidney Brooks, "I am well aware, and as to
which I am steadily trying to advance and perfect remedies." [55]
The President had come to experience in some way, at least,
the work of a proconsul, and he had acquitted himself well.

The occupation and administration of the Philippine Islands
concerned political issues primarily, in Roosevelt's estimate, but
policies there did reveal the main economic lineaments of his imperialist outlook. In the United States in the 1890's the feeling
was widespread that the Philippines were indispensable for
access to the markets of Asia (as islands in the Caribbean were
thought to be the means of facilitating the further commercial
penetration of Central and South America), and Roosevelt himself
shared in the anticipation of increased American wealth from

53. To Whitelaw Reid, September 3, 1908, *Letters*, VI, p. 1206.
54. To Joseph G. Cannon, March 2, 1907, *ibid.*, V, pp. 604–605.
55. To Sidney Brooks, November 20, 1908, *ibid.*, VI, p. 1370.

trade. If he found economic considerations less than congenial and beyond his expertise, he nevertheless enjoyed the advantage of a number of notable economic preceptors, especially Brooks Adams, to a lesser extent A. T. Mahan, and in a small way Frederick Jackson Turner. These men showed him that there was a meaning to be ascribed to economic forces in history that he otherwise might not have seen, and they interpreted current developments from the same point of view.

Theodore Roosevelt frankly despised the "economic man," the man who acted or who chose not to act chiefly out of economic advantage; but his very distaste in this regard led him to rely more and more on those whose judgments he much respected. For all his confidence in himself and in his imperialism he was not a completely self-contained hero. The main building stones of his imperialist philosophy had been hewn from family and frontier and later given increasing detail by his experiences in war and peace. The bent of his temperament encouraged him to look for advice in economic matters to those whose grasp of that measurement of history was intellectually respectable and generally consistent with notions already securely a part of him. A *weltpolitik* for the twentieth century, as he realized, would have remained incomplete without some appreciation of economic power.

Of those that helped to impart a specific economic character to Roosevelt's imperialism, Frederick Jackson Turner had some initial influence. Turner's concern with the significance of the frontier had been the personal and scholarly concern of T.R. as well. Turner's thesis seemed largely to confirm and formalize many of his own views. "I have been greatly interested in your pamphlet [*The Significance of the Frontier in American History*]," Roosevelt wrote to Turner as he prepared to write the third volume of *The Winning of the West*. "I think you have struck some first-class ideas, and have put into definite shape a good deal of thought which has been floating around rather loosely." [56] But

56. To Frederick Jackson Turner, February 10, 1894, *ibid.*, I, p. 363; see also to Turner, April 2, 1895, *ibid.*, p. 440; to Turner, April 26, 1895, *ibid.*, p. 446; to Turner, November 4, 1896, *ibid.*, p. 564.

Turner offered a thesis, not a challenge. T.R. noted his scholarly judgments and turned elsewhere, to the seminal Brooks Adams and to the familiar A. T. Mahan, for more provocative analyses of the economic forces at work in the world.

Theodore Roosevelt's understanding of the commercial value of the Philippines was necessarily part of his larger awareness of the future of the United States in Asia. This future became a component of his view of the imperial destiny of the American people. His debt to Brooks Adams in this regard was real enough. Adams's *The Law of Civilization and Decay* (1895) and the application of its main thesis in his timely essays on America's new role in world developments, gathered together and published under the title *America's Economic Supremacy* (1900), took on increasing importance in Roosevelt's thought after 1897. Though long a friend of Adams, it was while T.R. was serving as Assistant Navy Secretary that the two became intellectual confidants. In those years Roosevelt and Adams formed part of that small but persuasive coterie of American imperialist-patriots—Henry Cabot Lodge, A. T. Mahan, John Hay, and W. W. Rockhill, among others —whose individual and interrelated contributions account to no small degree for the American empire.

To Roosevelt, whose historical interests to that date possessed little conscious economic character, discussions in the "Adams seminars" not only confirmed in him a sense of national purpose and challenge, but enabled him to estimate that purpose from a novel perspective. The operation of economic laws that Adams had expounded in apocalyptic fashion in *The Law of Civilization and Decay* demonstrated to Roosevelt, among other things, how much the American nation had need of dedicated men of character.

In *The Law* Adams presented the thesis that was at the core of all his teaching. Long study of economic factors in history had convinced him that the center of trade, and with it wealth and power in the world, had consistently followed a western direction in its movement: from the Middle East to Constantinople, thence to Venice, Amsterdam, London. It appeared, furthermore, that

in the foreseeable future the trade center would gravitate
farther westward still, reaching America. If the theory had held
that much and no more, Americans like Roosevelt would have
reason to rejoice. But *The Law*'s continued operation was inexorable. To Adams, in 1895, it appeared that eventually power
would pass from America on to the Orient, for the entire movement in his view was keyed to the density of population and the
presence of modern centralizing techniques of trade and industry.
It was to China, where density of population would combine with
Russian and German technology, that the arrow of history pointed.
The Law struck Roosevelt as impressive enough in its erudition
and insights, but it was decidedly too gloomy for his temperament.
In his review of the book for *The Forum* he quarreled throughout with Adams's stress on the economic man, while recognizing the thoughtful and sobering thesis of the author.[57]

For Roosevelt, as it came to be for Adams himself, the larger
problem posed by this prophetic analysis was how to devise a
means of frustrating the economic forces at work, how to "repeal"
The Law. T.R. might well have been convinced that the gloomy
forecasts of his friend need never come true if only America remained strong in defense, steadfast in purpose, and self-dis-
ciplined in behavior, in short, followed the lessons of family and
frontier. Yet having once read *The Law*, he probably could never
have really been at ease in his imperialist outlook, even in the
expansive mood of his early Presidency, had not Adams himself
proposed an economic method for "repealing" *The Law*, a means
consistent with the other components of Roosevelt's imperialist
mind.

Between August 1898 and September 1900 Brooks Adams, in a
series of essays appearing in journals of opinion, made more
explicit the meaning of the operation of *The Law* in the contemporary world and how the United States must respond to events
if it was to avoid its own decay. The arguments presented by
Adams complemented the already well-defined imperialist views

57. Roosevelt, "The Law of Civilization and Decay," *Works*, XIV, pp. 129–
150.

of Roosevelt at so many points, it is no great wonder that T.R. accepted Brooks Adams as his senior tutor for the economic aspects of his *weltpolitik*. Specifically, Adams saw the Spanish War "as a link in a long chain of events" wherein the economic advantage passed to the New World.[58] England had reached the apogee of its power and had become stationary, whereas the United States continued to expand rapidly. Thus he argued that England and the United States should join forces "in the face of enemies who fear and hate us."[59] Who those enemies were Adams was impatient to indicate. He foresaw the time, a few years hence, when the Yangtze would be connected with Moscow and Berlin by rail. There were already numerous indicators that the great battle for China, where at the moment Anglo-American financial commitments far exceeded those of their rivals, was shaping up. The United States had to be in that struggle, for her very future depended on its outcome.

The Philippines, "rich, coal-bearing and with many fine harbors seem[ed] a predestined base for the United States," Adams wrote.[60] Manila was described as "lying where all the paths of trade converge, from north and south, east and west . . . the military and commercial key to eastern Asia."[61] Possession of the Islands would "keep the Chinese mainland open to us," making the United States "a greater seat of wealth and power than ever was England, Rome or Constantinople."[62]

Here was historical philosophy at its most apocalyptic, throwing down a challenge to be met. In the struggle envisioned by Adams "the fighting edge" so dear to Roosevelt's heart truly would be indispensable. American possession of the Philippines and the policies implicit in the Open Door notes, commitments Roosevelt inherited as President, were in part at least inspired and required by the arguments from economic factors put forth by Brooks

58. Brooks Adams, *America's Economic Supremacy* (New York, 1947), p. 65.
59. *Ibid.*, p. 71.
60. *Ibid.*, pp. 80–81.
61. *Ibid.*, p. 105.
62. *Ibid.*

Adams and listened to with increasing respect by Roosevelt after 1901.[63]

Only somewhat less influential on Roosevelt in these years were the ideas of A. T. Mahan, especially as they were expressed in his book *The Problem of Asia* (1901). Roosevelt's mind already owed much to Mahan for his earlier treatments of sea power and its role in history. In *The Problem of Asia* Mahan took up the argument for naval power less as a naval propagandist or historian and more as a geopolitical thinker. Like Adams he anticipated that China would be the imperialist arena of the new century.[64] There would be a contest between land power and sea power, between Russia and Germany, and Britain, Japan, and the United States, the latter group all possibly allied together.[65]

The United States had the most to fear from Russia, and Mahan in conjunction with Adams managed to give Roosevelt's imperialist outlook something of an anti-Russia bias. Russia could not be permitted to pre-empt the sea powers from the China trade, as Mahan thought her most likely to attempt to do. Instead, there might have to be some kind of accommodation by the powers in China, perhaps in the form of permanent spheres of influence. But it was imperative that the Yangtze "flowing out of the heart of China" have an "open door" to the commerce of all nations.[66] To Mahan retention of influence in the Yangtze area was essential; he referred to that part of China as "the decisive field where commerce, the energizer of material civilization, can work to the greatest advantage." [67] The advice of America's leading naval thinker blended smoothly with the counsel of Brooks Adams, providing Theodore Roosevelt with the guidelines needed to carry out the economic policy passed on to him at the demise of McKinley.

---

63. William A. Williams, "Brooks Adams and American Expansion," *The New England Quarterly*, Volume XXX, No. 2 (June 1962), pp. 217–232; p. 225. Arthur F. Beringause in *Brooks Adams* (New York, 1955) provides some excellent insights on the Adams-Roosevelt relationship; see especially pp. 143–170.
64. Alfred T. Mahan, *The Problem of Asia*, (Boston, 1901), p. 77.
65. *Ibid.*, p. 44.
66. *Ibid.*, p. 165.
67. *Ibid.*, p. 177.

This policy was one that Roosevelt had little difficulty agreeing with in principle. In the Pacific it aimed to retain Hawaii and the Philippine Islands as steppingstones to the China trade, policy based in a large degree on the influence of businessmen and business associations, business leaders in Government service, and the military with their strategy concepts.[68] Thanks chiefly to Brooks Adams, the President was able to listen with a sympathetic ear to the importunities of American capital investors and entrepreneurs, types he was not always ready to accede to for temperamental and political reasons. In his very first message to Congress in December 1901 he asked the legislature to consider commercial reciprocity between the United States and its possessions for the betterment of mankind, insofar as it was compatible with the welfare of domestic American producers.[69] Roosevelt instinctively linked the two purposes together. He admitted to Adams that for his purpose he had borrowed "one or two ideas" concerning reciprocity from him.[70] Thereafter, in private opinions and in policy pronouncements regarding his imperialist outlook insofar as they displayed an economic element, the presence of Brooks Adams could be generally sensed. Nevertheless, in the Philippines at least, the terms of the peace treaty with Spain, which provided for a ten-year period during which Spanish ships and goods would be admitted to Filipino ports on the same basis as ships and goods from the United States, limited to some extent the exclusive economic tie between America and the Islands desired by interested American enterprise.[71]

68. See Thomas McCormick, "Insular Imperialism and the Open Door: The China Market and the Spanish American War," *The Pacific Historical Review,* Volume XXXII, No. 2 (May 1963), pp. 155–169; p. 162. See also Charles S. Campbell, Jr., *Special Business Interests and the Open Door,* (New Haven, 1951).

69. Roosevelt, "First Annual Message" (1901), *Works,* XVII, p. 112.

70. Specifically, from "Reciprocity and Its Alternatives." To Brooks Adams, September 27, 1901, *Letters,* III, pp. 152–153.

71. *Foreign Relations of the United States, 1898,* pp. 831–840. Some slight trade concessions were made in the United States Revenue Act of 1902. In 1909, however, the United States Tariff Act and the parallel Philippine Tariff Act "instituted virtual reciprocal free trade between the two countries." Shirley Jenkins, *American Economic Policy Toward the Philippines,* (Stanford, 1954), p. 32.

In Theodore Roosevelt's eighth annual message to the Congress, his last report on the state of national affairs as Chief Executive, he left a summary judgment of conditions in the Philippines. He reviewed the methods and purpose, the limitations and the accomplishments of the American experiment there. And at the same time he articulated the constructive qualities of his imperialist rationale.

Real progress toward self-government is being made in the Philippine Islands. The gathering of a Philippine legislative body and the Philippine assembly marks a process absolutely new in Asia, not only as regards Asiatic colonies of European powers but as regards Asiatic possessions of other Asiatic powers; and, indeed, always excepting the striking and wonderful example afforded by the great empire of Japan, it opens an entirely new departure when compared with anything which has happened among Asiatic powers which are their own masters. Hitherto this Philippine legislature has acted with moderation and self-restraint, and has seemed in practical fashion to realize the eternal truth that there must always be government, and that the only way in which any body of individuals can escape the necessity of being governed by outsiders is to show that they are able to restrain themselves, to keep wrong-doing and disorder down. The Filipino people, through their officials, are therefore making real steps in the direction of self-government. I hope and believe that these steps mark the beginning of a course which will continue till the Filipinos become fit to decide for themselves whether they desire to be an independent nation. But it is well for them (and well also for those Americans who during the past decade have done so much damage to the Filipinos by agitation for immediate independence for which they were totally unfit) to remember that self-government depends, and must depend, upon the Filipinos themselves. All we can do is to give them the opportunity to develop the capacity for self-government. If we had followed the advice of the foolish doctrinaires who wished us at any time during the last ten years to turn the Filipino people adrift, we should have shirked the plainest possible duty and have inflicted a lasting wrong upon the Filipino people. We have acted in exactly the opposite spirit. We have given the Filipinos constitutional government—a government based on justice—and we have shown that we have governed them for their good and not for our aggrandizement. At the present time, as during the past ten years, the inexorable logic of facts shows that this government must be supplied by us and not by them. We must be wise and generous; we must help the Filipinos master the difficult art of self-control, which is simply another name for self-government. But we cannot give them self-government save in the sense of governing them so that gradually they may, if they are able, learn to govern themselves. Under the present system of just laws and sympathetic administration, we have every reason to believe that they are gradually acquiring the character which lies at the base of self-government, and for which, if it be lacking, no system of laws, no paper constitution, will in any wise serve as substitute. Our people in the Philippines have achieved what may legitimately be called a marvelous success in giving them a government which marks on the part of those in authority both the necessary understanding of the people and the necessary purpose to serve them disinterestedly and in good faith. I trust that within a generation the time will arrive when the Philippines can decide for themselves whether it is well for them to become independent, or to continue under the protection of a strong and disinterested power, able to guarantee to the islands order at home and protection from foreign invasions. But no one can prophesy the exact date when it will be wise to consider independence as a fixed and definite policy. It would be worse than folly to try to set down such a date in advance, for it must depend upon the way in which the Philippine people themselves develop the power of self-mastery.[72]

All in all, Roosevelt's response to the situation in the Philippines as he inherited it from McKinley provided reassuring confirmation of certain of his most deeply rooted convictions, a successful testing of the hypothesis of empire and of the world movement, an enterprise that had placed the United States among the world leaders. Though force had to be applied to achieve control of the Islands, the major emphasis of the experiment fell on the constructive purpose of human betterment.

Not that Roosevelt's mind was unclouded by doubt during these years. The Boer War presented him with a troublesome quandary. With respect to the whole American position in the China trade, as represented by the Open Door notes, he made a partial retreat in the face of stern realities in the Taft-Katsura

72. Roosevelt, "Eighth Annual Message" (1908), *Works*, XVII, pp. 631–633.

(1905) and the Root-Takahira (1908) agreements, actions which forced Brooks Adams to re-examine his own nationalist assumptions.[73] As he admitted late in his Administration, the Philippines might after all become, from a military standpoint, "our heel of Achilles." [74]

But these seemed more like imperfections than tragic inconsistencies. They were hardly more than suggestions that the world movement contained, potentially at least, a startling contradiction in that expansion could mean destruction and loss of values rather than a constructive promotion of human progress. Appropriately enough, in the working out of Roosevelt's philosophy of imperialism events and not speculation would test further his hypothesis of empire. In the years 1901–1909 the disaster of World War I appeared remote if not unlikely, while the necessity of governing the Islands wisely and of policing the Western Hemisphere was hard by.

II

The selfsame factors that prompted Theodore Roosevelt to encourage the American people to share the white man's burden also caused him to advocate the role of policeman of the American hemisphere, a policeman who did, as it turned out, walk softly enough while carrying a big stick. Many episodes in American diplomacy of greater or lesser importance occurring during Roosevelt's Presidency make up Big Stick diplomacy, and though the details varied with time and place there remained a singleness of motivation: Law and order must be maintained. In evaluating these police actions there is a danger of stressing their purely negative character—admittedly at times this is not easy or proper to avoid—and thereby ignoring the ultimate motivation, namely, the maintenance of law and order as the foundation and beginning of human prosperity.

Because this ultimate consideration often appeared far removed from the immediate controversy, because United States intervention in the internal affairs of small neighboring countries

73. William A. Williams, *loc. cit.*, p. 333.
74. To Silas McBee, August 27, 1907, *Letters*, V, p. 776.

seemed in the first instance of it to promote American advantage, because the President himself spoke and acted frequently with more indignation than dignity, American patrol of the Caribbean area left the impression of a mere display of power. In some respects this impression is no doubt accurate. But aside from Roosevelt's apologia for this policy of intervention, American national interests were vitally concerned in the use of the Big Stick. Even had Roosevelt not been President it is likely that some kind of United States supervision of the hemisphere would have evolved, once the expansionist mood of 1898 had become a settled state of the national mind. The United States had emerged in the Western Hemisphere as the power *sui generis*, it was recognized as such by all concerned, and it could be expected to supervise conditions to its own advantage within the bounds of reason and justice. One-dimensional national interest was a kind of reflex action of early twentieth-century western statesmanship.

In the actual program Roosevelt shaped for the Americas, United States national interest was his vital concern, and he went about securing it in an openly jingoistic fashion. But his nationalistic policies were always characterized by moral righteousness—justice obtaining between men and nations—as his patriotism was joined by a belief in the world movement. Roosevelt equated American national interest with progress for mankind, though national interest for its own sake, like conquest for its own sake, did not denote the limits of his conception of national interest. The promotion of American welfare was appropriate only insofar as this contributed to the good of mankind. The superior nations had the right to conquer in order that the world be stabilized; their very superiority and ability to control other peoples verified the right. The perpetuation of law and order Roosevelt looked upon as a duty of the great nations, and the failure to meet it would see the world revert to chaos. The national interests of the superior countries—and T.R. showed no reluctance in placing his country in the very forefront of the nations— and human well-being were inseparable elements of the world movement. To those who disagreed, for whatever cause, this identity of national interests and the world movement appeared as a particularly specious rationalization, suitable only to cloak accumulations of power. To those who were sympathetic, to Theodore Roosevelt himself, this line of reasoning constituted a historical principle akin to dogma and thus a powerful impulse to action.

Nonetheless, contemporaries who witnessed United States intervention in Cuba and Santo Domingo, those who damned the taking of Panama, and those who cheered the President's insistence on arbitration in the Venezuelan claims dispute had the strong impression that Roosevelt acted on a "might makes right" ethics not unlike the persuasions of social Darwinism. There was some parallel. The power political situation in the world at large was akin to the materialism of the evolutionary universe; the right of superior nations to rule appeared as a possible adaptation of survival of the fittest; the historical patterns inherent in the world movement evinced somewhat the same sense of inevitability as the determinism of the Darwinian account of life and death. Theodore Roosevelt was in fact an evolutionist to some degree, speaking, sometimes acting, and occasionally thinking like one committed to the postulates of natural selection. Although the evolutionary influences were present in his thought they were not decisive or essential, as subsequent discussion in Chapter 4 will make clear. He was an evolutionist largely because it was part of his immediate intellectual heritage. Evolution affected his outlook because he did not choose to reject evolutionary ideas as of no value whatever. Instead, he assimilated many such notions into his philosophy of imperialism, which had taken its major dimension from his conception of the world movement.

In the following critique of the various episodes that are commonly thought illustrative of the Big Stick, Roosevelt's words to William Bayard Hale on the occasion of United States intervention in Santo Domingo in 1904 are important to bear in mind. "The attitude of men like myself toward the weak and chaotic governments and peoples south of us is conditioned not in the least upon the desire for aggrandizements on the part of this Nation," he told Hale, "but solely on the theory that it is our duty, when it becomes absolutely inevitable, to police these countries in the interests of order and civilization." [75] Though the argument could be made, and was made by many critics of the Big Stick, that interference in the domestic affairs of smaller nations brought about aggrandizement as an unavoidable concomitant, it appeared otherwise to Theodore Roosevelt.

Cuba was an especially severe test of the President's optimism regarding the abilities of the backward peoples to rule themselves. Before the Spanish War he had been enthusiastic about Cuban independence, "a quietly rampant *Cuba libre* man." Though he doubted the Cubans would succeed very well in their own government, "anything would be better than a continuance of Spanish rule." [76] Certainly he did not want to annex the island to the United States. [77]

With the war over, the American position in Cuba became awkward. The United States was sincerely and officially in favor of Cuban independence but reluctant to leave the island without attempting to prepare the people for the realities of self-rule and without getting certain guarantees that American national interests would be safeguarded. The Platt Amendment incorporated into the Cuban constitution provided protection for United States interests in that part of the Caribbean. As for the preparation for self-government, Roosevelt believed the administration of Leonard Wood had fulfilled that need in singular fashion. In his judgment Wood created "in effect a civil government managed with an eye to the single benefit of the Cuban people, and so far as possible under the existing conditions it was conducted by the Cuban people themselves. . . . [This] enabled Cuba when she assumed her independence to start with the best possible chance of success." [78] In fact to Speck von Sternburg, the German ambassador in Washington, he described the American military rule in Cuba as "very nearly or quite the ideal of

75. To William Bayard Hale, February 26, 1904, *ibid.*, IV, p. 740.
76. To Anna Roosevelt Cowles, January 2, 1897, *ibid.*, I, pp. 573–574.
77. To Robert Bacon, April 8, 1898, *ibid.*, II, p. 814.
78. To Elihu Root, January 26, 1904, *ibid.*, IV, p. 711; see also Roosevelt, "First Annual Message" (1901), *Works*, XVII, p. 127.

what such a government should be in point of honesty and efficiency alike." [79] This was an optimistic assessment not altogether
warranted by the facts and evidence, furthermore, that T.R. often
saw what he wanted to see. Still, it is a reminder of the kind of
situation Roosevelt in his own way sought to bring about.

United States supervision in Cuba ended in May 1902 with
the election of a Cuban congress and a president. Meanwhile,
in giving some attention to economic relations between Cuba and
the United States, Roosevelt once again revealed the influence
of Brooks Adams. The President was agreeable to business demands for commercial reciprocity because it seemed to him to serve
the interests of both countries. He kept pressure on Congress for
such a trade arrangement, calling a special session of the legislature for that express purpose in June 1902. In his appeal to Congress, he characteristically subordinated economic to political
considerations. Thus he advocated reciprocity because the United
States was likely to play an increasingly important role in the
Caribbean, and economic ties with Cuba might be helpful in
facilitating that political objective.[80] The years after 1902 saw a
considerable economic prosperity on the island, and both Roosevelt and the American people were reassured concerning their efforts to enable Cuba to stand alone. At one point the President
was so optimistic concerning the success of Cuban independence
that he held it out as a model government of a kind to be enjoyed
eventually by the Philippines.[81] In summary, the result of America's Cuba policy was to make possible "a more prosperous
country than any other Spanish-American Republic of approxi-
mately the same size." [82]

Relations between Cuba and the United States in the years
between 1902 and 1906, with the exception of misunderstanding

79. To Baron Herman Speck von Sternburg, March 6, 1902, *Letters*, III, p.
239.
80. David Healy, *The United States in Cuba, 1898–1902* (Madison, 1963),
has a useful discussion of the fight for reciprocity and Roosevelt's role in it.
See pp. 195–205.
81. To Jacob Gould Schurman, August 26, 1904, *Letters*, IV, p. 906.
82. To Charles W. Eliot, April 4, 1904, *ibid.*, p. 770.

over health and sanitation regulations, which the Platt Amendment had required the Cuban Government to enforce carefully, went smoothly. But internal political matters were a different story. The Cuban congress failed to proceed in the spirit of sound constitutional government typical of a traditional republic. It did not act to make municipal offices elective, though this was required by the constitution; political minorities remained unrepresented in the congress despite protests; and rather obvious election frauds were perpetrated in 1905. The party offended by these malpractices, the Liberals, refused to take part in new elections and went into an open revolt against the authority of President Palma in August 1906.

Roosevelt's reaction to the new Cuban crisis was one of disappointment and indignation. "Just at the moment I am so angry with that infernal little Cuban republic that I would like to wipe its people off the face of the earth," was his oft-quoted remark to Henry White. "All we wanted from them was that they should behave themselves and be prosperous and happy so that we would not have to interfere." [83] Whatever legitimate grievances the Liberal Party may have had, they were, to the President, quite insufficient to justify a civil war. What had caused the revolution, in his judgment? He held it to be the inability of the Cubans to truly govern themselves. "These people have had for four years a decent, respectable government of their own. They are not suffering from any real grievance. Yet they deliberately plunged the country into civil war, and if they go on will assuredly deprive themselves of their liberty." [84]

These revolutionary events placed the United States in an embarrassing position, as well as jarring Roosevelt's confidence in the prospect of the Cubans effectively ruling themselves. He brooded over his dilemma. "On the one hand we can not permanently see Cuba prey to misrule and anarchy; on the other hand, I loathe the thought of assuming any control over the island. . . . We emphatically do not want it. . . ." [85] Yet it ap-

83. To Henry White, September 13, 1906, quoted in Allan Nevins, *Henry White, Thirty Years of American Diplomacy*, (New York, 1930), p. 255.
84. To Charles W. Eliot, September 13, 1906, *Letters*, V, p. 410.
85. To Sir George Otto Trevelyan, September 9, 1906, *ibid.*, V, p. 401.

peared the Cubans offered the United States very little choice but intervention, and those Cubans who fomented the civil strife were doing the most to force America's hand, Roosevelt held.[86]

On the strength of the Platt Amendment and the importunities of Cuban officials, but not without misgivings, the President assigned his Secretary of War, Taft, and Robert Bacon, Acting Secretary of State, as special commissioners to Havana. His aim was "to get some *modus vivendi* which would avoid the necessity of [military] intervention on our part, and would give the Cuban republic another chance for its life." [87] Upon arrival in Havana Taft and Bacon found President Palma firmly opposed to making any concessions to his opponents; the atmosphere was thick with political intrigue. They saw no alternative to cabling this evaluation of the situation to Roosevelt, and United States intervention was proclaimed on September 29, 1906. Fortunately, the use of troops was not required to regularize affairs after that date. Both the Government and the rebel group broke off their contention and accepted an American-sponsored provisional government headed by Charles E. Magoon, who succeeded Taft as the ranking American official in this *ad hoc* arrangement. Despite this sad train of events Roosevelt still felt there was a "good chance" for "giving Cuba one more trial of self-government." [88]

The President's summary of American policy relative to the Cuban insurrection, made to Congress in December 1906, stressed somewhat the negative aspects of the police activity undertaken to keep order and the need to intervene before "the representatives of the various European nations in the island would apply to their respective governments for armed intervention to protect the lives and property of their citizens." That the United States was able to act so quickly, he told Congress, was due to the preparedness of the American Navy, the vital instrument of power in the Mahan tradition.[89] Even with the insurrection destroyed by the presence of American officials and the occupation a continuing worry to him, Roosevelt was optimistic. "The path to be trodden

86. To Robert Bacon, September 10, 1906, *ibid.*, p. 402.
87. To Joseph B. Foraker, September 28, 1906, *ibid.*, p. 431.
88. To Henry Cabot Lodge, October 1, 1906, *ibid.*, p. 436.
89. Roosevelt, "Sixth Annual Message" (1906), *Works*, XVII, pp. 456–458.

by those who exercise self-government is always hard," Congress was reminded, "and we should have every charity and patience with the Cubans as they attend this difficult task. I have the utmost sympathy and regard for them. . . ." A year later his hopes were bearing fruit, and he was able to advise Congress that "our expectation is within the coming year to be able to turn the island over again to a government chosen by the people thereof." [90]

It was June 28, 1909, before the second provisional government could be brought to a close with inauguration of a new Cuban president and a new cabinet. Meanwhile, Roosevelt had occasion to reflect on the practical difficulties of teaching a less advanced people the skillful art of self-government. His conclusion was that the Cubans needed a very firm hand to superintend their renewed preparation for self-rule. The provisional government itself therefore proceeded to initiate reforms that included a stricter definition of presidential powers, a rejuvenated judiciary and more efficient administrative procedures, and an increase in the political weight assigned to the provinces. When elections for a president were finally held and full Cuban authority re-established, Roosevelt insisted that it be clearly understood by the Cubans that all reforms of the provisional government were to remain in effect. These laws could not be ignored unless they were formally and specifically rescinded by constituted authority. The reason for this caution was elemental: The first Cuban congress had been so inept that if the new was like the old it could not be trusted to enact proper legislation.

Once the new Government came into being it appeared appropriate to Roosevelt to leave some administrative assistants on the island to help the Cubans over the rough spots by insuring honest elections and keeping honest account books.[91] The mastery of self-government was a difficult art indeed, though as the President left office in 1909 he had reason to believe the Cubans could rule themselves after all. In this light police responsibilities by the great hemispheric power were not without some compensation. "At least," Roosevelt thought, "it is evident that we have done our

90. Roosevelt, "Seventh Annual Message" (1907), *ibid.*, p. 566.
91. To Elihu Root, July 20, 1908, *Letters,* VI, p. 1137.

best to put Cuba on the road to stable and orderly government." [92] In the years after 1906 his attitude toward Cuban affairs underwent a noticeable and meaningful moderation. Roosevelt's sincere desire to teach the ways of responsible rule had all but submerged his initial infuriation at the rebellion.

The political perplexities in Cuba and the articulation of United States policy they occasioned, which the President effectively managed, constituted a diplomatic episode that did not involve another major power. If it had not quite been a domestic contretemps, neither was it an international crisis. In contrast, the failure of responsible government in the independent nation of Venezuela in 1902 during the regime of Cipriano Castro had international implications of the first magnitude.

Castro's control of Venezuela which had begun in 1899 was simply one more phase in the history of a country widely reputed for civil unrest, property insecurity, and financial dishonesty. Since this particular trouble in 1902 touched the interests of Great Britain and Germany these two nations seemed determined to intervene to satisfy the claims of their citizens against Venezuela. Castro spurned offers of mediation, and the English and Germans jointly blockaded the principal ports in December 1902. Military action subsequently involved bombardment by naval guns of several ports and a brief flurry of troop activity before the blockade was lifted in February of the next year. The presence of the superior Anglo-German force left Castro no choice but to accept the arbitration he had previously refused.

The United States could not and did not remain insensitive to this crisis. In light of Roosevelt's strong support of the stand taken by President Cleveland in 1895 and his espousal of an extended meaning of the Monroe Doctrine on that occasion and frequently thereafter, the general reaction of Roosevelt as President to this new problem was easily predictable. In point of fact, however, it was somewhat more deliberate and diplomatic than

92. To Sidney Brooks, December 28, 1908, *ibid.*, p. 1445.

frenzied, though circumstances were no less provocative than they had been in 1895. Roosevelt's policy from the start in 1902 was one of watchful waiting as the crisis grew. Regarding possible German ambitions in Central or South America, fears concerning which he had confided to Lodge at a time when naval preparation was not progressing to his satisfaction,[93] his policy was not aggressively nationalistic. He had made a restrained and reasonable statement of the meaning of the Monroe Doctrine to the German ambassador, von Sternburg, in July 1901. "I do not want the United States territorially to aggrandize itself in South America, and neither do I want to see any European country so aggrandize itself. If any South American State misbehaves towards any European country, let the European country spank it. . . . My attitude is most emphatically one which is really for ultimate peace in this matter." [94]

As the crisis in Venezuela approached a flash point in November 1902 the policy of the Roosevelt Administration remained one of nonintervention. Both the President and Secretary of State Hay believed the United States should stand ready to provide good offices to facilitate a peaceful settlement, but apparently no direct pressure was applied to bring about this kind of solution prior to the decision of the British and the Germans to move in a naval force.

The utilization of naval power began on December 9 when the Anglo-German squadron seized four Venezuelan gunboats. On December 11 a blockade went into effect and on the 13th the United States submitted a Venezuelan proposal for arbitration to the Allied Powers. In this fashion the United States became directly but diplomatically involved in the claims dispute. It is unnecessary here to become entangled in the considerable historical controversy over the role of Theodore Roosevelt in forcing arbitration, upon the Germans especially, by threats of American naval action.[95] This much is beyond dispute. The Germans had

93. To Henry Cabot Lodge, March 27, 1901, *ibid.*, III, pp. 31–32.
94. To Herman Speck von Sternburg, July 12, 1901, *ibid.*, p. 116.
95. Howard K. Beale provides a useful summary of the historical debate as well as an impressive array of arguments to support the contention that Roosevelt indeed forced the Germans to arbitrate under threat of American naval action. Beale, *op. cit.*, pp. 395–432.

no solid reasons for refusing arbitration and had indicated their willingness to explore this avenue of settlement prior to the institution of the blockade.[96] President Roosevelt did inform "the German ambassador that . . . the Kaiser ought to know unless an agreement of arbitration was reached American public opinion would soon be at a point where [Roosevelt] would have to move Dewey's ships . . . south to observe matters along Venezuela." The President's later judgment of the matter was that because of his known opposition to German occupation of Venezuelan soil beyond a few days or a week the Germans, in the person of their ambassador, came "to terms at once." [97] He had acted, whether his conversations with von Sternburg constituted an ultimatum or a piece of judicious diplomacy, with the principles of the Monroe Doctrine fixed in mind.[98]

In his first annual message to Congress he had defined his position on the Monroe Doctrine. "The Monroe Doctrine is a declaration that there must be no territorial aggrandizement by any non-American power at the expense of any American power on American soil. It is in nowise intended as a hostile act to any nation of the Old World. . . . It is simply a step, and a long step, toward assuring the universal peace of the world by securing the possibility of permanent peace on this hemisphere." [99] In other words, he looked upon the Monroe Doctrine as a specific application of the principles directing the world movement, the general frame of reference for his historical outlook and for his imperialism. In purpose the Monroe Doctrine was not unlike the Open Door in China. Indeed to von Sternburg Roosevelt made that very comparison. "I regard the Monroe Doctrine as being equivalent to an open door in South America. That is, I do not want the United States or any power to get territorial possessions in South America but to let South America gradually develop on its own lines, with an open door to all nations. . . ." [100]

96. See Howard C. Hill, *Roosevelt and the Caribbean,* (Chicago, 1927), pp. 107 ff.

97. To Whitelaw Reid, June 27, 1906, *Letters,* V, p. 319.

98. For example, in a letter to Henry White, August 14, 1906, his own description of the interview with von Sternburg is a puzzling mixture of tact and forceful persuasion. *Ibid.,* p. 358.

99. Roosevelt, "First Annual Message" (1901), *Works,* XVII, p. 134.

100. To Herman Speck von Sternburg, October 11, 1901, *Letters,* III, p. 172.

The United States sponsored these two similar policies in the belief that they were necessary and wise as specific implementations of the major premises of beneficent western imperialism. The Monroe Doctrine, especially dear to the President, ought to be used in such manner as to show that it would never "become a pretense for self-aggrandizement at the expense of Latin-American republics," he once explained to Spring-Rice, "and on the other hand that it not be warrant for letting any of these republics remain small bandit nests of a wicked and inefficient type." [101] Neither of these alternatives would satisfy the cause of ultimate human betterment. Roosevelt seemed to wield the Big Stick in this Venezuelan crisis, threatening to chastise any power in order to protect the United States' advantage as represented by the Monroe Doctrine. This is an impression Roosevelt did little to alter, much less to rectify. It is simply not the whole of the story.

One final observation is appropriate. Roosevelt's apparent willingness to allow a nation or nations other than the United States to act to protect its interests in a Latin-American state—"if any South American State misbehaves towards any European country, let the European country spank it"—has some arresting implications for his later implementation of the Monroe Doctrine and for the working out of his concept of the world movement. And it provides a marked contrast in tone between the deliberate attitude in Venezuela and the passionate involvement in Panama. There is a time factor and a geopolitical factor to be weighed in this connection. Had this claims dispute occurred some years later Roosevelt, possessing greater self-assurance, would have proceeded more aggressively. Even more likely, had the dispute taken place in a matter where United States interests were better defined, was that the President would have been much less favorable to arbitration. His "taking of Panama" in 1903 was the first instance of his extreme sensitivity to real national advantage, while the very positive position he assumed in the long, drawn-out claims dispute in Santo Domingo from 1904 to 1907 illustrated both time and geopolitical considerations. The Big Stick was a developing

101. To Sir Cecil Spring-Rice, July 24, 1905, *ibid.*, IV, p. 1286.

instrument of policy and not a static frame of mind, as Roosevelt's action in Santo Domingo in 1904 and after showed.

Events in Santo Domingo in 1904 and the years following suggested to President Roosevelt that preventive medicine might be a wise prescription for alleviating the ills of some Latin-American republics and thus for maintaining the good political health of the entire hemisphere. Providing for the safety of the Americas in this way would avoid the excuse for interference by European nations seeking toe-holds in this United States sphere of influence. Equally significant in the perspective of the world movement, the Venezuelan incident of 1902 was potentially the kind of situation in which the superior nations might themselves clash with each other. This would be nothing especially new since European rivalry for empire had been lively for many decades, and very real areas of conflict, such as Fashoda in Africa (1898) and the Dardanelles, had appeared and would continue to do so.

But the United States was not so directly concerned in Africa or the Middle East as it had to be in the Americas. The Latin republics to the south were so frequently unstable that they offered a standing invitation for foreign intervention, should one of the superior powers determine to venture it. Though it might be agreed that the chances of this developing were slim in view of the more attractive and more accessible areas for imperialist expansion, nevertheless to Roosevelt and to the American people the possibility existed and hence must be guarded against. Though strict American enforcement of the Monroe Doctrine did prevent a rupture of the world movement in the Western Hemisphere, rivalry for empire in the world at large, where the United States could not be effective as a deterrent, harbored dangerous provocations within the world movement.

A fresh challenge to law and order in the hemisphere and to the Monroe Doctrine had reached the acute stage by the summer of 1904. The trouble spot was Santo Domingo; the problem, the financial irresponsibility of successive Dominican Governments. Although it had become an independent state in 1844, the Dominican Republic had been continuously under the control of reckless, corrupt politicians and military dictators. Civil unrest was the rule and revolutions frequent. Such a revolution was in progress in 1904. In Roosevelt's own words ". . . after a hundred years of freedom [Santo Domingo] shows itself utterly incompetent for governmental work." [102] This state of affairs made the role of policeman the inevitable if distasteful hemispheric duty of the United States. At first, in February 1904, Roosevelt preferred not to intervene in the political disasters of the country, "hoping and praying" that it would not be required, though it might come to a matter of "what a policeman had to do." As for annexing the area, he had "about the same desire to annex it as a gorged boa constrictor might have to swallow a porcupine wrong-end-to." [103]

A deteriorating situation in Santo Domingo, however, could gradually nudge him to positive action. By April he was writing that if he were motivated by "the spirit of altruistic humanitarian duty I would grant the prayers of the best people of the island and take partial possession of it tomorrow." That he did not act in this fashion was due, he added, to the misunderstanding of his purposes and motives likely to ensue at home. Respectful of public opinion, he also resented it, finding it necessary to delay until "even the blindest" could see the propriety of some kind of American intervention in Dominican affairs.[104] Although he was undecided and reluctant to act politically, in early 1904 he cabled Rear Admiral Wise at Guantanamo naval base to take precautions for protecting American lives and property in the disturbed area.

The demands of the European creditors, Italy, Germany, and Spain, became more insistent in the summer of 1904. During that same period, on July 14, the Dominican Government agreed to arrangements for paying the sum of $40,000 a month to the Santo

102. To Theodore Roosevelt, Jr., February 10, 1904, *ibid.*, p. 734.
103. To Joseph B. Bishop, February 23, 1904, *ibid.*, p. 734.
104. To Charles W. Eliot, April 4, 1904, *ibid.*, p. 770.

Domingo Improvement Company, a New York corporation; should the Dominican Government default on these payments an American representative of the company was to take over the collection of customs for the northern ports of the republic. The American agent—a private citizen, it should be noted—took up his duties in October because of the inability of the Dominican Government to pay the prescribed sum. This development jeopardized the continuance of the Government itself and reduced appreciably the likelihood that the European creditors would be able to collect their money claims. As the weeks passed it clearly was a situation that became more complicated and more dangerous.

Roosevelt chose to show his hand regarding Santo Domingo in his annual message of 1904. Disavowing any land hunger and offering reassurances that the United States desired only "stable, orderly and prosperous neighbors" he pronounced a warning and in effect a policy.

If a nation shows that it knows how to act with a reasonable efficiency and decency in social and political matters, if it keeps order and pays its obligations, it need fear no interference from the United States. Chronic wrong-doing, or an impotence which results in a general loosening of the ties of civilized society, may in America as elsewhere, ultimately require intervention by some civilized nations, and in the western hemisphere the adherence of the United States to the Monroe Doctrine may force the United States, however reluctantly, in flagrant cases of such wrong doing or impotence, to the exercise of an international police power.[105]

It remained only to implement the Roosevelt Corollary to the Monroe Doctrine.

The Dominican Government had sounded out the United States on the possibility of some kind of joint fiscal control in both 1903 and early 1904, only to be turned down on both occasions.[106] The worsening crisis late in 1904, in combination with Roosevelt's determination to intervene actively in Dominican affairs, reversed the previous United States position. The American minister to

105. Roosevelt, "Fourth Annual Message" (1904), *Works*, XVII, p. 299.
106. Hill, *op. cit.*, pp. 157–158.

Santo Domingo, on instructions from Secretary of State Hay, who was himself taking orders directly from the President, indicated to the Dominicans that a new request for help in the collection of revenues would be welcomed. The Dominican officials complied with this suggestion. The tone of the American inquiry was "in a perfectly friendly spirit." [107] Detailed arrangements were contained in the Dillingham-Sanchez protocol signed on January 20, 1905. This agreement committed the United States to guarantee the territorial integrity of the Dominican Republic and to supervise the collection of all customs, 45 percent of which was to be turned back to the Dominican Government and 55 percent used to pay the various creditors.

Opposition to this protocol, especially to its political provisions concerning territorial integrity, crystallized in Santo Domingo almost at once, so that the presence of U. S. naval vessels was the only sure guarantee of the continuance of the Dominican Government in power. Opposition in the United States Senate was no less pronounced, many critics pointing out that the President was supporting in power a government of dubious reputation. A new protocol was drawn up and submitted to the Senate in February. It failed of approval at that time and once again in a special session called by Roosevelt after his inauguration. This senatorial unwillingness to go along with the Chief Executive's policy put a further strain on the Dominican Government and thereby a further strain on the Monroe Doctrine, in Roosevelt's judgment.[108] He took the position that a vote against the protocol was a vote to refuse relief that Santo Domingo badly needed and sincerely wanted. Worse still, "every man who votes against this treaty by his vote invites foreign nations to violate the Monroe Doctrine." [109]

The arrival in island waters (March 14) of an Italian cruiser seemingly intent on pressing Italian claims presaged the fall of the Dominican Government and perhaps the confirmation of Roosevelt's fears about the Monroe Doctrine. What could not be

107. To Robert Bridges, March 21, 1905, *Letters,* IV, p. 1143.
108. *House Document I,* 59th Congress, 1st session, I, p. 298.
109. To John Spooner, February 25, 1905, *Letters,* IV, p. 1128.

formally arranged was now informally arranged. To Roosevelt the American policy stake in Santo Domingo, as underscored by the presence of U. S. warships there, was too great to be unprotected. An exchange of views between the Dominican minister of finance and the American minister, T. C. Dawson, produced a *modus vivendi*. By this most informal of understandings the Dominicans offered to name an American citizen as the one official responsible for the collection of customs, and the previously agreed-to 45–55 per cent split of revenues was to go into effect. Various creditors indicated their acceptance of this arrangement, according to information supplied by Dawson to the State Department.

The President's response to all this was prompt and unambiguous (and, his critics said, unconstitutional): "I direct that the Minister [Dawson] express acquiescence in the proposal . . . pending the action of the United States Senate upon the treaty. . . . This action is rendered necessary by the peculiar circumstances of the case." His reason for so acting was equally clear: "to maintain the *status quo*." [110] Both the pressure of the creditor nations for some sort of accommodation and the threat to the Monroe Doctrine could be obviated if some temporary device, backed by men-of-war, could be employed pending regularization by treaty. Though his action only gave more ammunition to those denouncing "executive usurpation," Roosevelt found some reassurance in the fact that certain of his leading opponents in the Senate "took for granted . . . some such action as that proposed" in the *modus vivendi*.[111] The President had not run as far ahead of public opinion as formal senatorial opposition suggested.

This *ad hoc* arrangement for American supervision of Dominican financial affairs went into effect April 1, 1905. Col. George R. Colton, formerly collector of customs for the Philippines, was named general receiver and Jacob H. Hollander, a Johns Hopkins professor who had had experience in Puerto Rico and in Indian territory, was named a special commissioner. It was an

110. To William G. Tiffany, March 14, 1905, *ibid.*, p. 1139.
111. To Alvey A. Adee, March 28, 1905, *ibid.*, p. 1149.

enterprise Roosevelt defended as being in the best interests of both the United States and Santo Domingo. "In Santo Domingo we have taken the necessary step," he told John Hay,[112] later adding that he was satisfied that the "solution has worked so well that the public is paying no heed to the matter whatever." [113]

But it was the preservation of national interest rather than special or private interest that concerned him. Typically, Roosevelt did not want to promote or to appear to promote the advantage of any individual or group. His attitude with respect to the claims of the American-backed improvement company in Santo Domingo exemplified this. Col. Colton had some doubts about the full validity of this corporation's claims against the Dominican Government. Accordingly, Roosevelt wrote to Special Commissioner Hollander on the matter: "I am always afraid of seeming to back any big company which has financial interests in one of these South American states and can only do so under the narrowest restrictions and most sharply defined conditions." [114] Such a comment reveals the indifference of the President to the economic argument of what was to become dollar diplomacy, as well as his constant political preoccupation.

The political considerations of Roosevelt's actions were plainly evident in the formal explanation he chose to make of his Dominican policy in his fifth annual message, parts of which were verbatim reiterations of previous public addresses. It was obvious in his address to Congress that he judged a continuance of the *status quo* in Santo Domingo to be essentially a measure for the maintaining of the Monroe Doctrine and that this doctrine was his central concern. He spoke of the "imminent danger of foreign intervention," of the need to prevent "the seizure of territory in Santo Domingo by a European power." He pointed out that by the *modus vivendi* "the mere fact that the collectors of customs are Americans . . . performing their duty with efficiency and honesty . . . gives a certain moral power to the government which it has not had before. This has completely discouraged all rev-

112. To John Hay, March 30, 1905, *ibid.*, p. 1150.
113. To John Hay, April 2, 1905, *ibid.*, p. 1156.
114. To Jacob H. Hollander, July 3, 1905, *ibid.*, p. 1259.

olutionary movements. . . ." Furthermore, Roosevelt claimed, "under the course taken, stability and order and all the benefits of peace are at last coming to Santo Domingo, danger of foreign intervention has been suspended. . . . Under the proposed treaty the independence of the island is scrupulously respected, the danger of violation of the Monroe Doctrine by the intervention of foreign powers vanishes." In keeping with the view that Roosevelt held of the Monroe Doctrine as a specific adaptation of national policy to the world movement, he concluded his remarks to Congress on a positive, constructive note. American policy, he declared, "will give the people of Santo Domingo the same chance to move onward and upward which we have already given to the people of Cuba. . . . If we fail to take advantage of this chance it will be of damage to ourselves and it will be of incalculable damage to Santo Domingo. Every consideration of policy, and above all, every consideration of large generosity" supported the Administration's position.[115]

The President had to wait many months, until February 25, 1907, for the Senate to adopt a treaty with Santo Domingo. Even then there were some significant omissions from the original protocol, all of them tending to lessen the prospect of future United States intervention in the internal affairs of the island republic. During that time of waiting for Senate action, Roosevelt continued to view his policy with undiminished confidence and to defend it with considerable vigor, for he was utterly convinced of the morality of what he had brought about, even though it required a show of force by the Navy.[116] To Andrew Carnegie the President argued that peace had been his aim for the Americas when he took action in Santo Domingo. "If only the Senate will ratify the Dominican treaty, we shall have taken another stride in that direction," he wrote.[117]

Conditions in Santo Domingo itself did much to support his confident assertions. When the informal arrangements went into

115. Roosevelt, "Fifth Annual Message" (1905), *Works*, XVII, p. 355.
116. To Charles J. Bonaparte, September 4, 1905, *Letters*, V, p. 10; to Joseph Lincoln Steffens, February 6, 1906, *ibid.*, p. 147; to Henry Cabot Lodge, April 30, 1960, *ibid.*, pp. 253–256.
117. To Andrew Carnegie, August 6, 1906, *ibid.*, p. 346.

effect in April 1905 the Dominican treasury was empty, public services nonexistent, violation of the law widespread. Upon the termination of the arrangement (July 31, 1907) the treasury held $3,223,000; the 45 per cent share of the receipts constituted a greater amount of money than the total collections at any time before American supervision commenced. In addition roads, schools, and other public improvements were under way. In Roosevelt's judgment he had "put the affairs of the island on a better basis than they had been for a century—indeed it would not be an overstatement to say on a better basis than they had ever been before." [118]

With the exception of the involvement with Colombia over canal rights in Panama, President Roosevelt wielded the Big Stick far more determinedly in Santo Domingo than in any other Caribbean crisis. The presence of the Navy was helpful if not critical during the first uncertain weeks of 1905. In a defense not unlike his classic justification for "taking Panama," he told the Harvard Union that "while the coordinate branch of the government discussed whether or not I usurped power and finally concluded that I had not . . . we collected more money than [the Santo Domingans] ever got when they collected one hundred percent themselves; and the island prospered as never before." [119] But even in this forceful example of power diplomacy he had been anxious to act in the best interests of the people of Santo Domingo as he judged them. If this implied that he knew better than many islanders what was good for them, it was merely another expression of his belief in the superiority of his race, one of the working principles of the world movement.

Chronologically speaking, it was the first instance of aggressive Rooseveltian diplomacy—the acquisition of canal rights in Panama—that stands as the best single example of the positive and negative effects of United States policy in Central American

118. To Sidney Brooks, December 20, 1908, *ibid.*, VI, p. 1445.
119. Roosevelt, "Athletics, Scholarship and Public Service," *Works,* XV, pp. 482–495; p. 493.

affairs. In the "taking of Panama" virtually every element in Theodore Roosevelt's conception of and contribution to the world movement stands out. Because of his highly personal and unusually decisive part in the Panama episode, it may be said to summarize various conflicting ingredients that must be placed in relationship one to another in evaluating Roosevelt's world movement frame of reference. Some of these elements were not easily reconciled. In theory probably there can be no satisfactory resolution of them. Yet Big Stick, and therefore United States, diplomacy over a number of years were both based on such a set of principles with divergent values. This indicates that in a particular crisis a collision of principles can be avoided by a statesman's response to the exigencies of a given moment. The progression of events resolves at the time and for the time being the inconsistencies upon which policy may be based, inconsistencies that in the case of the acquisition of canal rights in Panama were no more forgivable by opponents critical of the action than they were admissible by Roosevelt years after the events had taken place.

As was typical of the leading issues early in his Administration, Roosevelt did not inherit in Panama a general condition that he was relatively free to act upon, but a defined policy that already had received some implementation under President McKinley. As McKinley's successor and as a Republican President, he was to a degree committed to his predecessor's intentions to construct a canal somewhere in Central America.

Roosevelt personally was strongly in favor of the canal undertaking. Years before, in 1894, he had linked United States construction of an Isthmian canal to the right and necessity of national expansion into the Pacific. Samoa, Hawaii, a great navy, and a canal—these were all crucial to America's world position, and he wished his Republican Party would build the canal "with the money of Uncle Sam."[120] The Spanish War intensified interest in the prospect of an American-sponsored canal, and Roosevelt with his special concern for the Navy and his sense

120. To Anna Roosevelt, May 20, 1894, *Letters*, I, p. 379; to Henry Cabot Lodge, October 27, 1894, *ibid.*, p. 409.

of naval strategy as it affected national prestige wanted to be sure that if such a canal was built it would be fortified by the United States rather than in some manner internationalized. He told Albert Shaw that a canal was not enough, only a fortified canal would serve American interests. "Better have no canal at all than not give us the power to control it in time of war," [121] he wrote.

In the amplification of his canal views Roosevelt tended to emphasize several large considerations. First among them was the Monroe Doctrine. "If Germany has the same right we have in the canal across Central America," he observed to John Hay in expressing his unqualified disapproval of the first Hay-Pauncefote agreement, "then why not in the partition of any part of South America? . . . If we invite foreign powers to a joint ownership or a joint guarantee of what so vitally concerns us . . . how can we possibly object to similar joint action say in Southern Brazil . . . ?" [122] A second strategic aspect of the canal enterprise was the solidification of Anglo-American friendship that would no doubt result. In Roosevelt's opinion "it is really for England's interest that America should fortify the canal," [123] thus relieving the British of military responsibilities in the Western Hemisphere at a time when her world position faced the new German challenge. A greater identity of the superior Anglo-American peoples with each other was completely consistent with Roosevelt's historical premises, and when circumstances promoted what he accounted mutual advantage for England and the United States he very willingly lent his support. Roosevelt also chose to see the canal in terms of the ultimate purpose of the world movement—the betterment of mankind that could be expected from it—though at first he was inclined to stress this as resulting from the promotion of American national interest.[124]

Britain's formal acquiescence in the United States' intention to build an Isthmian canal made determination of the route the

121. To Albert Shaw, February 15, 1900, *ibid.*, II, p. 1187.
122. To John Hay, February 18, 1900, *ibid.*, p. 1192.
123. To Sir Cecil Spring-Rice, March 2, 1900, *ibid.*, p.
124. Roosevelt, *Autobiography, Works,* XXII, pp. 583 ff.

waterway would take the next step. Two routes were under serious consideration by the United States at the time. One was across Nicaragua, where the presence of natural lakes promised to facilitate the construction, and the other was in Panama, where a French company had tried and failed to link the two great oceans of the world. Roosevelt was especially concerned about doing the politically correct thing. Though he was not against a Nicaraguan canal in principle,[125] he was aware that the weight of engineering opinion favored the Panama route, and to him this figured as a very important plus factor for that route. His respect for expert engineering judgment was reinforced by his desire to avoid a disaster at the canal site and harm to his political career. With congressional approval of a canal across Panama (the Spooner Act, June 1902) the President was anxious to complete arrangements for construction in that area.[126] Panama or Nicaragua? The important thing was to make the dirt fly.[127]

Anticipating a successful arrangement with Colombia for Isthmian rights, the President in his second annual message to Congress played up the positive aspects of a great canal, linking human betterment with national advantage. "The Canal will be of great benefit to America and of importance to all the world," he declared. "It will be of advantage to us industrially and also as improving our military position. It will be of advantage to the countries of tropical America. . . . It will invite to their shores commerce and improve their material conditions by recognizing that stability and order are prerequisites of successful development.[128]

Unhappily, the negotiations between the United States and

125. Henry F. Pringle, *Theodore Roosevelt, A Biography*, (New York, 1931), p. 302.
126. *Ibid.*
127. The Walker Commission had estimated as follows:
$189,864,062 for a Nicaraguan Canal.
$144,233,350 for a Panama Canal.
$109,141,500 for rights and property of the New Panama Canal Company. However, the commission placed the real value of the French properties at no more than $40,000,000. The French corporation agreed to reduce its claims to that amount, making the Panama Canal slightly cheaper according to estimates.
128. Roosevelt, "Second Annual Message" (1902), *Works*, XVII, pp. 176–177.

Colombia ran a troubled course from the start. Talks between Dr. Concha, the Colombian minister in Washington, and Secretary Hay had begun as early as March, at a time when Congress was still debating the choice of routes. Roosevelt was in almost constant contact with Hay and thus knew daily the frustrations attendant upon Concha's refusal to accept American terms. "Terms" rather than "proposals" better describes the tone of the American attitude. Perhaps these frustrations experienced by men bargaining from a position of strength contributed to Roosevelt's determination to take Panama. Diplomatic decisions of great moment are not of necessity insulated from such personal factors.

American demands upon the Colombians were far-reaching. The United States insisted that Colombia renounce its sovereignty over a canal zone. This was the principal and most onerous proposal. In addition, however, Colombia was to be prohibited from dealing with the French company, the New Panama Canal Company as it was called, for cancellation of concessions previously granted. In return for these accommodations the United States agreed to pay an indemnity of $10,000,000, along with annual payments of $250,000. Dr. Concha considered the monetary arrangements grossly inadequate when compared with the surrenders of principle and territory asked of his country, for what the United States was seeking was no less than an infringement of Colombian sovereignty.

Only after months of conversations, during which Concha himself withdrew in protest over the American attitude, was an agreement of sorts reached. Concha had left Tomas Herran, the Colombian chargé in Washington, to continue representations to the State Department. When Hay informed the Bogotá government on December 30, 1902, that the United States intended to switch to a Nicaraguan canal, the pressure was sufficient to bring about agreement. The Hay-Herran Convention, granting the United States demands, was signed on January 22, 1903, and approved by the American Senate the following March 17. Thereafter the fate of the treaty rested with Bogotá.

The Colombian Government, in the hands of President Marroquin, a dictator who had come to power by a *coup d'état* in 1898, was opposed to the terms of the Hay-Herran Convention from the outset. Dispatches sent by the American minister at Bogotá, A. M. Beaupré, leave no doubt on this score, portraying the source of Colombian opposition as national pride rather than personal greed.[129] Marroquin convened a special session of the Colombian congress, which he had hitherto ignored, to consider the treaty. The congress merely became an additional source of virulent opposition to the proposed accord. The United States Government for its part was adamant and unyielding in its position; any change whatsoever in the provisions that Bogotá might suggest would be construed as a sign of bad faith and would be summarily rejected by Washington. If, as Roosevelt claimed, he was in direct, personal charge of guiding American policy toward Colombia during these months [130] he must be held responsible for the unrelenting pressure brought upon the smaller nation and the highhanded manner of its execution.[131] Despite this American insistence and Theodore Roosevelt to the contrary, the Colombian congress rejected the treaty on August 12. Events had now placed the American Government in a quandary. Secretary Hay advised the President that two courses of action remained open to the United States: reactivation of a Nicaraguan canal project or construction in Panama regardless of Colombia.

Meanwhile, in August, about the same time the treaty was rejected at Bogotá, Roosevelt was shown a memorandum written by John Bassett Moore, a professor of international law at Columbia University and himself a former Assistant Secretary of State. Acting Secretary of State F. B. Loomis was instrumental in placing the Moore critique before the President. Roosevelt read Moore's statement with consuming interest. It was Moore's professional opinion that an old (1846) treaty between the United States and New Granada (Colombia), guaranteeing to the United States "the right of way in transit across the Isthmus of Panama upon any modes of communication that now exist, or that may be here-

129. Hill, *op. cit.*, p. 51.
130. To Henry Cabot Lodge, January 28, 1909, *Letters*, VI, p. 1491.
131. Hill, *op. cit.*, p. 52.

after constructed, shall be free and open to the Government and citizens of the United States," still carried weight.[132]

While Professor Moore, reflecting the caution of his craft, contended only that this old treaty provided grounds for a serious continuation of negotiations, to Roosevelt it meant much more than that. It meant that the United States already had sufficient legal grounds to warrant action in the name of a Panama canal. "If under the Treaty of 1846 we have a color of right to start in and build the canal," he confided to Hay, "my off-hand judgment would favor such proceedings. It seems that the great bulk of the best engineers are agreed that that route is the best, and I do not think that the Bogotá lot of jack rabbits should be allowed permanently to bar one of the future highways of civilization." [133]

It is doubtful that the Moore memorandum and a subsequent meeting with Moore at Sagamore Hill in mid-September had yet convinced the President finally of the line of action to be taken; events had not as yet progressed so far. On September 10, for example, he told Jacob Gould Schurman of his canal dilemma. He admitted his fear that any public statement on his part "would undoubtedly be taken as equivalent to an effort to incite [in Panama] an insurrection" favorable to American ambitions. But he added he would "infinitely prefer to get title to the Canal outright" and did not "consent for one moment to the view that Colombia had the right permanently to block one of the world's great highways." Perhaps he hesitated in his decision because of his agreement with Schurman "that to wait a few months, or even a year or two, is nothing compared with having the thing done rightly." [134]

A week later, on the day of his meeting with Moore, he was still inclined to wonder which canal should be built. "No one can tell what will come out in the Isthmian Canal business," he observed to Taft. "This winter we may start the Nicaraguan Canal, or the *course of events* may force us to take action in Panama." [135] A letter to Hay dated the same day, September 15, added further

132. *Ibid.*, p. 39.
133. To John Hay, August 19, 1903, *Letters*, III, pp. 566–567.
134. To Jacob Gould Schurman, September 10, 1903, *ibid.*, p. 595.
135. To William Howard Taft, September 15, 1903, *ibid.*, p. 598 (italics added).

claim to his indecision, just as it left undisputed his contempt for the Bogotá Government. "At present I feel there are two alternatives. (1) To take up Nicaragua; (2) in some shape or way to interfere when it becomes necessary so as to secure the Panama route without further dealing with the foolish and homicidal corruptionists in Bogotá." [136] The overtones of these confidences to Taft and Hay are remarkably indicative of the President's willingness to keep his policy flexible enough to be able to respond most advantageously to a developing situation.

With no small amount of assistance from the Panama conspirators "the course of events" took a fortuitous turn: revolution in Panama against Colombian authority. The conspiracy, dominated at this stage by Bunau-Varilla, had no official assurances from Washington that the United States would support an uprising at the Isthmus, a *coup* that would have as its objective an independent Republic of Panama free to deal directly with the American Government regarding canal rights.

Neither did the conspirators receive any discouragement of their plans. In a conversation with the President, Bunau-Varilla heard from the Chief Executive such extreme expressions of hostility toward Colombia that he could not and did not assume that the United States would allow a Panama revolution to fail.[137] Furthermore, the President ordered the U.S.S. *Marblehead,* the U.S.S. *Dixie,* and the U.S.S. *Nashville* into the waters around the Isthmus to prevent any hostile force from occupying Panama. The legal basis of his instructions to his naval commanders was the provision of the Treaty of 1846 guaranteeing the "perfect neutrality" of the Isthmus. American forces successfully "neutralized" the area to the distinct benefit of the revolutionaries when the time was appropriate.

The nature and extent of Roosevelt's complicity in these swiftly moving events, however, is less germane than his reasons for acting or not acting.[138] As the rebels made their preparations, in which Roosevelt apparently had no direct part, he repudiated either

136. To John Hay, September 15, 1903, *ibid.,* p. 599.
137. Philip Jessup, *Elihu Root,* 2 volumes, (New York, 1938), I, pp. 403–404.
138. Roosevelt stoutly denied any complicity; see, for example, to John Bigelow, January 6, 1904, *Letters,* III, p. 689.

bribery or violence, as means unworthy of American ambitions in Central America.[139] But he was hemmed in by events, specifically the refusal of the Colombian Government to accede to American demands. A Nicaraguan canal was against the advice of the great majority of competent engineers, he complained at the time, leaving the United States little practical choice but to move in the direction events would take in Panama.[140] His official inaction, of course, helped to control these events while a formal pose of neutrality if not disinterest was maintained.

Roosevelt's ambiguous posture can be explained in terms of the conflicting elements in his world outlook: A nation, like an individual, must bear witness to the right; at the same time, law and order had to be observed and human betterment promoted. The benevolent Roosevelt and the ambitious Roosevelt were at odds once again. Events served to resolve this conflict. The interests of civilization must take precedence over those of "the little wildcat republic of Colombia [because it] behaved infamously about the treaty for the building of the Panama Canal." [141] The Colombians had forfeited their right to civilized consideration because of their inferiority as a people. Roosevelt pronounced them "not merely corrupt" but "governmentally utterly incompetent." Their inferiority was all the more unfortunate because their corruption and incompetence stood in the way of a great human achievement—the canal.[142] The President's mood of frustration can be gauged tolerably well by his denunciation of those who dared oppose him at this time as "shrill eunuchs." [143]

Roosevelt matched the march of events in Panama stride for stride. The revolution began on November 3 under the guns of American warships; the next day Panama declared itself an independent republic. The American Government at the direction of the President extended diplomatic recognition with uncommon haste (on November 6). By the 18th of the month an appropriate

139. To Albert Shaw, October 7, 1903, *ibid.*, p. 626; to Shaw, October 10, 1903, *ibid.*, p. 628.
140. To Albert Shaw, October 10, 1903, *ibid.*, p. 628.
141. To Kermit Roosevelt, November 4, 1903, *ibid.*, p. 644.
142. To Otto Gresham, November 30, 1903, *ibid.*, p. 662.
143. *Ibid.*, p. 663.

treaty had been drawn up committing Panama to United States canal requirements; approval by the American Senate came on February 23, 1904. Roosevelt defended these moves as "justified by the interests of collective civilization" inasmuch as the United States held a "mandate" from mankind to construct an interoceanic waterway.[144] In explaining matters to Spring-Rice he conveniently lumped together American national interest, the welfare of the people at the Isthmus as well as of all mankind, the benefits to law and order, and the political incapacity of the "Bogotá bandits" as the circumstances encouraging the United States to let events occur as they would.[145] He might well have added his determination to enter the presidential race with arrangements to build an American canal completed, for undoubtedly his political ambitions were a vital ingredient in his total policy. Any one of these considerations would have provided sufficient warrant in his judgment to proceed in Panama; combined, they enabled Roosevelt to defend his policy as not merely necessary but virtuous.[146]

The President undertook a full-dress defense of his handling of United States-Colombian relations in his third annual message. Although much of what he said was a review of happenings, beginning as far back as Colombian independence, certain of his arguments merit brief mention: As policeman of the hemisphere the United States by treaty right and by precedent was responsible for the neutrality of the Isthmus. The failure of the Colombian Government to ratify a treaty made by an official of that Government was evidence of the perfidy of the Colombians and of their incapacity to conduct political affairs with other nations in a proper way. The enormous benefit to the world that an Isthmian canal would bring about made it incumbent upon the United States to undertake the project. Equally compelling

144. Roosevelt, "Message to Congress," January 4, 1904, quoted in *Theodore Roosevelt Cyclopedia*, A.B. Hart and H.R. Ferleger, Editors, (New York, 1941), p. 404.
145. To Sir Cecil Spring-Rice, January 18, 1904, *Letters*, III, p. 099.
146. For example, to Joseph G. Cannon, September 12, 1904, *ibid*., IV, p. 992. Roosevelt, "Speech at Panama," November, 1906, quoted in Joseph B. Bishop, *Theodore Roosevelt and His Times*, 2 volumes, (New York, 1920), I, p. 452.

was American self-interest.[147] Here was the official apologia, an in-depth defense of American canal diplomacy, the details of which were subsumed by the world movement patterns of Roosevelt's thought.

No doubt Theodore Roosevelt acted as he had in the canal crisis in response to a developing situation. And one can be equally sure he saw in the results of his practical policy the first steps of a great human undertaking bound to effect the betterment of nations and people. As far as his own country was concerned he believed the building of the canal would "rank in kind, though not of course in degree, with the Louisiana Purchase and the acquisition of Texas." [148] In attempting to understand the influence of the world movement on Roosevelt's policy in Panama, or elsewhere in the Caribbean for that matter, it must be kept in mind that his was a highly personalized appraisal of what would serve the world best. This concept of the world movement was less a doctrine to believe in, which others could discern as an objective norm for action, and more a personal way of looking at things, an evaluation of what the situation demanded that was substantially in keeping with one or several of its major propositions. The world movement idea did not shackle Roosevelt in his approach to decision-making. It liberated him by offering him a variety of purposes for acting in the solution of problems that events foisted upon him, answers he was impelled to discover by his own temperament and by his high public office.

In each of the diplomatic actions reviewed—Cuba, Venezuela, Santo Domingo, and Panama—though in Roosevelt's own view he acted for the improvement of mankind, he was able to act because public opinion at home supported him. Without public opinion behind him he realized his power position would have been a

147. Roosevelt, "Third Annual Message" (1903), *Works*, XVII, pp. 235–249 *passim*.
148. To Samuel W. Small, December 3, 1903, quoted in Bishop, *op. cit.*, I, p. 295.

weak one and his intervention policies less effective. The need for intervention in the various Caribbean crises was great and the people of the nation on the whole were made to understand this. But Roosevelt insisted it was a question at all times of leadership, of the education of public opinion, a task that was not always certain of accomplishment.[149]

This leadership quality was equally apparent in his Philippine program. The reluctance of the American people—perhaps it was an incapacity stemming from their traditions—to continue a constructive occupation of the Islands worried Roosevelt. The United States had stayed in the Philippines during his presidential years largely, he felt, because he had continually reminded the American people of their duty to the backward peoples there. On this issue, among others, he went before the electorate in 1904 and thereafter believed that the American people stood in support of his Philippine program. Toward the end of his presidency, however, he was not sure that "a duty-loving spirit . . . to control the Philippine Islands for the good of the Filipinos" would survive his generation.[150] Such thoughts made him aware of the difficulty of leadership in an increasingly democratic republic. He observed, in commenting on the "kaleidoscopic political affairs" in 1907, that "the public is very short-sighted . . . and is not interested in the Philippines or the Canal." [151] The success of his implementation of the world movement principle through the use of American power and American idealism is therefore all the more remarkable, a testimony to Theodore Roosevelt's influence on events and on history.

149. To William Bayard Hale, December 3, 1908, *Letters*, VI, p. 1408.
150. To William Howard Taft, August 21, 1907, *ibid.*, V, 761.
151. To William Howard Taft, September 3, 1907, *ibid.*, p. 782.

4

The Place of Evolution

Theodore Roosevelt was an uncommon man, an attribute obscured by the applause of his fellow citizens for his public service. His rarity consisted in this: Though a storied man of action he remained thoughtful, respectful of the past and the lessons it offered, fond of learning old and new, sometimes in awe of the scientific promises of his own day. He was a cowman who wrote a scholarly account of how the West was won. He was an imperialist statesman, sometimes shooting from the hip, who was guided, if not rigidly determined by, a philosophy of history. The juxtaposition of thought and action in Roosevelt is an absorbing and a provocative one, so much so that one is at last led to probe secondary avenues of his experience in order to arrive at a more complete awareness of his uncommon dimension.

He was also a complex man, and neither he nor his confident imperialism is likely to be explained in simple or general terms. To see him as an American is merely to suggest his patriotism and his practicality in public affairs. To say that he was an imperialist is to denominate him and not to define him or his work. To describe his value code as Judaeo-Christian does not locate him in the spectrum of that moral system. He thought he belonged to a superior people, but his racism was unconventional and inconsistent. Though he treated Orientals generally as inferiors, he respected the Japanese the same way he feared and respected the Slavs. His racism has been related to a larger proposition, evolution and the tenets of social Darwinism that were derived from it. The record is clear. Theodore Roosevelt can be termed an American or an imperialist or a Christian or a racist or an evolutionist, all with ample justification. But because in his public years he was all of these, simultaneously rather than successively, because he adhered to a composite of principles not easily reconciled, his policies and especially his imperialism often struck contemporaries and later critics alike as the compulsive acts of a man intent on power, devoid of any other purpose.[1]

In a unique way Roosevelt's imperialism can be understood from its relationship to the world movement and as an expression of it. This was a consistent guide and a constant reference in his own personal evaluation of policies and their particulars. It was the central theme of his imperialism, frontal, immediate, obvious. But despite what it may clearly depict, it offers a limited view like a photograph of a man taken full face. No matter how graphically Roosevelt's imperialism can be rendered by focusing on the world movement rationale, there remains an incomplete visualization because such an analysis presumes a synthesis, or at least an accommodation, of the various allegiances that came to him in his formative years.

Those early years witnessed the growth of two pre-eminent influences. One was the sense of right and justice that young Roosevelt found so well exemplified in his father, the original source of the rule of righteousness for nations and for men alike; the

1. Only slight attention, and that indirectly, is given Roosevelt's evolutionary disposition in Pringle's *Theodore Roosevelt,* for example. Carleton Putnam suggests it in terms of Roosevelt's urge to physical fitness in *Theodore Roosevelt: The Formative Years, 1858–1886,* pp. 224–225. Howard K. Beale sees it largely as part of the race thesis, Beale, *op. cit.,* pp. 72–74; 160–162; 181. A better characterization of his Darwinism as modified by other factors has been offered by John M. Blum in *The Republican Roosevelt,* (Cambridge, 1954), pp. 22–28; see also his essay "Theodore Roosevelt: Years of Decision," *Letters,* II, pp. 1484–1494. Blum's essay has influenced the full-length study of Roosevelt, *Power and Responsibility: The Life and Times of Theodore Roosevelt* (New York, 1961), by William Harbaugh. Typical of general commentaries, Richard Hofstadter's *Social Darwinism in American Thought, 1860–1915,* (Philadelphia, 1945) points to Darwinism in Roosevelt's imperialism; see Chapter 8, "Racism and Imperialism," pp. 146–173; also Ralph H. Gabriel, *The Course of American Democratic Thought,* (New York, 1940), pp. 351–354.

second critical experience of his youth was his bout with nature and the success he scored in the struggle to make his body. The former imparted to him a respect for the ethical code of Protestant Christianity, the latter provided him with a will to action difficult to dissociate from the sociology of Herbert Spencer.

Such distinct and potentially disruptive allegiances, together with Roosevelt's appreciation of the frontier in American history, were the watershed of his world movement ideology. His confident imperialism was an outgrowth of that larger phenomenon. United States expansion in the late nineteenth and early twentieth centuries was promoted in significant fashion by Roosevelt's insistence that right must prevail, with right a concept broad enough to include peace, order, and human progress. Linked to this was the conviction that the superior nations, whose superiority was evidenced in stable governmental systems and unmatched technological accomplishments had clear title to world domination. In the acting out of Roosevelt's imperialism in the Philippines and in the Caribbean both right and might were recurring and competing criteria. Granting his very personal and sometimes controversial judgment of right and wrong for other nations as well as for his own, Roosevelt thought of himself as consistently pursuing a righteous end. Because this is so fundamental a consideration of confident imperialism—the very heart of it—it is imperative to trace to the origins of these implications of righteousness.

In his formal religious outlook Roosevelt stressed that the believing man must be a "doer" of the Word. "In business and in work, if you let Christianity stop as you go out of the church door, there is little righteousness in you," he once told a church group.[2] By righteousness he meant "justice between man and man, nation and nation, the chance to lead our lives on a somewhat higher level, with a broader spirit of brotherly good will for one another."[3] He spoke of "the ethical and spiritual as the truly religious element in life."[4] Theology and dogma interested him less

2. Roosevelt, "At Trinity Reform Church," Chicago, September, 1901, quoted in Hart and Ferleger, *op. cit.*, p. 76.
3. Roosevelt, "International Peace," *Works*, XVIII, p. 411.
4. Roosevelt, *Through the Brazilian Wilderness*, *Works*, VI, p. 56.

than conduct. There was only one test that he applied to the professors of all creeds, "the test of conduct"; this was termed "the ultimate test of the worth of belief." [5] While he harkened to the message of the Bible his religion remained worldly, rather than other-worldly. "The religious man who is most useful is not he whose sole care is to save his own soul," he advised undergraduates at the Harvard Union on one occasion, "but the man whose religion bids him to strive to advance decency and clean living and to make the world a better place for his fellows to live in." [6]

Such views as these when read in conjunction with the oft-repeated "ultimate purpose" of American imperialism leave no doubt of Roosevelt's commitment to the "social gospel" of nineteenth century American Protestanism. What needs to be evaluated, however, is the nature and extent of his attraction to the tenets of Darwinian evolution and its social ramifications. The notes of inner conflict that have been observed in Roosevelt's imperialist accomplishments are due in the main to his fondness for features of these two systems of thought that are not likely to be compatible. An examination of the place of evolution in the mind of Roosevelt makes possible an evaluation of its importance in his intellectual makeup; at the same time it may capture the outlines of his world movement philosophy from a fresh and novel perspective.

Consideration of the place of evolution in Theodore Roosevelt's imperialism convincingly exposes his uncommon quality. The man of action was also a man with a strong philosophical disposition. Not a philosopher, he was nevertheless reflective enough to want to move with the main intellectual currents of his time because of his deep-seated conviction that action was worthy only of a well-defined system of thought. Part of that definition is to be found in his interest in evolutionary principles. Some of these principles strongly attracted him and others repelled him, but

5. Roosevelt, "The Bible and the People," *Realizeble Ideals, ibid.*, XV, p. 613.
6. Roosevelt, "Athletics, Scholarship and Public Service," *ibid.*, p. 490.

he continued to display a scholarly and intellectually honest respect for all of them throughout his lifetime. No other system of thought received so much of his formal attention and serious concern, not only because its theories were the common coin of his intellectual realm but also because of his genuine sympathy for struggle as a means and justification for survival. His devotion to American political principles and to Christian ethical standards went unquestioned within him as his mind took shape. They were so interwoven into his time and place as to be neither arguable nor very interesting areas in which honest, intelligent men might seriously differ or the truth of a proposition might be tested.

With the theory of evolution it was otherwise. Though evolution was widely accepted as a valid explanation of the physical universe, the application of its laws to the psychic world or to man in society had been sharply challenged. Evolution had any number of formal apologists and a whole host of convinced practitioners, but there were also schools of dissent organized around religious fundamentalism or based on scientific methodology. Theodore Roosevelt grew up and came to maturity at a time when the claims of the social Darwinists flooded to their highest stage, breaking over the ramparts of traditional cultural attitudes. Publication of *The Origin of Species* (1859) and Roosevelt's birth failed to coincide by only one year, and the application of the evolutionary thesis—first to individuals and later to groups—had a scholarly and a popular vogue well into the twentieth century. The milieu, social and economic, in which Roosevelt moved and with which he came to share convictions was permeated with Darwinism. Education at Harvard accepted Christian ethical values and taught Darwinism, blithely, gracefully; in this it resembled Roosevelt's own mentality. Such ambivalence was quite proper, for it was an era full of change (more talked of than realized as it turned out for Roosevelt's morality). After Harvard Roosevelt studied under John W. Burgess at the Columbia University Law School, where his Darwinism received a positive stimulus for Burgess openly expressed the conviction in his course on law and government that only a few races were fit to rule.

In the course of his education and experience Theodore

Roosevelt became an evolutionist of sorts. The label fits easily because of his insistence that struggle produced progress, that there were superior and inferior peoples with differing rights and responsibilities, that force was frequently appropriate to accomplish good among men and among nations—all these views usually uttered with dramatic, pungent confidence. The pertinent consideration is the extent of his evolutionary commitment and a determination of the persuasions that were wrought upon his public philosophy. Roosevelt was disposed to speak warmly of the place of struggle in life, a theme he stressed in his writings on natural history; his temper encouraged him to use the catch phrases of the evolutionists in public addresses and in offhand remarks. But is his choice of language an accurate index to his authentic attitude toward evolution as the fundamental historical proposition? An unqualified Darwinist label is misleading, confirming a distortion of the popular image Roosevelt created of himself and complicating the effort to understand the influence of evolutionary ideas on his confident imperialism.

Whatever the nature of his Darwinism, at no significant juncture in his public life did it appear to be, even temporarily, the dominant strain in his motivation. The evolutionary influences were present but only in competition with other persuasive forces. As his imperialism unfolded, an American sense of what was patriotic and practical, the social gospel of nineteenth century Protestantism, the folklore of western man each made its telling contribution to Roosevelt's intellectual self and offered its peculiar challenge to the possible hegemony of Darwinism.

Though the span of years during which Theodore Roosevelt possessed great political power was a short one—less than a decade even if his time as Assistant Navy Secretary is included—his philosophy of imperialism was elaborated over a much longer period of time. It is on the total content of his thought that he must finally be judged. The outlines of his historical rationale began to appear in the early 1880's with the first volume of *The Winning of the West,* and it was not completely stated until the lessons of World War I had made their impact. For the better part of forty years until his death in 1919 events combined with his own scholarly instincts to test continuously the hypothesis of the world movement.

All of this brings up the problem of growth or change in the public man. For example, can the opinions expressed in 1895 be linked validly to the policies of 1905, and if so with what qualifications? Or did the years after he had enjoyed the immense power of the Presidency reveal an alteration of his views on the righteousness of western imperialism? Ordinarily the judgments of a statesman may be expected to change, even drastically, after years of exposure to political situations constantly in flux. But Roosevelt was an exception to that rule, and the place of Darwinism in his outlook underscores his singularity. The deeply embedded features of his thought could perhaps be expected to remain unbending under the strong winds of change and challenge; but surprisingly his thoughts on Darwinism, which itself was then undergoing development and refinement, were in 1918 substantially what they had been in the 1890's.

"The rivalry of natural selection is but one of the features of progress," he wrote in 1895. There were others but by all odds the most important feature of progress was what he spoke of as *character*, an attribute not effected by rivalry in nature.[7] By 1900 "the strenuous life" had become a household phrase, yet in that year in *The Outlook* he offered some advice on "Character and Success." "Bodily vigor is good, and vigor of the intellect is even better, but far above both is character. . . . In the long run," he continued, "in the great battle of life, no brilliancy of intellect, no perfection of bodily development, will count when weighed in the balance against that assemblage of virtues, active and passive, of moral qualities, which we group together under the name of *character*." [8] In the Romanes Lecture for 1910 character, not force, was urged as the solution to national and international problems alike.[9] One of his last review-essays, "The Origin and Evolution of Life" (1918), contained a final rejection

7. Roosevelt, "Social Evolution," *ibid.*, XIV, p. 109; p. 126.
8. Roosevelt, "Character and Success," *ibid.*, XV, p. 496 (italics added).
9. Roosevelt, "Biological Analogies in History," *ibid.*, XIV, p. 102; p. 104.

of evolution as an intellectually acceptable explanation of man in society.[10] If there was a change apparent in Roosevelt's estimate of the place and purpose of evolution it was an accumulated certainty that when its laws were applied to social conditions they were inadequate. A lifetime of reflection on man's social condition found him reliant on traditional values rather than scientific conclusions.

Evolution performed a two-fold function in Roosevelt's thought. Because it was intellectually exciting and attractive he adopted some of its propositions as undeniably valid, and for this reason he was in certain respects an evolutionist. But if the evolutionary thesis had not been enunciated in his generation Roosevelt might not have been forced to define so certainly his traditional ethic, his espousal of it might have been less vigorous, and his faith in the ultimate purpose of expansion by the western powers less steady. The second, but not the secondary, function performed by evolution as a system of thought was to require Roosevelt to consider the respective claims of religion, history, and science with equal seriousness. He had subscribed to tenets of each of these as providing meaning in life. Instead of his being allowed to proceed undisturbed with the assurances afforded by religion and history, the theories of evolution forced him into a comparative analysis, providing insights into man in history that otherwise might have gone unappreciated and unarticulated and thus would not be characteristic of him as conscious or unconscious norms of conduct.

Charles Darwin was to Theodore Roosevelt both a revolutionary and a seminal thinker. Darwin, along with Huxley, "succeeded in effecting a complete revolution in the thought of an age" [11] so that Roosevelt came to believe that "the acceptance of the fundamental truths of evolution are quite as necessary to sound

---

10. Roosevelt, "The Origin and Evolution of Life," *ibid.*, p. 33.
11. Roosevelt, "History as Literature," *ibid.*, pp. 9–10.

scientific thought as the acceptance of the fundamental truths of the solar system." [12] Yet he was inclined to set Darwin and his work in a historical perspective. Writing to Oliver Wendell Holmes, Jr., in 1904 Roosevelt allowed that Darwin was "the chief factor in working a tremendous revolution" but went on to speculate that in the future he would be read "just as we read Lucretius now; that is, because of the interest attaching to his position in history, in spite of the fact that his own work will have been superseded by the work of the very men to whom he pointed out the way." [13] Roosevelt believed that Darwin had opened a new era but that it would fall to others to exploit his contribution in succeeding generations. He was exceedingly anxious that the world avoid revering Darwin in repetition of the medieval acceptance of Aristotle, for the consequences would be intellectual stagnation. He found this had already happened with Darwin and Darwinists in some quarters, and the resulting extreme dogmatism he deplored as nonscientific.[14]

Roosevelt's attitude toward Darwinism, however, was not simply the posture of the man of science who stood ready to reject Darwin or any part of his work should later investigation advance a stronger case. He was always prepared to tailor evolutionary modes of thought whenever they did not fit comfortably with the demands of his total and somewhat varied intellectual heritage. This dual position of scientific detachment and cultural involvement was evident in Roosevelt's first serious consideration of the meaning and implications of evolution for society, his review-essay of *Social Evolution* by Benjamin Kidd, which appeared in *The North American Review* for July 1895, under the title "Social Evolution."

The center of Roosevelt's disagreement with Kidd's espousal of social Darwinism was that it was faulty scientific method, reflecting a dangerously narrow orientation, for anyone to argue

---

12. Roosevelt, "The Foundations of the Nineteenth Century," *ibid.*, p. 198; p. 202.
13. To Oliver Wendell Holmes, Jr., October 21, 1904, *Letters*, IV, p. 989.
14. To Francis H. Herrick, January 15, 1912, *ibid.*, VII, p. 478.

that the single postulate of natural selection could alone explain social progress. There were other factors along with a notable body of contrary evidence to be taken into account. Roosevelt took particular issue with Kidd's assertion that there was no rational sanction in progress, that "it is a deliberate verdict that the conditions of life in advanced societies of today are without any sanction from reason for the masses of the people." [15] Roosevelt's objection to this was on the grounds that it made evolution out to be exclusively materialistic and the singular principle of life as well. "Side by side with the selfish development in life," Roosevelt thought, "there has been almost from the beginning a certain amount of unselfish development too; and in the evolution of humanity the unselfish side has on the whole tended steadily to increase at the expense of the selfish, notably in the progressive communities." [16] This was not to deny that in the attainment of progress some individuals are penalized. "The nations that make the most progress may do so at the expense of ten or fifteen individuals out of a hundred whereas the nations making the least progress or even going backward may sacrifice almost every man out of the hundred." [17] In this manner Roosevelt dismissed the contention that there was no rational sanction for progress. The sanction lay within the progressive community itself where "the conflict between the interests of the individual and the organism of which he is a part . . . is at a minimum." [18]

A second factor he insisted upon for understanding man in society, one that had no place whatsoever in Kidd's discussion, was what he termed *character*. Character was a quality not to be confused or identified with reason, though by no means was it inimical to reason. Rather than render a definition of character in his rebuttal of Kidd he chose to exemplify its meaning. Character was unselfishness, courage, devotion to duty, honesty, feelings that were in keeping with the nature of man. Character was "the

---

15. Benjamin Kidd, *Social Evolution*, (New York, 1894), p. 78.
16. Roosevelt, "Social Evolution," *Works*, XIV, p. 114.
17. *Ibid.*, p. 113.
18. *Ibid.*

women who watches over the sick child and the soldier who dies at his post." [19] Thus understood, character was vital to social progress, and so much emphasis was Roosevelt willing to place upon it that he judged it more important than intellect to the person and to the race. "We need intellect," he concluded, "and there is no reason why we should not have it together with *character;* but if we must choose between the two, we choose *character* without a moment's hesitation." [20]

Throughout the history of western man Roosevelt found religion and character to be closely related. He took issue with Kidd's avowal that the ultrarational sanctions of religion related to conduct in the individual, where "his interests and the interests of the social organism are antagonistic." This was simply not so in his judgment. Admitting that any religion that stressed ascetic behavior as an ideal was socially antagonistic, he nevertheless protested that "most of the present-day creeds of Christianity, both Protestant and Catholic, which do very noble work for the race [do so] because they want the individual to subordinate his own interest to the interests of mankind."

What were the implications of this position for a social evolutionary principle like survival of the fittest? Roosevelt believed quite the contrary of that principle in cultural matters. He wrote "undoubtedly, in the race for life, that group of beings will tend ultimately to survive in which the general feeling of its members, whether due to humanitarianism, to altruism, or to some form of religious belief proper, is such that the average individual has an unselfish—what Kidd would call an ultrarational—tendency to work for the ultimate benefit of the community as a whole." [21] The individualism Roosevelt was advocating in passages such as this was not the "rugged individualism" of the school of Spencer and Sumner, but the much older, indeed the traditional, individualism of the western European experience, in which the all-important individual would fulfill himself, satisfy his conscience or

19. *Ibid.,* p. 119.
20. *Ibid.,* p. 128 (italics added).
21. *Ibid.,* pp. 112–113.

his reason, and attain heaven, or whatever that fulfillment had come to mean to him, by serving others. While at times Roosevelt acted more in the fashion of the rugged individualist and thought like one as well, his best judgment favored *character* at the expense of either physical prowess or intellect.

In addition to these considerations, which worked to restrain the adoption of a one-dimensional view of evolution, there was in Roosevelt's opinion a sizable body of historical evidence to underscore how facile evolutionary oversimplification could be. For one thing he did not agree with Kidd that if man were left to himself and presumably were guided by his reason "the average of each generation would continually fall below the average of the generation which preceded it." [22] Roosevelt conceded that this "is undoubtedly true of the world taken as a whole. It is in all probability entirely false of the highest sections of society. At any rate there are numerous instances where the law does not work. . . ." [23] Roosevelt was insisting upon a distinction between the geological and the animal world, as opposed to the historical, social world. Concretely, the hypothesis that progress advanced farthest where competition or rivalry was keenest was not substantiated by certain cultural facts. If this were so "the European peoples standing highest in the scale would be the south Italians, the Polish Jews, the people who live in the congested districts of Ireland. As a matter of fact, however, these are precisely the peoples who made the least progress when compared with the dominant strains among, for instance, the English and the Germans." [24] This was not a denial of the function of competition, but an indication that Roosevelt thought its value could be overstressed if taken as the only consideration or if the competition became so severe as to wear out the race involved.

Respecting the role of competition Roosevelt suggested an additional distinction that had to be made between classes within the same nation or racial group. The leaders of society, philos-

22. Kidd, *op. cit.*, p. 39.
23. Roosevelt, "Social Evolution," *Works*, XIV, p. 114.
24. *Ibid.*, p. 110.

ophers, statesmen, judges, soldiers, successful businessmen, "all these come from the classes where the struggle for the bare means of subsistence is less severe . . . than in the class below." [25] Progress was sustained in such communities, Roosevelt held, because though the least fit survive "they and their children often tend to grow more fit" as they are taught by the superior if less numerous class above them.[26]

This argument points up an additional factor that militated in Roosevelt's mind against the theory of natural selection as the single law of social evolution: Since acquired attributes of *character*—love, duty, courage—could be passed along through efforts of individuals and institutions, through laws and ideals, men could learn from other men, with progress the likely result. He had stressed this very conclusion just prior to "Social Evolution" in a review of *National Life and Character*.[27] "Even though the best people of society do not increase as fast as the others," he had written, "society progresses, the improvement being due mainly to the transmission of acquired characteristics, a process which in every civilized society operates . . . [against] the baleful law of natural selection." [28] Roosevelt made use of this same reasoning in "Social Evolution" because it plainly appealed to him as a way out of the cultural dilemma posed by an unqualified social Darwinism. It was a practical restriction of natural selection in keeping with his reading of history and his adherence to traditional western morality.

"Social Evolution," written some years before Roosevelt assumed the Presidency, was at most a guarded endorsement of evolutionary principles. Though he saw no sense in questioning the fundamentals of evolution as scientific fact, he had large and critical reservations concerning the propriety of social applications. Such an approach was at once too simple and too much in conflict with other convictions he firmly held. Yet as a practitioner of imperialism many of his policies took on, in his own

25. *Ibid.*, p. 112.
26. *Ibid.*
27. This was a book review of *National Life and Character: A Forecast,* by Charles H. Pearson; it appeared in *The Sewanee Review,* August, 1894.
28. Roosevelt, "National Life and Character," *Works,* XIV, p. 249.

mind at times and rather more often in the judgment of others, a Darwinist coloration. In the pursuit of empire Roosevelt had not abandoned the tempered philosophical attitudes expressed in "Social Evolution," however. Quite the contrary, he was remarkably loyal to them, so much so that "Social Evolution" provides a sure if somewhat generalized guide for understanding the influence of evolution on Roosevelt's imperialist thought and action.

When Theodore Roosevelt brought out *The Winning of the West* during the decade or so prior to writing "Social Evolution," he produced in effect a study of American imperialism as it had possessed much of the continental mainland. Knowledge of the dynamism of an expanding people gained from this considerable historical investigation enabled him to appreciate more readily the colonialist urge gripping the western world in his own era. Elements of the Darwinist ethic were evident in his analysis of the westward-moving frontier. Pre-eminent among them was the superior-race argument as justification for military conquest and occupation. Roosevelt spoke of war against the savages as "the most ultimately righteous of all wars"; [29] he refused to accord the native peoples the "same rules of international morality which obtained between stable and cultural communities." [30] He defended the cruelty inflicted upon the Indians by the conquering race on the grounds of "the extraordinary conditions of life on the frontier" [31] and gloried in the right of conquest itself.[32] His entire conception of the history of the frontier was predicated on the right and necessity of conquest,[33] and on occasion he digressed to scold those of his readers who refused to acknowledge the applicability of his judgments to the imperialist conditions of the late nineteenth century.[34]

29. Roosevelt, *The Winning of the West*, Allegheny Edition, III, p. 45.
30. *Ibid.*, III, p. 45.
31. *Ibid.*, II, p. 117; III, pp. 100 101.
32. *Ibid.*, III, p. 1.
33. *Ibid.*, I, pp. 1–5 *passim.*
34. *Ibid.*, III, pp. 175–176; see also Roosevelt, *Thomas Hart Benton*, pp. 1–4 *passim;* pp. 51–52; pp. 175–176.

Aside from the evolutionary ingredients of *The Winning of the West,* the study also revealed the author's belief that expansion by a people had a purpose outside the process itself, that "the conquest and settlement by the whites of the Indian lands were necessary to the greatness of the race and to the well-being of civilized mankind." [35] There was involved here not some vague, romanticized notion of "civilization," but specifically the initiation of free government wherein men would learn to rule themselves.[36] This constituted progress in a tangible and a worthy sense, for by the successful exercise of self-rule a people displayed *character,* the quality Roosevelt prized most highly in men as individuals or in a group. Whatever cruelty or bloodshed or temporary injustice had to be endured or countenanced to achieve conditions conducive to self-government, this kind of political progress was sufficient warrant for it.[37] Though the means might remain starkly brutal, suggestive of the unrelenting operation of the laws of natural selection, the purpose or outcome of the process as interpreted by Roosevelt marked a decided break with a logical social reduction of the tenets of evolution. The Anglo-Americans after generations of struggle had reached a level of civilization unequaled in human history because they had acquired the requisite ability for self-rule. In a word, they as a people had come into possession of *character.* Because *character* was artificial and not innate, western expansion had its justification in the spread of free government that would enable many more men to enjoy liberty as promised by nature and by history.

The total lesson of the West had the same expression in one of Roosevelt's famous and most widely quoted speeches, "The Strenuous Life." No other single address early in his national career did so much to identify him with Darwinism and its code. The speech fairly breathed the hard struggle from which alone progress resulted. But it was more popularly misunderstood than any other of T.R.'s famous and oft-quoted addresses. Few would deny, on rereading it, that the speaker was swept along by

35. Roosevelt, *The Winning of the West,* Allegheny Edition, III, p. 175.
36. *Ibid.,* II, p. 381.
37. *Ibid.,* IV, p. 218.

a passion for "the life of strenuous endeavor," calling upon his fellow Americans to "boldly face the life of strife," imploring them—"let us not shrink from strife, moral or physical," suggesting by his tone an identification of Darwinism and jingoism. It was a fighting speech.

In the swirl of oratory the message was often overlooked, however, and in no small way was Roosevelt himself responsible for this. The message was a call to the strenuous life not for its own sake, but to advance the cause of civilization. Thus in describing the man worthy of admiration he chose to portray him as "the man who embodies victorious effort, the man who never wrongs his neighbor, who is prompt to help a friend, but who has those virile qualities necessary to win the struggle of actual life." In attempting to evaluate fairly the strenuous life ideal, it would be absurd to deny the martial spirit. "The army and the navy are the sword and the shield which the nation must carry if she is to do her duty among the nations of the earth," Roosevelt proclaimed. It would be equally foolish to confound the means with the end. Granting that the end was "true national greatness," it must be remembered that his norms for judging greatness were duty, honesty, service, summed up in *character*. He applied his values to American history as a yardstick for judging the policies of the American Government in 1899. Just as the Civil War was justified by the high purpose of saving the Union, so the imperialism of his own time was right, for it was "our part in the great work of uplifting mankind," a responsibility that a leading nation could not fail to honor.[38]

Not surprisingly in view of the mingled elements of right and might, as graphically exemplified in "The Strenuous Life" speech, there is a strong coloration of evolutionary thought frequently encountered in Roosevelt's response to the actualities of American imperialism. He was perceptive enough and sufficiently objective to point out in his review-essay "National Life and Character" that

38. Roosevelt, "The Strenuous Life," *Works*, XV, pp. 267–281.

the term "higher races" was a relative and not an absolute one, the so-called higher races having led the world for only the previous twenty-five hundred years. Another indication of his evolutionist perspective was his recognition that such material conditions as climate could have a controlling effect on culture. He believed, for example, the higher races of the contemporary era could not prosper in the tropics, but "only under conditions of soil and climate analogous to those obtaining in their old European homes." [39]

Years later, after Japan had stirred from its past and had come forth as a significant nation-state in the western manner, the same evolutionary judgment appeared. In a letter to an American missionary-educator residing in Japan, Rev. David B. Schneder, Roosevelt wrote a reminder that two thousand years ago "to Greeks and Romans the most dreaded and yet in a sense the most despised barbarian was the white-skinned, blue-eyed and red- and yellow-haired barbarian of the North. . . . It would not seem possible to the Greek or Roman of that day that this northern barbarian should ever become part of the civilized world—his equal in civilization. The racial differences seemed too great." [40] But an evolutionary process of some sort had taken place. Just what had happened, though certainly not why it happened, Roosevelt on one occasion described in a particularly revealing way. "Think of the people of Europe stumbling upward through the Dark Ages," he said, "and doing much work in the wrong way, sometimes falling back, but ever coming forward again, forward, forward, forward, until our great civilization as we now know it was developed at last out of the struggles and failures and victories of millions of men who dared to do the world's work." [41]

All this bore directly upon the realities of American imperialism insofar as it possessed an evolutionary dimension. Reflecting on the achievement made possible by a genius for self-rule by the Anglo-Americans, he was at pains to emphasize that "our people are now successfully governing themselves because for more than

39. Roosevelt, "Expansion and Peace," *ibid.*, p. 286; pp. 287–289 *passim.*
40. To David B. Schneder, June 19, 1905, *Letters, IV,* 1240.
41. Roosevelt, "America's Part in the World's Work," *Works,* XVI, p. 475.

two thousand years they have been slowly fitting themselves, sometimes consciously, sometimes unconsciously, toward this end." [42]
A similar gradual unfolding of a capacity for self-government
was to be expected in the Philippines, which is why Roosevelt,
as has been noted, would not pledge himself to a definite date
for granting the Islands their independence. Furthermore, a failure by the United States to maintain firm control over the area
might foster a regression to chaos and savagery. Decline as well
as growth was an evolutionary principle that merited respect in
the affairs of men. But without doubt the central theme in Roosevelt's consideration of United States involvement in the Philippine Islands was his concern for doing an effective job of preparing
the Filipinos for eventual self-government, a purpose he derived
from Anglo-American political experience to which social Darwinism made no contribution.

The interplay of might and right was a prominent aspect generally of Big Stick diplomacy, revealing both the Darwinist and
the humanitarian attributes of Roosevelt's policies. In 1904 during
the Santo Domingo crisis he spoke of "a hundred years of freedom
so far from teaching the Santo Domingans how to enjoy freedom
and turn it to good account, has resulted so badly that society
is on the point of dissolution," and said that American intervention was required for the safety of Santo Domingo and the hemisphere. [43] Santo Domingans, Cubans, Colombians—it made little
difference; Roosevelt was inclined to lump them together with
other backward peoples across the world. Regarding internal problems in Haiti, some years after he had left the Presidency, he
pointed to the failure of self-rule there as typical of all backward
races. The reason was simple and simply stated: Democracy was
"much the highest ideal of government" and the Haitians were
"preposterously unfit" to exercise it. [44]

But in each instance of American action or intervention in the
Caribbean for which Roosevelt was responsible, the mere superior
power of the United States constituted the means of promoting

42. To Raymond Reyes Lala, June 27, 1900, *Letters*, II, p. 1343.
43. To Charles W. Eliot, April 4, 1904, *ibid.*, IV, p. 769.
44. To William T. Denison, August 3, 1914, *ibid.*, VII, p. 792.

what he estimated to be progress. Progress came about not mechanistically and inevitably because some unknown or knowable force determined it but by conscious, directed effort on man's part. In this effort some peoples were better equipped at a given time to lead and control the movement than were others. Roosevelt's fondness for certain evolutionary ideas faced him with a dilemma common to all adherents of that system of thought: how to fit the conscious striving of man into a universe that was inexorably unfolding. It was a quandary not unlike that of the strict Calvinist who had to square predestination with his everyday consciousness of free will. Unlike the Calvinist, Roosevelt was not bound to one scheme of belief; his eclectic mind had slight difficulty in composing differences, since other of his intellectual allegiances spared him submission to a logical social application of the evolutionary principle.

The Romanes Lecture for 1910, which Lord Curzon as Chancellor of Oxford University had invited Theodore Roosevelt to deliver, was entitled "Biological Analogies in History." For an awareness of evolution in Roosevelt's considered judgment of history and its influence on his imperialist philosophy, the address is of the highest value. Though coming after the presidential years, the power years when he frequently seemed a Darwinist in imperial matters, years likely to affect his reflections on history, "Biological Analogies in History" nevertheless strictly qualified the role of evolution in human affairs.

Much of this speech bespoke a mind conversant with the phenomena of nature to be expected of an ardent naturalist, and of course one sympathetic with the general propositions of evolutionary science. As Roosevelt observed, "he who would fully treat of man must know at least something of biology . . . and especially of that science of evolution inseparably connected with the great name of Darwin." [45] The definition and use of such terms as "new species," "extinction of species," and "specialization"

45. Roosevelt, "Biological Analogies in History," *Works*, XIV, p. 69.

were in keeping with an organic notion of life, physical and social, between which there were certain parallels:

As in biology, so in human history, a new form may result from the specialization of a long existing and hitherto very slowly changing generalized or non-generalized form; as for instance, occurs when a barbaric race from a variety of causes suddenly develops a more complex cultivation and civilization. This is what occurred, for instance, in western Europe during the centuries of the Teutonic and later the Scandinavian overflows from the north.[46]

Since this parallel applied to death as to life and growth, the analogy was complete.[47] With regard to the death of a civilization Roosevelt recognized that there were certain differences, as was also the case in the biological order. Ancient Babylon and Nineveh as well as the New World Indians disappeared, whereas the Roman way never became extinct in blood or culture because much of it was successfully transmitted to the barbarians and survived with them in an altered form.

Looking to the period after 1500 Roosevelt also discerned the phenomena of growth and decay. The gathering momentum of the European advance marked one of the most spectacular examples in history of the social growth process. Though similar to the expansion of ancient Rome, it had surpassed the Roman achievement by the range of its proliferation and its inherent power of cultural synthesis. He also noted instances of decay in the modern era. The Dutch of the seventeenth century enjoyed a healthy social organism, but like other civilizations that had gone into decline they failed to observe struggle as a law of life.[48]

Despite a definite biological flavor in the Romanes Lecture, Roosevelt agreed with both anthropologists and historians as to "how artificial most great nationalities are and how loose the terminology usually employed to describe them." [49] He went on to offer his own evaluation that "most of the great civilizations which have developed and have played a dominant part in the

46. *Ibid.*, p. 78.
47. *Ibid.*, p. 82.
48. *Ibid.*, pp. 82–92 *passim.*
49. *Ibid.*, p. 82.

world have been—and are—artificial; not merely in social struc-
ture but in the sense of including totally different types. A great
nation rarely belongs to any one race. . . ." It might seem otherwise, however, because "the curious fact remains that these great
artificial societies acquire such unity that in each one all parts
feel a subtle sympathy and move or cease to move, go forward or
go backward all together, in response to some throbbing very
powerful, and yet not to be discerned by our senses." [50] He was
also prepared to recognize the existence and importance of the
races, "the half dozen great ethnic divisions of mankind," though
ethnic divisions as such had not usually remained unified and had
not produced cultures. "National unity was far more apt than
race unity to be a fact to reckon with." [51] Again one notes the
tension, typical of Roosevelt's imperialism, provoked by the conflict between an evolutionary explanation of man and other mean-
ings that history and tradition provided.

That Roosevelt found evolution alone to be unconvincing is
demonstrated by the concluding portions of "Biological Analogies
in History"; the emphasis on *character* significantly appears
once more. For advice to the contemporary world he drew upon a
lesson from the past, that "free people can escape bing mastered
by others only by being able to master themselves. We Americans
and you people of the British Isles alike need ever to keep in
mind," he went on, "that among the qualities indispensable to the
success of a great democracy, and second only to a high and
stern sense of duty, of moral obligation, are self-knowledge and
self-mastery. . . .[52] Just as in private life many of the men of
strongest character are men of the loftiest and most exalted
morality, so I believe in national life, as the ages go by, we shall
find that the permanent national types will more and more tend
to become those in which, though intellect stands high, *character*
stands higher." [53]

It followed that national problems must be approached in "the

50. *Ibid.*, p. 84.
51. *Ibid.*
52. *Ibid.*, p. 97.
53. *Ibid,* p. 101 (italics added).

spirit of broad humanity, of brotherly kindness, of acceptance of responsibility. . . . And at the same time a spirit as remote as the poles from every form of weakness and sentimentality [must prevail]. . . . The only effective way to help any man is to help him to help himself. . . . True liberty shows itself to best advantage in protecting the rights of others, especially the minorities. . . ." [54] Might was not right in the relationship of man to man or of conqueror to conquered. "In the long run there can be no justification for one race managing or controlling another unless . . . in the interests and for the benefit of that race." [55] This was the main lesson of "Biological Analogies in History," which Roosevelt recommended that Anglo-Americans continue to give heed to as he felt he had done in his imperialist policies while President. [56]

The steadily more explicit character of Roosevelt's attitude toward evolution in relationship to other facets of his intellectual makeup can be illustrated by contrasting aspects of "Social Evolution" (1895) and "Biological Analogies in History" (1910). In the earlier essay he had written that while the principle of natural selection is "undoubtedly true taken of the world as a whole . . . in all probability [it was] entirely false of the highest sections of society." [57] The inference was that in the physical universe, the realm of matter, evolution is a sound and acceptable law, but with regard to the conscious world, the human condition, the principle and its corollaries are applicable hardly at all. In "Biological Analogies in History" this distinction was presumed and treated as fundamental. Roosevelt wove into his discussion the essential difference between material and conscious, between prehuman and human history, between nations composed of races with blood ties and nations that were artificial entities, between what he knew little of (the remote past) and history, which he had read thoroughly.

Was his reliance on the evolutionary thesis a substitute for

54. *Ibid.*, p. 102.
55. *Ibid.*, p. 104.
56. To Edmund R.O. von Mach, November 7, 1914, *Letters*, VIII, p. 834.
57. Roosevelt, "Social Evolution," *Works*, XIV, p. 108.

knowledge, genuinely enough avowed but all too likely to be limited and refined by history and tradition, by inherited mores and moral precepts? In both his major writings dealing with Darwinism, "Social Evolution" and "Biological Analogies in History," Roosevelt assumed, loftily, the unquestionability of evolution; it was as indisputable as the solar system. Yet consistently, as he brought the theory to bear on the real human conditions he was close to and striving to understand and master (particularly the problems of imperialism, where evolutionary tenets presumably had application), Darwinism was less and less decisive, even less and less pertinent.

In light of the seriousness with which Roosevelt approached his Romanes Lecture, the formal circumstances of its delivery before the Oxford community of scholars gathered in the Sheldonian Theatre, and the extent and detail of its argument, "Biological Analogies in History" can well stand as Theodore Roosevelt's definitive statement of the place of evolution in human history and the distinction between it and social Darwinism.

But it was not his last word, and brief notice of some later remarks serves to deepen an awareness of his resistance to the inclusive assertions of science. In the *Outlook* in December 1911 he observed, "the claims of certain so-called scientific men as to 'science overthrowing religion' are as baseless as the fears of certain sincerely religious men on the same subject. The establishment of the doctrine of evolution in our time offers no more justification for upsetting religious beliefs than the discovery of the facts concerning the solar system [does] . . . and the materialistic scientists who gleefully hail the discovery of the principles of evolution as establishing their dreary creed might with just as much propriety rest upon the discovery of the principles of gravitation." [58] Though he expressed these thoughts, he nonetheless admired Darwin and other scientists as "seekers after truth." "The debt of mankind to the modern scientific movement is incalculable," he concluded, but he saw grave danger in

58. Roosevelt, "The Search for Truth in a Reverent Spirit," *ibid.*, p. 424.

giving "to each passing and evanescent phase of materialistic scientific thought a dogmatic value." [59] He was prompted to warn how "foolish we should be to abandon our adherence to the old ideals of duty toward God and man without better security than the most radical among the new prophets can offer us." [60]

Roosevelt's address to the American Historical Association Convention in 1912, entitled "History as Literature," made the same point. "Scientific writers of note had grasped the fact of evolution long before Darwin and Huxley," he reminded the historians, "and the theories advanced by these men to explain evolution were not much more unsatisfactory, as full explanations, than the theory of natural selection itself." [61]

It was still later, in his last important review-essay, "The Origin and Evolution of Life," that Roosevelt offered his final reservations regarding the evolutionary hypothesis, while at the same time retaining his regard and respect for science in its quest for learning of the origin of life. "All the theories hitherto propounded to account for evolution, even if taken together, fail to account for it," he commented. "It is possible that our intelligence is not such as to enable us to account for it. . . . But other scientific investigators believe that at least there is a chance the cause may be found . . . that *energy* and not *form* lies at the beginning of life."

Roosevelt was sufficiently scientific in his intellectual disposition and historically conversant enough to agree that what was not then known could someday in the future become known. His was an open universe of the mind. On the other hand, he was not willing to concede that any discovery of the principle of material life necessarily and perfectly would have application to man as man. "The tracing of an unbroken line of descent from the protozoan to Plato does not in any way really explain Plato's consciousness, of which there is no vestige in the protozoan. There has been a non-measurable quantity of actual creation," he went on.

59. *Ibid.*, p. 423.
60. *Ibid.*, p. 430.
61. Roosevelt, "History as Literature," *ibid.*, pp. 9–10.

"There is something new which did not exist in the protozoan. It has been produced in the course of evolution. But it is a play on words to say that such evolution is not creation." [62] Fascinated by the awesome potential of science, Roosevelt was still traditional enough in his thought to suggest that understanding creation itself might involve a preternatural order of intelligence, beyond the ken of man. And there was no mistaking his judgment of the application of evolutionary science at the time to the social order. For him Spencerian individualism, which scientific Darwinism had spawned, was too noxious to survive.

It is possible to derive different conclusions from the refusal of Theodore Roosevelt to hew to a social Darwinist line, given his evolutionary predisposition. A pragmatic man, he may have embraced some aspects of the doctrine of natural selection out of expediency because they could justify actions he judged to be in order practically. The pragmatic way, however it may be viewed, is historically American and in some ways typical of Roosevelt's approach to any problem.[63]

Philosophy aside, in many of his policies Roosevelt appeared as an old-fashioned individualist, a character type well known before the tide of Darwinism began to run high. No doubt the cult of the individual as it came to be honored from the time of the Renaissance had a strong claim upon him. For example, in his treatment of *character* he made an easy transference of personal qualities from the individual to the national community, arguing that just as it was the honest, diligent, and upright man who possessed *character* and achieved personal fulfillment, so also was greatness in the nation constituted; the honest, diligent, upright nations would inherit the earth. Darwinism offered parallels more striking than causal. The difficulty with such conclusions is that they ignore Roosevelt's deep and continuous involvement

62. Roosevelt, "The Origin and Evolution of Life," *ibid.*, p. 36.
63. See for example, Howard C. Hill, *op. cit.*, pp. 198 ff; Edward Wagenknecht, *op. cit.*, pp. 181 ff.

with evolution as a historical principle, to which his writings attest.[64]

A final appraisal of the influence of Darwinism on Roosevelt and his imperialist philosophy might well settle upon the meaningful distinction drawn between evolution and social Darwinism. It was a distinction he himself made and maintained. In his last essay, which dealt with natural selection, he spoke of accepting "evolution as a natural law no more disputable than the law of gravity," of considering the universe as having gone through phases preparatory to the advent rather than the descent of man.[65] But Darwin and Darwinists hardly had all the answers. Human consciousness and the creation of man remained beyond the Darwinian theories and their social corollaries; likewise the ultimate purpose of his imperialism was to be found in traditional values. However, without the challenge of Darwinism, which forced him to consider carefully its social and ethical implications only to reject them in areas crucial to man in society, Roosevelt's own code of values would have been less well defined, less intellectualized, and perhaps less a controlling influence on the uses he made of power.

64. Roosevelt cannot be seriously considered as a "reform Darwinist" in view of the nonscientific qualifications he applied to evolution; nor did he particularly favor economic interpretations of history, which were among the favorite analytical tools of the "reform Darwinists."

65. Roosevelt, "The Origin and Evolution of Life," *Works*, XIV, p. 34.

5

On Its Own Sword

The years during which Theodore Roosevelt enjoyed the great prerogatives of the American Presidency were promising ones for the world movement. The Great Powers continued to extend their authority by force over the waste spaces, which according to the Rooseveltian formula brought about an advance of civilization for the backward peoples. In his judgment the United States had offered its cooperation and promoted the cause of peace and human betterment in the Philippines and in the Caribbean; in so doing it had established a reputation for colonial administration and national self-discipline unsurpassed by that of any of the European powers.

President Roosevelt was intensely proud of what the United States had accomplished. He was not, on the other hand, a foolish optimist. As he once described himself to Owen Wister, "I am an optimist, but I hope a reasonably intelligent one" who saw the evil in the world but who believed that "on the whole the good will come out ahead." [1] One of his last pieces of advice to President elect Taft before leaving office bespoke his caution. "Dear Will," he wrote, "One closing legacy. Under no circumstances divide the battleship fleet between the oceans prior to the finishing of the Panama Canal." [2]

1. To Owen Wister, February 25, 1895, quoted in Owen Wister, *Roosevelt, The Story of a Friendship,* (New York, 1930), p. 39.
2. To William Howard Taft, March 3, 1909, *Letters,* VI, p. 1543.

His over-all mood as he departed the White House was nonetheless one of confidence and of satisfaction. "I have done my
work; I am perfectly content; I have nothing to ask; and I am
very grateful to the American people for what they have done for
me"; these comments aptly summed up his frame of mind in March
1909.[3]

The decade after Roosevelt left office—the last ten years
of his life—witnessed not the fulfillment of the world movement
but an end to it. In the war of 1914 the world movement was run
through with its own sword. The use of force by the Great Powers,
which Roosevelt had so ardently believed was productive of
civilization, convulsed man's social, economic, and political orders
instead. The ex-President was brave enough to face what had
happened. Alert to the last of his days, he watched the slow tor-
ture of the war; he lost his youngest son, Quentin, in the ordeal
of battle. With respect to his world movement philosophy he was
forced by the causes and the coming of the war to offer some final
verdict on it. He came to see that the expansive quality of the
western people might well be a means of civilization, but at Arma-
geddon the preservation of civilization took precedence over the
mere physical prowess that had served so well in lesser battles.

The potential for conflict in Roosevelt's mind, that is, antagonism between his adherence to both traditional and scientific
modes of thought, did not materialize in a deeply critical fashion
because when faced with a choice of ethical norms he was
prepared to elect the old verities. The conflict was more apparent
than real when the moral choice was clear-cut. But regardless of
Roosevelt's view of the world movement, the interplay of appearance and reality was almost the opposite. The likelihood that
internal contradictions would effect a destructive end to the
movement was quite real, though not readily apparent. If, as
happened, warning signs flashed, these were often disregarded or
viewed as strains within the movement denoting nothing more than
the need for adjustment. Only a general war among the Great
Powers would bring the world movement to disaster and though

3. To Paul Morton, March 2, 1909, *ibid.*, p. 1541.

omens accumulated to portend it, Roosevelt, like many men, could not bring himself to accept this as a probability. Again, care must be exercised to distinguish between what might be called in the Rooseveltian phrase a "flabby optimism" and realistic optimism. Writing to Arthur James Balfour in 1908 he pronounced "a very firm faith in the general forward movement [of European civilization] considering only men of our own race for the past two score centuries, and I hope and believe that the movement will continue for an indefinite period to come; but no one can be sure; there is certainly nothing inevitable or necessary about the movement." [4]

Not a few warning signs Roosevelt certainly did read with some accuracy. "I do not see how any thinking man can fail to feel now and then ugly doubts as to what may befall our modern civilization—the civilization of the white race," he confessed to Balfour. But since each sign indicating trouble involved a specific problem, he did not understand, in his practical way, why that one issue could not be settled reasonably. "The important thing is generally the 'next step'. . . . We should not hesitate to take it once we are sure; and we can safely take it without bothering . . . overmuch as to any somewhat fantastic theories [concerning] the two hundredth step, which is not yet in sight." [5] Roosevelt's step-by-step methods worked well enough for a long while, if only because the Great Powers for the most part continued to be arrayed against the weaker peoples rather than against each other.

As the world movement worked itself out in both depth and breadth there were two areas of potential danger, one lesser and one greater, which if carried ineluctably forward could spell the end of the movement. The lesser of these was the conflict between imperialism and native nationalism. The presence of westerners and influence of modern western notions on politics and economics, whether in British India or in the American-controlled

4. To Arthur James Balfour, March 5, 1908, *ibid.*, p. 961.
5. Roosevelt, "Socialism," *Works*, XVIII, p. 565.

Philippines, invariably stimulated the native peoples to an emulation and an envy of the ruling foreigners. The more deeply and more thoroughly the western ways penetrated, the greater was the awareness by the local peoples of their own identity, and the greater their dissatisfaction with their status as colonial dependencies.

Roosevelt saw this development in India before the nineteenth century was out, and his reaction to it was stern and straightforward. As a knowledgeable historian he sensed the impermanency of European control in Africa and in Asia. In "National Life and Character" he had early envisioned the time when the English power in India would meet the same fate as that of the ancient Greek kingdoms, but he added that for the good of mankind he "sincerely hoped and believed that it would occur in the very remote future." [6] The issues in India by the 1890's were immediate ones. It was the "next step" that was called for—what ought to be done in the name of civilization now, not decades hence. In India, therefore, he advised that the English rule firmly and not be intimidated by irresponsible native agitation.[7] His position he clearly stated, the force at hand being more than sufficient to the demands of the specific occasion. What happened eventually in India might perhaps develop from "some fantastic theories" but these had no immediate relevance. It would be unfair to imply that Roosevelt had no appreciation at all of the complex social problems the English faced in India,[8] but he remained convinced that "if English control were now [1909] removed from India, the whole peninsula would become a chaos of bloodshed and violence. . . . The great salient fact is that the presence of the English in India has been for the advantage of mankind." [9] The "here and now" demanded that Britain's position in India be maintained undiluted.

The greater of the perils involved in a working out of the world movement was the possible clash between superior peoples, even

6. Roosevelt, "National Life and Character," *ibid.*, XIV, p. 239.
7. To Sir Cecil Spring-Rice, August 13, 1897, *Letters*, I, p. 648.
8. See for example to Whitelaw Reid, September 3, 1908, *ibid.*, VI, p. 1206.
9. Roosevelt, "The Expansion of the White Race," *Works*, XVIII, pp. 345–347.

on a very local level. The size of such a war might not be so important as the principle concerned. Trouble between Boer and Britisher in South Africa gave serious warning of this. Both parties to the conflict represented the expansive dynamism of the white race; both served the cause of civilization by wresting land from the ignorant barbarian and rendering it productive; both brought European law and order to the waste spaces of Africa. Yet in South Africa white men opposed each other in a long-standing controversy over the control of territory that eventuated in a full-scale war.

The Boer War was an actualization of the tragic contradiction within the world movement and a prophecy of more compelling evidence to come. Though sympathetic to the arguments that both Boer and Britisher advanced to justify their respective positions, Roosevelt was greatly distressed by this rupture within the ranks of the superior peoples. The choice of war in South Africa, he wrote his sister, Anna Roosevelt Cowles, "makes me really sad." [10] The Boers appealed to him as "belated Cromwellians with many fine traits." [11] The policy of Rhodes and Chamberlain in seeking to maintain British dominion in the area had been in method rather than in purpose "one huge blunder." [12] Furthermore, he felt that the resistance of the Boers to British expansion was "perfectly right from their standpoint, and also [they] had the technical right in the case." [13] Despite all this, he favored a British victory. As he had written to Henry White several years before the war erupted, "I feel it is in the interests of civilization that the English-speaking race should be dominant in South Africa." [14] With the war in progress "England was really fighting the battle of civilization" and because of that fact alone deserved to win.[15]

10. To A.R. Cowles, December 17, 1899, Letters, II, p. 1112.
11. To Sir Cecil Spring-Rice, September 2, 1899, quoted in Stephen Gwynn, The Letters and Friendships of Sir Cecil Spring-Rice, 2 volumes, (Boston, 1929), I, p. 305.
12. To William W. Sewall, April 24, 1900, Letters, II, p. 1270.
13. To A.R. Cowles, February 5, 1900, Letters from Theodore Roosevelt to Anna Roosevelt Cowles, 1870–1917, (New York, 1924) p. 235. (Hereafter cited as Cowles Letters.)
14. To Henry White, March 30, 1896, Letters, I, p. 523.
15. To A.R. Cowles, February 5, 1900, Cowles Letters, p. 235.

The Boer War presented to Roosevelt a choice between centering his world movement philosophy around a physical factor—the power of a people to expand—and a moral one, the good of mankind to be achieved. His decision favored the moral consideration. In this case it was made easier by his admiration for Britain's historic role as civilizer, his close personal friendship with numerous influential Englishmen, and the obvious determination of England to prevail in the matter. These reasons, however, should not obscure that it was an essential, if supremely personal, judgment that guided Roosevelt's preference for a British victory.

The aftermath of the Boer War may have reassured Roosevelt about the contradictions that the killing by the Boers and the British had made plain. It had been his hope that once the war was over the British and Dutch races would fuse in South Africa as they had once done in America, and in this he was not disappointed. Conqueror and conquered came to live together peacefully and to build another bastion of white power in Africa. The Boer farmers really had small choice but to accept the military verdict, especially since at first many hundreds attempting to flee alien rule had been decimated by disease and forced to return to British-occupied territory.

The English were conciliatory and generous in their treatment of their former foes. When Roosevelt visited South Africa in 1909 he remarked that "it was pleasant to see the good terms on which Boer and Briton meet. . . ." The Boers "were being treated precisely on an equality with the British settlers," he learned. The result was a significant step forward for the world movement because there were "no better or manlier people, [and] the English and the Dutch [were] engaged in the great and difficult task of adding East Africa to the domain of civilization." [16] Such sound, judicious statesmanship would not prevail in the years after 1914, but the healing of wounds in South Africa helped to account for the continued optimism Roosevelt placed in the constructive character of the world movement in spite of the Boer War itself.

When there is light, there are also shadows. The nature of the

---

16. Roosevelt, *African Game Trails, Works*, V, pp. 39–40.

new British settlements in East Africa that Roosevelt visited on tour in 1909 did not reassure him regarding the vitality of the world movement. He wryly called many of the British he encountered there "make-believe settlers . . . not one in ten intending to stay in the country or to make it a permanent home in which he and his wife and his children should live." With the Boer farmers, the very men defeated by the British in the war, it was quite the contrary. They had put their roots down with the purpose of making East Africa their home, much like the old American frontiersmen who had conquered the West. It was the Boers and not the British who were making an ethnic rather than a mere political conquest. Had Roosevelt preferred the wrong side in the Boer War after all? Had the British as a people succumbed to materialism, or perhaps to success? Was this not an early hint of the waning of the world movement? The situation in South Africa remained unclear to Roosevelt despite his reassertion during World War I of the propriety of British dominion there.[17]

Three particular controversies during his Presidency, which Theodore Roosevelt took a personal interest in, threatened the continued progress of the world movement. By helping to remove or to lessen the source of friction in each case an adjustment was made possible that relieved the strain of international tension between certain of the superior nations. The first of these was the Alaskan boundary dispute between the United States and Canada. American purchase of Alaska in 1867 had had little impact on U.S.-Canadian relations until the discovery of gold in the Klondike in 1896. Shortly thereafter the Canadian Government advanced the claim that the boundary between Canadian territory and that of the United States in the Alaska Panhandle region lay close to the coast and not some miles inland, as had been presumed by the United States. United States admission of this Canadian claim would have virtually cut the Panhandle district off from the rest

17. To H. Rider Haggard, August 22, 1911, *Letters*, VII, p. 330.

of Alaska by a land route. Furthermore, it was possible that new gold deposits might be located in the disputed region.

A *modus vivendi* without prejudice to the prior claims of either party had been arranged by Secretary Hay in 1899 and was operant when Roosevelt came into the presidential office. Of course the new President had kept himself informed of the controversy before September 1901. In March of that year, in a letter to his British friend Arthur Hamilton Lee, he wrote: "I have studied that question pretty thoroughly and I do not think the Canadians have a leg to stand on," arguing that the Canadian claims originated some fifteen years after the United States had acquired Alaska.[18] Still he did not propose an abrogation of the temporary agreement at that time. Writing again to Lee in April he expressed his "horse-back judgment" that the *ad hoc* arrangement should stand. The territory he estimated to be of small worth, though more pertinent to his judgment was the high value he placed on Great Britain's friendship with the United States. This friendship, typically, he did not allow to interfere with his concern for the best interests of his own nation in the dispute. He was not prepared to arbitrate, he told Lee, referring once again to the "entirely modern" character of the Canadian claims.[19] As Vice-President his attitude was friendly toward the disputing party but firm: "We would not yield on the Alaska business."[20]

The temporary nature of the *modus vivendi*, fear of an incident should gold be discovered in the disputed area—a worry sufficient to cause President Roosevelt to direct Secretary of War Root, in March 1902, to dispatch additional troops to prevent disturbances along the boundary,[21] and the diplomatic representations of the British ambassador in Washington all encouraged a final solution to the controversy. Nonetheless, the President was in no mood to accommodate the Canadians at American expense. He made his position clear in a letter to Secretary Hay. The Canadian-claimed boundary was an invention of the past few years, he re-

18. To Arthur Hamilton Lee, March 18, 1901, *ibid.*, III, p. 20.
19. To Arthur Hamilton Lee, April 24, 1901, *ibid.*, p. 65.
20. To Nicholas Murray Butler, June 3, 1901, *ibid.*, p. 85.
21. Jessup, *op. cit.*, I, pp. 390–392; to John Hay, July 16, 1902, *Letters*, III, p. 294.

iterated. American maps, Russian maps, British Admiralty maps, and all but the most recent Canadian maps as well always represented the disputed territory as non-Canadian. The claim therefore was not one subject to compromise, the likely outcome of any arbitration. The Canadian position Roosevelt pronounced "an outrage, pure and simple." [22] His friendly but firm tone of a few months before had turned less friendly, no doubt, but an open clash with Great Britain was still to be avoided. He placed the blame for worsening relations on Canada, whose "spirit of bumptious truculence" England had resisted for years.[23] This deterioration was arrested by a successful negotiation of a treaty signed in January 1903 that provided for a tribunal of six "impartial jurists of repute," three from each country, to decide the validity of the rival claims. Roosevelt was unhappy with this treaty. "Nothing but my earnest desire to get on well with England and my reluctance to come to a break made me consent to a Joint Commission," he told Oliver Wendell Holmes, Jr.[24]

President Roosevelt chose Secretary Root, his personal friend Cabot Lodge, an Anglophobe of special notoriety, and outgoing United States senator from the State of Washington, George Turner, as the American members of the tribunal. The judicial qualifications of these appointees have been earnestly questioned, but they reflected Roosevelt's determination to protect American interests under any circumstances, since he felt he could rely on the patriotic good sense of his choices. The President's instructions to them, dated March 17, 1903, reveal his attitude. "I feel I should briefly call your attention to my view of the question," he wrote. "You will of course impartially judge the questions that come before you for decision," but, he went on, "the question is not in my judgment one in which it is possible to consider a reconciling of conflicting claims by mutual concessions." [25]

Deliberations did not get under way in London until Septem-

22. To John Hay, July 10, 1902, *ibid.*, p. 286.
23. To John Hay, July 16, 1902, *ibid.*, p. 294.
24. To Oliver Wendell Holmes, Jr., July 25, 1903, *ibid.*, p. 529.
25. To Elihu Root, Henry Cabot Lodge, and George Turner, March 17, 1903, *ibid.*, pp. 448–449.

ber 1903, a delay that only added to the President's testiness.[26] In point of fact, the American commissioners were not absolutely unyielding. Roosevelt gave his permission to concede two small islands, Wales and Pearse, to Canada, "using them as make-weight" [27] sufficient for Britain to save face and bring about the desired adjustment in Anglo-American relations.[28] When the commission sustained the American contention by a vote of four to two, Lord Alverstone, the Lord Chief Justice of England, siding with the Americans against the two Canadian members, Roosevelt was immensely pleased, not least of all because it relieved strained relations with London. As he told Spring-Rice, "it has been a very happy and fortunate thing to get the question definitely settled and out of the way." [29]

The Alaskan boundary settlement sometimes has been interpreted as "big sticking the British," [30] and no doubt it had some of the flavor of that aspect of Roosevelt's diplomacy. He combined veiled threats with a firm hand in bringing the issue to a favorable conclusion for his country. But his policy in this case lacked the rancor and the contempt so notoriously associated with his Colombian canal policy, which was conducted simultaneously. The difference was not that the United States had a better moral right in the Isthmus than in Alaska; nor was it merely that the Colombians were weak and Britain a great power. Ultimately it can be accounted for by those considerations that had made Britain a power, the manifest superiority of the British as a people. As determined as Theodore Roosevelt was to satisfy American demands, he remained anxious to avoid an open split with a leading people of the world movement. Perhaps in the long view the Alas-

26. To John Hay, June 29, 1903, *ibid.*, p. 507.
27. To John Hay, September 15, 1903, *ibid.*, p. 601.
28. To Henry Cabot Lodge, October 15, 1903, *ibid.*, p. 616.
29. To Sir Cecil Spring-Rice, November 9, 1903, *ibid.*, p. 650.
30. This is the judgment of Thomas A. Bailey in "Roosevelt and the Alaska Boundary Dispute," *The Canadian Historical Review*, XVIII, No. 2 (June 1937), pp. 123–130. See also C.C. Tansill, *Canadian-American Relations, 1875–1911*, (New Haven, 1943), pp. 191–265 for an altogether exhaustive treatment of the controversy and its settlement. Tansill stresses Roosevelt's strongly nationalistic attitude.

kan boundary episode ranks as only a slight threat to the peace of the world, but for a time it was a pressing, immediate issue that required settling.

A graver threat to the peace of the world had developed in far-away Morocco hard on the heels of the Anglo-French entente of April 8, 1904. That famous understanding sought to establish Anglo-French hegemony in North Africa by a mutual recognition of Britain's primary position in Egypt and France's primary position in Morocco. France was anxious to bring all of Morocco within her sphere of influence. This arrangement conflicted with German ambitions in North Africa. It occasioned German Chancellor von Bulow's Moroccan policy of forcing the French and English to reveal what those powers might have done in violation of the Madrid Convention of 1880, an older agreement concerning Morocco that had promised "most favored nation" treatment to all signatory powers, of which Germany was one. The visit of the Kaiser to Tangier on March 31, 1905, was part of von Bulow's strategy, for it was intended to dramatize Germany's determination not to be supplanted in North Africa without consideration or compensation. After the Kaiser's appearance in Tangier, von Bulow proposed the calling of an international conference of all the powers signatory to the Madrid Convention in order to review the Moroccan state of affairs.

Since the United States was also a signatory to the agreement, Germany aimed to bring off the international meeting through the good offices of the American Government. The handle that the Germans hoped the Americans would grasp was the future of United States economic interests in Morocco. Von Bulow represented French intentions as a violation of the general principle of the Open Door, properly applicable to backward or underdeveloped areas whether in Asia or in Africa.[31] The Germans counted on Roosevelt's inclination to be at the center of things and his

31. A.L.P. Dennis, *Adventures in American Diplomacy, 1896–1906,* (New York, 1928), p. 487.

genuine concern for the peace of the world to spark American participation. German Ambassador von Sternburg's personal friendship with the President was expected to expedite the venture. Meanwhile, on the European diplomatic front von Bulow played a deliberate waiting game, a policy that eventually brought about the downfall of Delcassé, the French foreign minister chiefly responsible for the entente of 1904. This cleared the way for the long-awaited conference.

At first Roosevelt was not receptive to German overtures. In early March, some weeks before the Kaiser went to Tangier, von Sternburg had delivered a message from the Kaiser to the President asking that Germany and the United States pronounce in favor of the independence of the sultan of Morocco from outside (that is, French) advisers and requesting a continuation of the Open Door principle there. Roosevelt replied that United States commitments in the area were not sufficient to warrant intervention, but he went on to express friendliness for Germany and his conviction that German policy stood for peace.[32] This guarded American response was not adequate to German purposes, and several times in April and May von Sternburg continued to press Roosevelt for United States support of the proposed conference. One memorandum transmitted from the Kaiser through the ambassador spoke of war as an alternative to some agreement to be brought off by a conference.[33] The Germans were convinced that it was England who blocked French acquiescence to a conference. Under pressure exerted through von Sternburg, Roosevelt, while on a hunting trip in Colorado, did agree to permit Taft to sound out Great Britain in this regard because he was "sincerely anxious to bring about a better state of feeling between England and Germany."[34]

When the President returned to Washington from the West at the end of May he found both von Sternburg and the French am-

32. To Whitelaw Reid, April 28, 1906, *Letters*, V, p. 230.

33. *Ibid.*, pp. 230–232. Eugene N. Anderson's *The First Moroccan Crisis, 1904–1906* (Chicago, 1930), gives a balanced account of the crisis and Roosevelt's role with respect to the Algeciras Conference.

34. William Howard Taft, April 20, 1905, quoted in Roosevelt to Whitelaw Reid, April 28, 1906, *Letters*, V, p. 230.

bassador, Jules Jusserand, "greatly concerned lest there should be a war between France and Germany" and "sincerely anxious to avert such a possibility." [35] Still Roosevelt was reluctant to act. On June 11 another memorandum from the Kaiser emphasized the threat of war and interpolated the idea that in such a war Russia might well be in a position to have a freer hand in the Far East, perhaps trying to cede a portion of China as her war indemnity to Japan.[36] It should be realized that the summer of 1905 saw Roosevelt busy trying to arrange an end to the Russo-Japanese War. It was the German Government's argument that what Roosevelt did or did not do in Morocco might detrimentally affect his role as a peacemaker between Russia and Japan. The Kaiser was not unaware of the President's hostility toward Russia, and he pleaded knowingly that peace could come to the Orient and be preserved in North Africa if Roosevelt "could give a hint now in London and Paris that [Roosevelt] would consider a conference as the most satisfactory means of bringing the Moroccan question to a peaceful settlement." [37] By this time the President had come to the conclusion that "there might be a war" and he "felt in honor bound to try to prevent the war." The reasons he advanced for this change of attitude are of the utmost importance for understanding the ramifications of his world movement philosophy. "Such a war [would be] a real calamity to civilization, a conflict that might be a world conflagration," he was later to tell Whitelaw Reid. It might be noted in addition that he confessed to Reid he acted also "for the sake of France." [38]

The decision made, the President proceeded to promote the Algeciras Conference. In his own words he took "active hold of the matter with both Speck [von Sternburg] and Jusserand . . . [and] got things temporarily straightened out." [39] His major appeal was to the French, whose interests in Morocco were vitally concerned. He had already indicated to von Sternburg that there was strong sentiment in Washington favoring France's role as the

35. *Ibid.*, p. 234.
36. *Ibid.*, p. 235.
37. *Ibid.*, pp. 235–236.
38. *Ibid.*, p. 236.
39. *Ibid.*

civilizing power in Morocco.[40] With genuine feeling for France and her future, he addressed Paris with the argument that war meant a very grave danger to her at home and abroad and that a conference would hardly sanction any unjust action by Germany against France.[41] Whether or not Roosevelt was explicit in the belief that a German attack on France would be a calamity for civilization is not so important as his thought that any war between the powers would be a setback to the world movement.[42] As he expressed it to von Sternburg after he had taken the initiative for a conference, "I felt the extreme importance of doing everything possible to maintain the peace of the world," a direct and consistent explanation of his purpose.[43] The Germans and the French agreed to a meeting on July 8, with Britain and the other powers signaling approval soon after.

Roosevelt believed that he had done what he could to help preserve the peace, showing his "anxiety for peace" as he phrased it, and that the absence of American interests in Morocco would limit United States participation accordingly.[44] Such was not the case. The President found it necessary to "save the conference," for public failure of a meeting so much heralded could have had dire consequences for international accord. The powers assembled at Algeciras in Spain, their usual suspicions and animosities barely concealed. French insistence upon having a decisive influence in the Moroccan police force was countered by a German-inspired Austrian demand for a division of the country's ports among certain of the powers. Deadlock ensued, prompting Roosevelt to oppose the German position. The United States regarded the proposal of a distribution of Moroccan ports as "an essential departure from the principle declared by Germany and adhered to

40. Dennis, *op. cit.*, p. 496.
41. To Whitelaw Reid, April 28, 1906, *Letters*, V, p. 236.
42. Roscoe Thayer in *Life of Roosevelt* (New York, 1919) maintains that Roosevelt's Moroccan policy was dictated by his early recognition of Germany as a menace to civilization while A.L.P. Dennis denies it. See Thayer, p. 228, and Dennis, *op. cit.*, p. 495.
43. To Herman Speck von Sternburg, June 25, 1905, *Letters*, IV, pp. 1256–1257.
44. Dennis, *op. cit.*, p. 496.

by the United States," namely, an Open Door in Morocco. In a series of exchanges between the State Department and the German Government, Secretary Root, at the direction of the President, remained unalterably opposed to a division of Moroccan commerce and the rigid spheres of influence likely to result.[45] Von Sternburg was informed that should the conference break up by reason of German rejection of the American position the President would feel obliged to publish the entire correspondence . . . [which would] make our people feel a grave suspicion of Germany's justice and faith."[46] Roosevelt later spoke of his threat to von Sternburg as "the vital feature" of his campaign to persuade the Kaiser to behave.[47]

Very probably the German decision to accede to American pressure helped to "save the conference," though there are ample reasons besides United States persuasion why the Germans did not choose to fight at that time over that issue. Whether it saved the peace for a few years or merely added to German grievances is another matter. Roosevelt for his part was convinced that he had worked successfully for peace. As he summed it up, justice was done, international good will promoted, friction between the powers decreased, and improved conditions for Moroccans themselves brought about. Finally, he judged the conference to be a harbinger of friendlier Franco-German relations, which he described as "my hope and wish, as it must be the hope and wish of every sincere well-wisher of humankind."[48] All these conclusions are familiar enough as elements of the world movement philosophy.

Roosevelt's widely acknowledged role in sponsoring the Treaty of Portsmouth (September 1905), which concluded the Russo-Japanese War, ironically occupies a smaller place in an account

45. Elihu Root to Herman Speck von Sternburg, quoted in Roosevelt to Whitelaw Reid, April 28, 1960, *Letters*, V, p. 247.
46. *Ibid.*, p. 249.
47. To Whitelaw Reid, June 27, 1906, *ibid.*, p. 319.
48. Roosevelt, "Speech to German Veterans," quoted in Roosevelt to Whitelaw Reid, April 28, 1906, *ibid.*, p. 250.

of his contribution to the world movement than, for example, his part in the Moroccan crisis. The President had a great deal of admiration for the Japanese, looking upon them as the superior Oriental people because they had "the fighting edge," and he suspected and disliked the Russians in equal measure, though at Portsmouth his primary purpose was peace, irrespective of personal likes or dislikes. The immediate problem of peace affected the United States, since American interests in China and in the Far East generally were large and growing each year. A continuation of hostilities could disrupt the *status quo;* armies mobilized and fighting anywhere in the Orient posed a threat to the Open Door in China. Roosevelt's exertions in the cause of peace were founded to no small degree on the fear of a multipower conference that might proceed to a solution of the larger problem of China in a manner detrimental to the United States. His leadership in securing a treaty acceptable to the contending parties was mostly a work of realistic American diplomacy in which the world movement rationale was a presumed rather than a pronounced element.

The fact of the war was a bad omen for the world movement. It demonstrated that by the twentieth century the extension of the various imperialist domains and the soaring dreams behind them were more likely to produce a destructive war than a continuation of progress. If the prize was attractive enough and the determination to obtain it firm enough there might be little opportunity for the good offices of disinterested powers to avert armed conflict, perhaps on a widening scale. The Russo-Japanese War suggested in unmistakable fashion the prospect of superior peoples at war against each other on a vast scale, with the underdeveloped areas of the world the source of discord. Obviously powerless to prevent the outbreak of war between Russia and Japan, Roosevelt was able only to try to end hostilities and to restore peace. His efforts in this respect were exceptionally effective and recognized as such by the award of the Nobel Prize for Peace in 1906.[49] But the world movement itself had suffered a defeat.

49. "I did not consult him [Hay] at all in any of the movements that led to the peace of Portsmouth." To Henry Cabot Lodge, January 28, 1909, *ibid.,* VI, p. 1498; see also to Andrew Carnegie, February 26, 1909, *ibid.,* p. 1538.

Optimistically, he sought to reverse this verdict by playing the peacemaker. He succeeded only in promoting a solution to an immediate issue and not in excising the root causes of the war, which were a natural outgrowth of the world movement itself. When the Great War of 1914 came and with it the end of this cherished concept, Roosevelt himself was finally struck by the internal contradictions that a maturation of the movement forced into the open. Refusing to take the theory of imperialism to a logical conclusion in a speculative way, he was convinced only by the fact of World War I. But for the time being—the spring of 1905, when the Japanese made their first overtures to Roosevelt to act as mediator—these contradictions remained unarticulated.

In considering President Roosevelt's part in the Russo-Japanese negotiations we shall narrow an examination of it solely to a determination of the possible influence of his world movement outlook.[50] His admiration for the Japanese and his hostility toward the Russians are well known. What were the sources of his differing evaluations? An answer to that question explains the relationship of the world movement idea to his mediation in the affairs of the two warring nations. In Roosevelt's judgment the Japanese were to be welcomed "as a valuable factor in the civilization of the future." [51] "I believe that Japan will take its place as a great civilized power of a formidable type," he told Spring-Rice, "with motives and ways of thought which are not quite those of the powers of our race." [52] The Japanese were a race who could teach the West as well as learn from it.[53] Looking to the future he thought that Japan "will play her part honorably and well in the world's work of the Twentieth Century," [54] because the Japanese had mastered the industrial and commercial technology of the West, were able to

<hr/>

50. For a full treatment see Tyler Dennett, *Roosevelt and the Russo-Japanese War*, (Gloucester, Mass., 1959). It is the burden of Dennett's study that Roosevelt's motivation was to maintain in the Orient a balance of power favorable to the United States.

51. To Sir George Otto Trevelyan, May 13, 1905, *Letters*, IV, p. 1174; to Henry Cabot Lodge, June 5, 1905, *ibid.*, p. 1205.

52. To Sir Cecil Spring-Rice, June 16, 1905, *ibid.*, p. 1233.

53. To David B. Schneder, June 19, 1905, *ibid.*, p. 1240.

54. To Sir George Otto Trevelyan, September 12, 1905, *ibid.*, V, p. 22.

maintain a stable government, and had retained the fighting edge.[55]

And what of the Russians, who belonged to the white race? It is well to remember what, in Roosevelt's opinion, constituted character in the individual and that he ascribed somewhat the same standards of judgment in determining the worth of a nation or a people, if one is to appreciate his estimate of the Russians as the peace negotiations went forward. Though he professed regard for the Russian people, under the circumstances he found Russian officials "hopeless creatures . . . utterly insincere and treacherous . . . having no conception of truth."[56] On one occasion he described Russia as "so corrupt, so treacherous, so shifty and so incompetent, that I am utterly unable to say whether or not it will make peace";[57] on another, he remarked on the "extraordinary duplicity, shiftiness and insincerity of the Russians."[58] The character of Russian officialdom being what it was, the Government could hardly be expected to rise above its source. "Did you ever know anything more pitiable than the condition of the Russian despotism in this year of grace?" he asked John Hay. "The Czar is a preposterous little creature as the absolute autocrat of 150,000,000 people."[59] Czardom was a system of government to be abhorred,[60] "an amorphous affair."[61] The internal problems then troubling the country in combination with the military defeat at the hands of the Japanese occasioned Roosevelt to predict both internal disaster and loss of Great Power status unless the Czar made peace abroad and undertook reforms at home.[62]

Throughout the course of the peace talks between the representatives of the two countries the President's purpose remained the conclusion of a workable peace. He did not allow his personal

55. To Sir Cecil Spring-Rice, June 16, 1905, *ibid.*, IV, p. 1233.
56. To Henry Cabot Lodge, June 5, 1905, *ibid.*, p. 1205.
57. To Henry Cabot Lodge, June 16, 1905, *ibid.*, p. 1230; to Sir George Otto Trevelyan, May 13, 1905, *ibid.*, p. 1174.
58. To George L. von Meyer, July 18, 1905, *ibid.*, p. 1276.
59. To John Hay, April 2, 1905, *ibid.*, p. 1156.
60. To Sir George Otto Trevelyan, May 13, 1905, *ibid.*, p. 1174.
61. To Whitelaw Reid, June 30, 1905, *ibid.*, p. 1257.
62. To George L. von Meyer, July 7, 1905, *ibid.*, p. 1263; to Whitelaw Reid, July 7, 1905, *ibid.*, p. 1266.

attitudes to divert him from that purpose. When the Japanese persisted in their demands for a large indemnity, to the point of jeopardizing a settlement, Roosevelt was readily capable of applying pressure upon them to forgo such a provision. The Japanese were "of course entirely selfish, though with a veneer of courtesy," he once remarked to Lodge,[63] and he had no intention of permitting their greed to wreck a treaty of peace. He predicted that Russia would refuse to pay a money indemnity and would remain in the war, commenting further that "the civilized world" would back the Czar in his stand. The Japanese were warned that "every interest of civilization and humanity forbids the continuation of the war," [64] and while the argument of self-interest undoubtedly appealed more strongly to the Japanese leaders, to the President the benefits of peace for the world loomed larger.[65]

The Treaty of Portsmouth realized but one of the objectives Roosevelt had in assuming the responsibility of mediation, however; a war between the powers was terminated and peace was restored. But the more demanding task, that of maintaining the American Open Door policy intact was served only temporarily. The fact is that a balance of power in the Orient, which was a precondition for a successful maintenance of the Open Door, was a less prominent feature of international politics in the Far East after the Russo-Japanese War than it had been before the conflict, and American capital did not see fit to commit heavy investments there for that very reason.[66] Roosevelt himself had been not unwilling to indulge in some diplomatic horse trading where an American sphere of interest was concerned. The Taft-Katsura agreement of 1905, by which the United States recognized Japanese suzerainty over Korea in return for Japan's promise to respect the American position in the Philippine Islands, demonstrated this, even though Roosevelt chose to see the arrangement as helping to preserve the peace of the Far East.[67]

63. To Henry Cabot Lodge, June 16, 1905, *ibid.*, p. 1230.
64. To Kentaro Kaneko, August 22, 1905, *ibid.*, p. 1309.
65. To Kentaro Kaneko, August 23, 1905, *ibid.*, pp. 1312–1313.
66. George Mowry, *The Era of Theodore Roosevelt*, (New York, 1958), pp. 190–191.
67. To William Howard Taft, October 7, 1905, *Letters*, V, p. 59.

And then in 1908 came a dramatic retreat from the original Open Door policies in the Root-Takahira understanding. Confident imperialism was showing dangerous signs of strain. The anti-Japanese demonstrations on the American West Coast, which were an outgrowth of the school segregation crisis, had some bearing on the understanding. But, as Roosevelt was to concede in 1910, Japan's vital interests lay in Manchuria and in Korea, a fact that the United States had to recognize. Considering developments in the Orient the former President was less inclined to see Japan as one of the superior nations claiming its place of leadership than he was to judge the situation as one of power politics. He pointed out to President Taft that "Our vital interest is to keep the Japanese out of our country, and at the same time to preserve the good will of Japan. The vital interest of the Japanese, on the other hand, is in Manchuria and Korea. . . . The open door policy in China is an excellent thing [but] as a matter of fact [it] completely disappears as soon as a powerful nation determines to disregard it, and is willing to run the risk of war rather than forgo its intention." [68] The future of confident imperialism in that part of the world seemed uncertain after all.

The ambivalent values typical of the world movement had been hinted at by the Anglo-American dispute over the Alaskan boundary and by the first Moroccan crisis. But the demonstrable fact of conflict between superior peoples and Great Powers in Africa and in Asia, with which Theodore Roosevelt had become concerned, he fully comprehended only with the onslaught of

68. To William Howard Taft, December 22, 1910, *ibid.*, VII, pp. 189–190. According to Raymond A. Esthus, in "The Changing Concept of the Open Door, 1899–1910," Roosevelt practically handed responsibility for Chinese affairs over to Secretary of State Root after 1905. Esthus dates Roosevelt's retreat from the Open Door as early as 1903. Esthus, "The Changing Concept of the Open Door, 1899–1910," *The Mississippi Valley Historical Review*, Vol. XLVI, No. 3 (December 1959), pp. 435–454, p. 445. For a fuller treatment of Roosevelt's policies as they affected Japan see Raymond A. Esthus, *Theodore Roosevelt and Japan*, (Seattle, 1966). Another recent book of importance is Charles E. Neu, *An Uncertain Friendship: Theodore Roosevelt and Japan, 1906–1909*, (Cambridge, Mass., 1967).

World War I. There were any number of indications of a new, more violent era in world affairs, presaging the denouement of the neoimperialistic drama that had begun in the nineteenth century. Restive native nationalisms were symptomatic of this no less than the elaboration of a system of rival alliances in the fore-dawn of the Great War. Roosevelt's personal experiences in Egypt during his Afro-European tour of 1909–1910 illustrated the former President's reaction to the difficult problem of imperialism vis-à-vis native nationalism. An examination of the events of his Egyptian visit convincingly brings out two facts: the very real contradictions within the world movement as it reached maturity, and Roosevelt's own stubborn refusal to admit that as a principle of international affairs it had lost a great deal of its vitality.

On March 14, 1910, Theodore Roosevelt, fresh from the African game trails, arrived at Khartoum in the Sudan; by the end of the month he and his party had cleared Egyptian waters for Naples and the next leg of the famous "Teddyssey." During this fortnight sojourn in Egypt and the Sudan he found himself in searing contact with the developing problems of imperialism and local nationalism in the Middle East. These were problems that, not unnaturally, he was confident he had sure and useful knowledge of, and he was prompted to deliver a number of speeches— both impromptu remarks and formal addresses—concerning British policy for administering these colonial areas.[69] The former President was not altogether able to appreciate the large implications of tensions steadily mounting between the imperialist powers and the colonial peoples. His contradictory attitude was based on a conflict between the best interests of the imperialists and the nationalists, as he understood Egypt and its future. Roosevelt's firsthand observations of the people of the Nile exposed him to young nationalism in the raw. The experience confused him.

---

69. Roosevelt made three formal speeches on the Egyptian question: "Peace and Order in the Sudan," (Khartoum, March 16, 1910); "Law and Order in Egypt," (Cairo, March 28, 1910); and "British Rule in Africa," (London, May 31, 1910). These addresses are reprinted in Roosevelt, *African and European Speeches*, (New York, 1910), hereafter cited as *Speeches*. In addition, he made a number of shorter talks to various groups in Egypt and the Sudan. The texts of these talks have been gathered from various sources.

The result was that his public pronouncements became exhortations to the native population to be better and more useful citizens of their country, not better subjects of the British Crown, and admonitions to the British to "govern or go" from Egypt.

The Egypt of 1910 like other areas of the colonial world was experiencing the birth pangs of modern nationalism. It was a nationalism its advocates sought to bring to fruition in a national self-government. When as cautious a critic as Lord Cromer could write seriously of rendering "the native Egyptians capable of eventually taking over their share in the government of a really autonomous community" [70] it is not surprising that nationalist opinion demanded independence from the control of Europeans forthwith. It was a nationalism that in a large sense was expressed in terms of "Egypt for the Moslems." It was a nationalism whose extremist elements did not scruple to commit political murder. On February 10, 1910, Boutros Ghali Pasha, the Coptic prime minister, who had a long record of amicable relations with the British agency, was assassinated by a young Moslem fanatic. Nationalist agitation for a time threatened to disrupt the political balance of khedive, middle class, and British officialdom that ruled in Egypt. In the backwash of this smoldering unrest aggravated by the assassination, Theodore Roosevelt arrived in the Sudan.

For any enthusiastic young Egyptian who heard Theodore Roosevelt as the voice of one of the great nations it would have been impossible not to glimpse a vision of the new Egypt, the new nation, of which the former President spoke and which he urged his listeners to help create. Basic to the new Egypt was a new westernized Egyptian, an individual capable of helping himself and thereby performing the role of a good citizen. Roosevelt wanted to see the graduate of Egyptian schools "prepared to do his work in some capacity in civil life, without regard to any aid whatever received from or any salary drawn from the Govern-

70. Lord Cromer, Evelyn Baring, *Modern Egypt*, 2 volumes, (New York, 1908), II, p. 569. Cromer, in the concluding chapter entitled "The Future of Egypt," emphasized the necessarily gradual assumption of self-government by the Egyptians and the need to prepare the natives to assume power eventually. See II, pp. 563–571 *passim*.

ment. If a man is a good engineer, a good mechanic, a good agriculturist, if he is trained so that he becomes a really good merchant, he is, in his place the best type of citizen." [71] This was the way of Europe and America and it must be the way of Africa.[72] There were unmistakable echoes of Roosevelt's classic western American as he encouraged the youth of the Nile to become "men who will be able to shift for themselves, to help themselves and to help others, fully independent of all matters connected with the Government." [73] "There is only one way a man can permanently be helped, and that is by helping him to help himself," he warned the young people of Africa.[74] The active life of constant growth and increasing knowledge, the stock in trade of T.R. at home, was readily declared to a people yearning to assert itself. He asked the members of one audience at Khartoum, for example, not to close their minds or books once they had left school behind, but to keep training, keep educating so that instead of their standing still great progress—"good work, better work"—could be accomplished.[75] This was a familiar western creed which, as practiced in Europe and especially in the United States, had contributed much to the making of the nation-state.

One of the truly decisive means available to the Egyptians for bringing about a new nation was education. Roosevelt took occasion to remind the Egyptians of the function of education in the larger sense and the place of the university as the best means of expressing a country's ideals. For one thing they must not simply imitate western universities; rather, Egyptians must "copy what is good in them but test in a critical spirit whatever you take, so as to be sure that you take only what is wisest and best for yourselves." [76] A critical spirit of inquiry was not calculated to enhance British popularity in many quarters of the Egypt of 1910, however. The former President had in mind a university whose impact should be felt in many phases of the people's lives, as was

---

71. Roosevelt, "Peace and Order in the Sudan," *Speeches,* p. 5.
72. *Ibid.,* p. 6
73. *Ibid.,* pp. 5–6.
74. Roosevelt, "At the Luxor Mission," *New York Times,* March 22, 1910, p. 5.
75. Roosevelt, "Peace and Order in the Sudan," *loc. cit.,* p. 9.
76. Roosevelt, "Law and Order in Egypt," *Speeches,* p. 19.

amply borne out by the following words of the address at the National University in Cairo.

This university should have a profound influence on all things educational, economic and industrial throughout this whole region, because the very fact of Egypt's present position is such that this university will enjoy freedom hitherto unparalleled in the investigation and testing out of all problems vital to the future of the peoples of the Orient.[77]

It was to be a university "fraught with literally untold possibilities" for the good of the country.[78]

Closely tied to the free National University advocated by Roosevelt was the free status of the country's press. Western struggles for liberty very often had revolved around freedom of the newspapers to criticize the Government. Roosevelt, good democrat that he was, did not insist upon a free press for Europeans and Americans and remain complacent about a muzzled press for the native Egyptians.[79] At Shepheard's Hotel where he stayed in Cairo he held a press interview to which representatives of the local newspapers were invited. Some fourteen editors attended. Suitably, the group included various shadings of nationalistic political opinion. In discussing their responsibility as editors Roosevelt addressed them as he would have spoken to a similar gathering of newspapermen in, say, the American Midwest.

I always tell the newspapermen in my own country that they are using one of the most formidable weapons of modern life, and that it is vital to see that they use it for good purposes and not for bad purposes. The correspondent or editor of a newspaper is in reality a public servant.[80]

Yet a free press in Egypt would have certainly included elements agitating for the withdrawal of British forces from the country

77. *Ibid.*, p. 17.
78. *Ibid.*, p. 16.
79. The Press Law of 1881 enabled the Government to suppress newspapers for criticism unfavorable to it. This law went into effect after the death of Boutros Pasha.
80. *New York Times*, March 28, 1910, p. 1. *The Daily Mail* (London) carried a glamourized account of the same interview, March 29, 1910, p. 5.

and the establishment of a national government. Many Egyptian editors would have felt remiss in their duty as public servants and as Egyptians to have written otherwise. According to a firsthand account furnished by Ali Youssef, editor of *El Garida,* one of the moderate nationalist organs, Roosevelt expected any rebuke he gave the nationalists over the death of Boutros Pasha to receive adverse comment from the press.[81] But as an American nurtured on the tradition of an uncontrolled press this did not disturb him. On the contrary it was natural to him. In Africa as in America! His vision of the modern Egypt included as a matter of course a responsible press free to criticize.

The kind of society the modern Egyptian should expect to find himself in was western in many of its aspects. Before the National University Roosevelt insisted on the practical, technical, industrial foundation of a healthy country. "The base, the foundation of healthy life in any country, in any society, is necessarily composed of men who do the actual productive work of the country, whether in tilling the soil, in handicrafts, or in business. . . ."[82] The economic objective of the modern Egyptian should be, in other words, the development of a nation of productive workers who could by their own efforts add to the security and welfare of their country. And in this regard Roosevelt reiterated that his doctrine for Americans and for Africans was one and the same.[83]

There were other attributes of a great community modeled on western lines that Roosevelt urged on his Egyptian audiences. One of these was a Christian respect for womanhood. Stopping at the Luxor Mission on his journey to Cairo he commented favorably on the training given the native girls at the mission school. The women as well as the men must be elevated to a new status based on respect for the individual. This could be achieved in part by instructing the girls in the domestic arts to be sure, but

81. Ali Youssef has quoted the former President as remarking at the press interview: "I do not want newspaper men to dictate to me. I am going to speak tomorrow in the Egyptian University. Wait until you hear what I shall say and then say what you wish to say." "Egypt's Reply to Colonel Roosevelt," *The North American Review,* June 1910, p. 732.

82. Roosevelt, "Law and Order in Egypt," *loc. cit.,* p. 23.

83. *Ibid.,* pp. 23–24.

their literary education should not be neglected.[84] Another western idea discussed briefly by the former President was predicated
on what he considered sound American experience: a mutual
respect for the religious beliefs of all Egyptians. Moslems, Copts,
and Jews were mingled with native converts to Christianity.
Learn to live together regardless of differences was the practical
advice he offered to overcome the dangers inherent in the religious
pluralism of Egypt.[85] Nor must the Egyptians allow the Government to become dominated by the military. "Woe to the people
whose army tries to play a part in politics," Colonel Roosevelt
admonished the new Egypt.[86] Control by a military *junta* would
preclude the establishment of the very kind of society he envisioned for Egypt; generals too frequently had been the death of
freedom and criticism. Ali Youssef, for one, was in agreement.[87]

It was an easy matter for the Egyptians to accept Roosevelt's
encouragement of their nationalistic ambitions. Americans were
the exemplars of freedom and prosperity from whom they had
learned much without having to pay them tribute in suffering and
humiliation.[88] A remarkable example of the nature of the feelings
of the Middle East peoples for Americans was seen in a testi-
monial presented to the former President by a committee representing the Syrian community of the city of Khartoum. The
document was eloquent in its presentation of the aspirations that
motivated the inhabitants of that part of the world, whether in
Syria, the Sudan, or Egypt. In part it read:

The chief reasons which the Syrians have to be grateful to
America are the introduction of a system of education which is free, of
education on terms within the means of the masses, and the broad and
liberal lines of American policy in welcoming immigration. . . .

Schools were opened in almost all important centers of Syria [by
Americans], a printing press was established at Beirut, and a genuine
yearning for the acquirement of learning animated the whole popula-

84. *The Times* (London), March 24, 1910, p. 5; "Mr. Roosevelt in Egypt,"
Outlook, April 30, 1910, p. 981.

85. "Peace and Order in the Sudan," *loc. cit.*, p. 6.

86. *The Times* (London), March 18, 1910, p. 5.

87. "Egypt's Reply to Colonel Roosevelt," *loc. cit.*, p. 730.

88. *Ibid.*, p. 729.

tion . . . instilling into the minds of the rising generation the true principles of liberty, and inspiring them with American, English and French ideals of life.[89]

Roosevelt proudly accepted this accolade from a grateful people. After all, these were the ideals of life he cherished as civilized man's highest aspiration. There were no better models to guide native peoples in constructing their societies for the future.

For the present Roosevelt concerned himself with the fact and, as he saw it, the necessity of British control in Egypt and the Sudan. This defense of the British occupation the former President made at a time when violent feelings of political unrest in Egypt were rife. To match the murder of Boutros Pasha there was the terrible memory of Denshwai, with its death sentences and floggings of Egyptian villagers.[90] At the time it might have seemed that the final crisis in Anglo-Egyptian affairs was at hand. The incumbent agent-general, Sir Eldon Gorst, was not made of the stern stuff of Lord Cromer, and the Liberal ministry in London was divided as to its policy for Egypt. Very probably these circumstances intensified Roosevelt's antagonism to the nationalist political factions and threw into more visible relief the contradictions of "democratic nationalism," as Roosevelt chose to term imperialist control of Africa at the time.

There were two major reasons in Roosevelt's thinking why Great Britain must not be disturbed in her occupation of the Nile provinces, both reasons consistent with his world movement philosophy. Britain was a vessel of civilization, carrying western ideas across the world. In each of his major speeches on the Egyptian question,[91] in his extemporaneous remarks delivered to

89. "Address Presented to Colonel the Honorable Theodore Roosevelt by the Syrian Committee of Khartoum," March 17, 1910, Roosevelt *Mss*.

90. In 1906 at Denshwai a British officer was killed by villagers during a misunderstanding over hunting privileges in the area. Three death sentences and several floggings were ordered by a special court. Popular reaction among Egyptians was violent in denunciation of this judgment and penalty. Boutros Pasha had served as president of the special court.

91. *Speeches*, p. 3, pp. 26–27, p. 159.

informal groups,[92] and in his private correspondence,[93] Roosevelt tirelessly insisted upon Britain's historic role as the agent of western culture. Equally important was his conviction that the Egyptians were themselves incapable of self-government at the time; the continuance of British power was its logical complement. According to Rooseveltian criteria it would be years, generations perhaps, before this deficiency in the Egyptians would be overcome. Writing to Sir George O. Trevelyan he characterized nationalist agitation as centering in two groups: "Levantine Moslems . . . of the ordinary Levantine type, noisy, emotional, rather decadent, quite hopeless material on which to build, but also not really dangerous as foes" and "the real strength of the Nationalistic movement . . . the mass of practically unchanged, bigoted Moslems to whom the movement meant driving out the foreigner, plundering and slaying the local Christians, and a return to all the violence and corruption which festered under the old style Moslem rule, whether Asiatic or African." [94] Under these circumstances the Egyptians, however keen they might be for self-government at once, could not be trusted with it. Years of further political apprenticeship under British direction had to intervene.[95]

92. "He [Roosevelt] gave two little addresses, one to the boys in the Government school, and the other to the principal merchants. Upon each group he urged the necessity of doing everything in their power to perpetuate the rule of peace and justice in the Sudan. To the merchants he said: 'Uphold the government which has given you prosperity and upon which your further prosperity depends.'" *The Times* (London), March 17, 1910, p. 5. In commenting upon the Gordon College as an example of a great civilizing institution Roosevelt exclaimed: "Think of it! The sons of the Khalifa El Mahdi are studying in a college which perpetuates the name of the man originally responsible for the destruction of their father's power." *New York Times*, March 16, 1910, p. 4.

93. For example, Roosevelt to Sir Percy Girouard, July 21, 1910, Roosevelt *Mss*: to Lay Delamere, September 22, 1910, *ibid.*

94. To Sir George Otto Trevelyan, October 1, 1911, *Letters*, VII, p. 351.

95. An extreme version of Roosevelt's estimate of the level of Egyptian political maturity is included in the following news story that appeared in the *New York Evening Journal*. "At Tantah Colonel Roosevelt was reminded that it was the spot where in 1882 the Moslems pulled the Christians out of the trains and massacred them. 'Yes,' said Colonel Roosevelt, 'and it is just what should happen again if they had self-rule in Egypt.'" *New York Evening Journal*, March 31, 1910, p. 21. Although one may hesitate to give credence to this report, its chief source being the somewhat sensational *Evening Journal*, the former President in effect said the same thing in his London address. It is also necessary to point out that whether authentic or not, the story circulated among the Egyptians. See "Egypt's Reply to Colonel Roosevelt," *loc. cit.*, p. 736.

The full expression of Roosevelt's doubts about an immediate self-contained Egyptian government was prominent in his speech before the National University, the same address giving so much encouragement to the spirit of nationalism. In part the audience was advised:

. . . the training of a nation to fit it successfully to fulfill the duties of self-government is a matter not of a decade or two but of generations. There are foolish empiricists who believe that the granting of a paper constitution, prefaced by some high sounding declaration, of itself confers the power of self-government upon a people. This is never so. Nobody can "give" an individual "self-help". . . . With any people the essential quality to show is, not the haste of grasping after a power which it is only too easy to misuse, but a slow, steady, resolute development of those substantial qualities such as love of justice, love of fair play, the spirit of self-reliance, of moderation, which alone enable a people to govern themselves.[96]

In light of the foregoing it is not surprising that during the course of his journeying along the Nile he frequently insisted upon the wisdom of maintaining British power and that in his final address on the future of Egypt, delivered in London, he called for a strong arm to rule. In these passages of his speeches he assumed the attitude of a hardfisted soldier intent on keeping order, rather than that of the patient colonial administrator concerned with demonstrating the reality of Anglo-American justice. The "thing, not the form was vital"; it was England's "first duty to keep order." [97]

On the evening of his arrival in Khartoum Colonel Roosevelt was entertained at the palace of the governor-general. His host was Slatin Pasha, the sirdar, the senior British military officer in the Sudan, and his fellow diners were British military and civil officials. Roosevelt was not expected to speak formally but in the course of the dinner conversation the subject of the assassination of Boutros Pasha came up. He was asked what he would have done had he been the agent-general. His reply was a forceful ex-

96. Roosevelt, "Law and Order in Egypt," *loc. cit.*, pp. 24–25.
97. Roosevelt, "British Rule in Africa," *Speeches*, p. 171.

ample of Roosevelt's "tough" policy as a reaction against strong nationalist pressure to achieve self-rule.

It is very simple. I would try the murderer at drum head court martial. As there is no question about the facts, for his own faction do not deny the assassination, he would be found guilty. I would sentence him to be taken out and shot; and then if the home government cabled me, in one of their moments of vacillation, to wait a little while, I would cable in reply: "Can't wait, the assassin has been tried and shot." The home government might recall me or impeach me if they wanted to, but *that* assassin would have received his just deserts.[98]

This conversational remark largely set the tone for all of Roosevelt's more formal addresses when his theme gravitated to the demands of the Egyptians for immediate self-rule. Many of the British audience were pleased to have this "tough" answer and he was urged to speak out for law and order whenever possible.[99] Two days after the dinner, in a formal address before British officialdom at the Sudan Club, Roosevelt paid tribute to the work of the British and insisted that any attempt to dislodge them from their Nile occupation would be criminal.[100] As he was to remark later in London, self-government in the hands of the Sudanese had been the self-government of the wolf pack, a situation no civilized power could permit to continue unchecked.[101] Native press reaction to these opinions concerning the political future of the Egyptian people was highlighted by repeated demands for local autonomy and even a warning to Roosevelt that he must refrain from speaking out again in a pro-British vein.

Nothing daunted, the day after the Sudan Club speech he addressed at their invitation the Egyptian Officers Club, where nationalist feeling was understandably strong. Slatin Pasha had asked him in advance to urge the native officers to maintain their "absolute and unflinching loyalty to English rule" and Roose-

98. Lawrence F. Abbott, *Impressions of Theodore Roosevelt*, (New York, 1919), pp. 154–155.
99. *Ibid.*, p. 155.
100. *The Times* (London), March 18, 1910, p. 5.
101. Roosevelt, "British Rule in Africa," *loc. cit.*, p. 165.

velt "very gladly" consented to do so.[102] The speech warned the officers of the dangers of involving in politics. "The soldier who mixes politics with soldiering becomes a bad politician and a poor soldier. In the Spanish War," Roosevelt continued, "most of the men in my regiment differed from me in politics. I didn't care a particle. I knew they felt so long as they were in uniform, that their duty and pride bade them to be soldiers and nothing else, and that they devote all their thoughts, will and energy to working for the greatness of the flag under which they fought." [103] This appeal for loyalty to British rule at the expense of nationalist aspiration, with the curious analogy of the Spanish War only adding a note of obscurity, must have seemed ill-founded to many of the native officers. In any case, his remarks tended to emphasize that Roosevelt frequently did not relate his theory to the facts at hand. That he was inclined to persist in this attitude is illustrated further when two days later at Aswan he repeated his warning about the dangers of mixing politics and soldiering to a group of native officers informally gathered to greet him.[104]

The unsettling effects of Roosevelt's widely circulating opinions upon the Egyptians may be judged from Sir Eldon Gorst's initial desire that he say nothing of the assassination of Boutros Pasha in his scheduled speech at the National University. Roosevelt refused to do this, and his outspoken opposition apparently convinced Gorst that some good might come of an admonition to the Egyptians to forgo violence in their fued with Great Britain.[105] Thus while the greater portion of this address was devoted to praise and encouragement of the university with the nationalistic appeal, it also included a stinging rebuke to the assassins:

All good men, all men of every nation whose respect is worth having, have been inexpressibly shocked. . . . The type of man who

102. To Sir George Otto Trevelyan, October 1, 1911, *Letters,* VII, p. 350.
103. *The Times* (London), March 18, 1910, p. 5.
104. *Ibid.,* March 21, 1910, p. 5.
105. To Sir George Otto Trevelyan, October 1, 1911, *Letters,* VII, p. 351. Sir Eldon Gorst (consul general for Egypt, 1907–1910) wrote "how glad I am that you consented to speak to these people. If anything can bring them to a more reasonable frame of mind your words should have that effect." Gorst to Roosevelt, March 26, 1910, Roosevelt *Mss.*

turns out the assassin is a type possessing all the qualities most alien to good citizenship. . . . Such a man stands on a pinnacle of evil infamy.[106]

Perhaps this publicly administered reprimand was the most stinging phrase of the address, given the circumstances of tension and bad feeling. British approval certainly was not lacking, Roosevelt's words having been edited and approved in advance by Gorst.[107] But *Almo,* one of the organs of the Constitutional Nationalists, seemed to think that Roosevelt had also come out for more self-rule for the Egyptians.

Some criticism is due to the bad translation [it told its readers] made in reference to the strategic position of Europe, which seemed to indicate that he [Roosevelt] desired England always to remain in Egypt. But he has insisted that the Egyptians are as fit for a Constitution as the people of Turkey, which movement Mr. Roosevelt has approved.[108]

It depended upon which part of the speech was studied and by whom. The Cairo address is of critical significance in Roosevelt's analysis of the Egyptian question because the cleavage in his thinking was so palpable within the passages of the same speech.

Perhaps the most widely known of Theodore Roosevelt's addresses on Egyptian issues was "British Rule in Africa," delivered at the Guildhall in London on May 31, 1910, on the occasion of granting the freedom of the City of London to the former President. There was little in it conducive to a favorable interpretation by the nationalists. It has been termed the "govern or go" speech, an apt summation of its most forceful passage.

Now either you have the right to be in Egypt or you have not; either it is or it is not your duty to establish and keep order. If you feel that you have not the right to be in Egypt, if you do not wish to establish and keep order there, why, then, by all means get out of Egypt. If, as I hope, you feel that your duty to civilized mankind

106. Roosevelt, "Law and Order in Egypt," *loc. cit.,* p. 26.
107. Sir Reginald Wingate to Roosevelt, March 30, 1910, Roosevelt *Mss.* Wingate to Roosevelt, June 8, 1910, *ibid.* (Wingate was the British governor-general in the Sudan.)
108. *New York Times,* March 30, 1910, p. 3.

and your fealty to your own great civilization alike bid you stay, then
make the fact and the name agree and show that you are ready to meet
in very deed the responsibility which is yours.[109]

Roosevelt also pointed out the dangers of self-government for a
people such as the Egyptians had been demonstrated amply
in the Sudan. Under Sudanese rule "great crimes were committed
. . . crimes so dark that their very hideousness protects them
from exposure. . . . Then the English came in; put an end to
independence and self-government which wrought this hideous
evil, restored order, kept the peace and gave to each individual
. . . liberty. . . ." [110] To Roosevelt the murder of Boutros Pasha
proved this. "The attitude of the so-called Egyptian Nationalist
Party in connection with this foul murder has shown that they
neither are desirous nor capable of guaranteeing even that
primary justice the failure to supply which makes self-government not merely empty but a noxious farce." [111] British power
and the duty to use it to effect law and order, along with native
incapacity to rule, were reasons enough to require Great Britain
to remain undisturbed in Egypt and the Sudan.

No amount of criticism, and he was roundly challenged in
England and in Egypt for his remarks, dissuaded Roosevelt from
the view that in North Africa he discovered Britain doing "a great
work for empire" and "a great work for civilization." [112] Years
before he had come to admire Lord Cromer's colonial administration of Egypt, and what he saw there in person confirmed his
prior judgment. It would be bootless to charge Roosevelt with
hypocrisy or democratic cant in light of his Egyptian speeches,
for such allegations would ignore the whole pattern of his conception of modern history and his sincere avowal of it. The mis-
fortune was that he was unable to appreciate the world movement as a dynamic force, not a static condition, and to see that by
his words and actions in Egypt he was adding to the momentum

109. Roosevelt, "British Rule in Africa," *loc. cit.*, p. 171.
110. *Ibid.*, p. 165.
111. *Ibid.*, p. 170.
112. *Ibid.*, p. 159. To Sir Percy Girouard, July 21, 1910, *Letters*, VII, p. 104;
to David Gray, October 5, 1911, *ibid.*, p. 402.

of that force, at the same time stiffening resistance to it. He knew
well enough the dynamism of an expanding western nation, but
he remained unsympathetic to that same quality when it touched
a native people. No doubt part of his impatience with native nationalism was his temperamental need to command. "I should
greatly like to handle Egypt and India for a few months," he confidentially boasted to Whitelaw Reid. "At the end of that time I
doubtless would be impeached by the House of Commons, but I
should have things moving in fine order first." [113] Fundamen-
tally, however, his failure was an intellectual one rather than a
failure of temperament.

The war of 1914 brought the world movement to a dramatic
halt. The faith Theodore Roosevelt had placed in the civilized
nations and their consciences as a means and guarantee of human
progress was tested and found misplaced. The luxury of right and
might as component parts of a single creed could no longer be enjoyed without fatal embarrassment. Some of the fundamentals of
the old belief had to be rejected, the faith purified as it were in
the fires of a great holocaust. Those doctrines that survived included the higher or spiritual elements of the world movement
confession along with an altered dynamic of belief, but they were
somehow incomplete, standing naked in the innocence of their
ideals. What was left no longer constituted the classic rendering of the world movement rationale of modern history. The purpose of that movement, the betterment of mankind, was still to
be cherished; the theory about the means to achieve it, the expansive abilities of superior peoples, was exploded by an inter-
necine struggle for nationalistic advantage.

The World War forced upon Roosevelt a re-examination of
the sources of his imperialism. He felt fully able to honor the traditional values. His nationalism too stood firm but it became, under
the impact of total war, more narrow, more doctrinaire, lacking
generosity and breadth of spirit. As for his racism, that was dead

113. To Whitelaw Reid, March 24, 1910, *ibid.*, p. 63.

indeed. His belief in the white race—defined by European origin, the Christian religion, the cultural link with Greece and Rome, and a kinship of blood—no longer endured.[114] Something that had been essential was not now tenable, change had set in, the older order had passed away.

Roosevelt lived long enough to understand all of this, in general terms at least, and though his last years unhappily lacked the large view of his days of power and responsibility, he managed a realignment of his thought that merits consideration if only because it reveals quite emphatically what counted most to him. Not that his wartime pronouncements and judgments are the best or truest representation of Theodore Roosevelt's outlook. They are not; as a body they are, perhaps, the least attractive. During the war he became rancorous, totally impatient of any save those who agreed with his views completely, and increasingly frustrated by a lack of power, hating Wilson, hating "peace at any price" men, hating the Germans. Segments of his wartime reflections deserve review if only to show more clearly the rule of righteousness in his judgment of history. They can be treated in a limited manner here, for Roosevelt's wartime utterances have come down to posterity not as a fitting climax to a progressively more ordered system of historical interpretation, but as acrimonious comments of a man to a great degree disappointed by the failure of his world movement philosophy.

"The intense fear felt by each nation for other nations and the anger arising from that fear" seemed to Roosevelt "the real and ultimate causes" of World War I.[115] The fear had been generated by the rivalry of nations both in Europe and in the world at large. The rivalry had sprung from the expansive character of the superior peoples involved. Years before he had put himself for a moment in the Kaiser's shoes and had concluded that "If I were a German I should want the German race to expand . . . as a German I should be delighted to upset the English in South Africa and to defy the Americans and their Monroe Doctrine." [116] He

114. Roosevelt, "Biological Analogies in History," *Works*, XIV, p. 68.
115. *New York Times*, October 18, 1914, p. 11.
116. To Sir Cecil Spring-Rice, August 13, 1897, *Letters*, I, p. 645.

did not believe in expansion for its own sake, however, but for the advance of civilization. Long before World War I this factor occasioned him to make certain distinctions regarding expansion as a national characteristic. With particular reference to imperial Germany he said he "should hail with delight" German control over Asia Minor, for the Turk would thereby be put down. He would equally "regret to see Germany take Switzerland or Holland or Denmark" because they were already responsible and self-regulating countries with their own modest contributions to the world's work.[117] Interestingly enough, Roosevelt made no objection to Austrian control in the Balkans, where the Slavic Europeans in his judgment were politically backward. "No better bit of governmental work has been done in Europe than the work of the Austrians in governing Bosnia and Herzegovina," he told William Howard Taft at the time of the Austrian annexation of those provinces. "I hope and believe that the Southern Slavs will ultimately grow able to stand by themselves but . . . at present, independence or annexation to Serbia would work . . . very much as Bryan's theory of immediate independence would work for the Philippines."[118] Preparation for self-rule, it was again made apparent, was not a matter of race or of geography but of ability and experience, a matter of *character*. The world movement was based ultimately not on power but upon righteousness.

Ironically, it was to the Germans that Roosevelt spoke most explicitly about "The World Movement," the title of an address he gave at the University of Berlin while he was in Europe in 1910. "This world movement of civilization," he said, "should link the nations of the world together, while leaving unimpaired that love of country in the individual . . . essential to the world's well being."[119] His confidence in the movement at that time was stronger than ever; presumably he refused to admit that rival patriotisms might be one of the most hazardous sources of war between the Great Powers.

117. To Frederic R. Coudert, July 3, 1901, *ibid.*, III, p. 106.
118. To William Howard Taft, December 29, 1908, *ibid.*, VI, p. 1447.
119. Roosevelt, "The World Movement," *Works*, XIV, p. 284.

For Theodore Roosevelt the precise moment of his loss of faith in the world movement was the day the Germans invaded Belgium in August 1914. His shock at this event was profound; he never recovered from it and never ceased to refer to it as proof of German barbarism, though it took him several months to appreciate this fully. As the war dragged on wearily his hatred for those responsible for the crime against Belgium and his contempt for those who stood idly by, content to be mere spectators, grew daily. Belgium, he told Sir Edward Grey, was "the crux of the situation." Had England or France acted in such fashion, he insisted to Grey, he would have "opposed them exactly as I now oppose Germany." [120] What the Germans had done in Belgium was to deliver a "deep and lasting wound upon civilization by the blow struck at international law and international righteousness. . . . It is to this act of unforgiveable treachery that every succeeding infamy is to be traced. . . ." [121]

Convinced as he was that the German attack had been carefully planned for several years,[122] Roosevelt felt the Germans had forfeited their rights as a civilized nation, much as the Colombians had done when they failed to ratify the canal treaty with the United States. The war continued to reveal for Roosevelt a Germany "without pity, mercy, humanity and international morality," [123] with the kaiser "one of the leading conspirators, plotters and wrong-doers." [124] All this and more the war had prompted him to say of a people whom a few years before he had extolled so generously. "I believe in you and your future" he had said in the conclusion of "The World Movement" address at the University of Berlin. "I admire you and wonder at the extraordinary greatness and variety of your achievement in so many and so widely different fields." [125] But that had been in 1910, before the loss of confidence.

120. To Sir Edward Grey, January 22, 1915, *Letters,* VIII, pp. 786–877.
121. Roosevelt, *Fear God and Take Your Own Part, Works,* XX, p. 333.
122. *Ibid.*
123. To F.W. Whitridge, December 15, 1916, quoted in Bishop, *op. cit.,* II, p. 460.
124. To Arthur Hamilton Lee, November 19, 1918, *Letters,* VIII, p. 1396.
125. Roosevelt, "The World Movement," *Works,* XIV, p. 285.

One of the inevitable consequences of the war for Roosevelt, as for many of his contemporaries, was a reinforced and impregnable kind of nationalism. "Nationalism is the keynote of your attitude as it is of mine," he wrote to Albert Beveridge in 1918. "I have never known an internationalist who was worth his salt." [126] In the postwar era, after the great victory had been won over the forces of barbarism, he thought nationalism rather than internationalism should be the dominant motif in world relations. The war had demonstrated that international commitments, like the Hague convention's solemn pledge guaranteeing Belgian territory, were all too likely to be treated as scraps of paper by irresponsible leaders. Nationalism could be expected to achieve justice for mankind in a way internationalism based either upon a common bond of race or upon the pious sentiments of Wilsonian idealism had not been able and could never hope to accomplish.

Allied victory brought with it three great postwar problems: a reorganization of Europe made necessary by the destruction of the German and Austro-Hungarian empires, the disposition of Germany's colonial holdings (and the larger problem of colonialism in general), and the question of how the postwar settlement might be maintained intact. Roosevelt's views and proposals in each of these areas provided some further evidence of the traditional and historical as the more durable segments of his world outlook; at the same time they underscored his nationalism, so that there is no doubt of his abandonment of the original racist premise of the world movement. In Europe he favored self-determination for those people adequately prepared to assume political responsibility. While this included most Europeans in the eastern as well as in the western regions of the continent, he did have one or two reservations. He suggested to Lord Bryce that among other arrangements "the Czecho-Slovak, Polish and Jugo-Slav commonwealths must be created entirely independent" but

126. To Albert Beveridge, July 18, 1918, *Letters,* VIII, pp. 1352–1353.

"Albania should be a cantonal state under the protection of France, England or perhaps the United States." He also had qualifications to offer concerning the nationalities of Russia, speaking of their independence as only probable.[127]

As for the colonial world after 1918, the superior race thesis was replaced by the superior nation thesis. Roosevelt's prejudice against any international administration of colonies was pronounced; "it was tried in Samoa and in the Congo and it worked uncommonly badly." [128] He told Lord Bryce that "England and Japan must keep the colonies they have won." [129] To deprive the victors of gains would be a crime; in fact this was the only way to dispose of the colonies since to give to the various native peoples the power of self-rule "would be worthy of Bedlam were it not so transparently dishonest." [130] The war had not secreted some magic elixir whereby the aboriginal populations acquired the *character* needed to rule themselves. The old backwardness persisted, so that for African savages to have anything more than a consultative and subordinate share in their own affairs he termed "simply silly." He scored the Wilson Administration for planning to preach self-determination at the peace conference while ruling Haiti and Santo Domingo with marines, putting this forth as proof of the evil of an indiscriminate policy of self-determination.[131] A sharp distinction still had to be made and adhered to between those people with *character* and those who had yet to acquire it.

Nationalism was also a salient consideration in Roosevelt's outlook for maintaining the peace brought about by victory. Early in the war he expressed the view that "to advocate international peace not based on might" was ridiculous. "The civilized states . . . [must] guarantee to use their force to keep the peace." [132] Thus Wilson's proposal for a League of Nations did not engender much hope in him or elicit his support. It appeared

127. To James Bryce, August 7, 1918, *ibid.*, p. 1358. For a variation of this basic proposal see to L. Michailovitch, July 11, 1918, *ibid.*, pp. 1349–1351.
128. To Charles R. Van Hise, November 15, 1918, *ibid.*, VIII, p. 1393.
129. To James Bryce, August 7, 1918, *ibid.*, p. 1359.
130. To Arthur Hamilton Lee, September 8, 1918, *ibid.*, p. 1368.
131. To James Bryce, November 19, 1918, *ibid.*, pp. 1400–1401.
132. To Susan D.D. Cooley, December 2, 1914, *ibid.*, p. 853.

to be a mere cure-all not grounded on the realities of national interest.[133] At best the League could be looked upon as an addition to and "not as a substitution for thorough preparation and intense nationalism on our part," he wrote in one of his pieces in the *Kansas City Star*.[134] Why create a League of Nations, he asked, when there already existed a League of Allies? In his judgment, power in the nation and not some international commitment would achieve real justice.[135]

Perhaps no better sign that the world movement ideal was dead in Roosevelt's thought can be discerned than his avowal that force stood back of law and that the success of the League depended on the will to use force to back up its principles. In his prewar elaboration of the world movement theory Germany, Austria, and Russia all had had important and constructive parts to play. But the Central Powers, by their repeated violations of "every rule of civilized warfare and of international good faith," and Russia under the Bolsheviks were now unworthy of any trust which honest men might wish to place in them.[136] Yet without these important nations as members of the League, how could that proposed body keep the peace? Roosevelt was dubious that it could. In truth, he objected to the League mostly because it seemed to be based on the kind of solidarity within the community of nations that Roosevelt believed to have been destroyed in the war.

The war had simply shattered for him the concept of the so-called civilized nations working together. The world still needed justice and it still called out for it, but in the ashes of 1918 a nation that was strong, prepared, and dedicated to the cause of righteousness appeared to be its sole guarantor, at least within its own sphere of influence. Nationalism, which had always figured essentially in Roosevelt's world outlook, had become an obsession by the end of the war, a shutter closing out much of the rest of the world and darkening portions of his own once-

133. To H. Rider Haggard, December 6, 1918, *ibid.*, p. 1414.
134. Roosevelt, *Roosevelt in the Kansas City Star*, (Boston and New York, 1921), p. 248.
135. *Ibid.*, p. 293.
136. Roosevelt, "The Terms of Peace," *Works*, XXI, p. 411.

confident thought. Had Roosevelt lived on into the twenties it is no idle speculation to suggest that his atomistic view of the world community would have impelled him to become an extreme isolationist, willing to accept a more narrow national jurisdiction in return for a possibly higher ideal of justice.

It is unfair but unavoidable, understandable though misleading, to close a commentary on Theodore Roosevelt's confident imperialism with the distressing loss of confidence that was its fate. In a way the tragedy of World War I, however necessary to explain the fullness of Roosevelt's views, is something of an anachronism, its inclusion best justified on negative grounds. An examination of his wartime pronouncements is not unlike an autopsy to determine where and how the failure that brought death to the once-living world movement principle occurred. The war and its implications added nothing to the dimensions of the world movement; they only underscored in a kind of perverse way the more durable qualities of a theory of history. This is not to say it would have been more suitable if Roosevelt had predeceased the outbreak of the conflict; no man should go before his time or linger long after it, and his earlier death would have, among other things, left less evidence of what he held most dear.

But if his reaction to World War I was his last great political experience, it ought not stand as a final vision of his confident imperialism. Always granting the supremely personal, and therefore not infrequently controversial, nature of his conception of modern history—that of the superior nations acting in the best interests of mankind in a world movement and when necessary using force—the constructive contributions of confident imperialism are better remembered than its final failure. The finest of these contributions without doubt was the work done in the Philippines for the Filipino people, where Roosevelt's leadership came into full bloom. For the United States, the Islands became the prime subject in the work of civilizing, and it is by that enterprise that American imperialism may best be judged. Shadows were cast upon United States imperialism in Roosevelt's time by police action in the Caribbean and by the suppression of the Filipino nationalists, indications of the undeniable deficiencies and evils in the condition of man. Confident imperialism consciously sought to render that condition somewhat less flawed. It is on its success or failure in this regard that a final judgment of Theodore Roosevelt's confident imperialism should be made.

Index

201